The Criminal Law Library

SENTENCING

The Criminal Law Library

Editor-in-Chief:

Rt. Hon. Lord Elwyn-Jones, PC, CH

General Editor:

Gavin McFarlane, LLM(Sheffield), PhD(Lond),
Barrister and Harmsworth Scholar of the Middle Temple

1. *Fraud* by Anthony J. Arlidge and Jacques Parry
2. *Misuse of Drugs* by Patrick Bucknell and Hamid Ghodse
3. *Forensic Medicine* by Evan Stone and Hugh Johnson
4. *Criminal Evidence* by John A. Andrews and Michael Hirst
5. *Sentencing* by Eric Stockdale and Keith Devlin

The Criminal Law Library—No. 5

SENTENCING

ERIC STOCKDALE, MSc(Cranfield), LLM, PhD(Lond),
Circuit Judge

and

KEITH DEVLIN, LLB, MPhil(Lond), PhD(Brunel),
Circuit Judge

WATERLOW PUBLISHERS

First edition 1987
© E. Stockdale and K. Devlin 1987

Waterlow Publishers
Oyez House, PO Box 55
27 Crimscott Street
London SE1 5TS
A division of Hollis Professional and Financial Services PLC

ISBN 0 08 039248 2

British Library Cataloguing in Publication Data

Stockdale, Eric.
    Sentencing.—(The Criminal law library).
    1. Sentences (Criminal procedure)—England
    I. Title   II. Devlin, Keith   III. Series
    344.205'772   KD8406

Printed in Great Britain by
A. Wheaton & Co Ltd, Exeter, Devon

Foreword

BY THE RT. HON. LORD ELWYN-JONES, P.C., C.H.

Sentencing policy and practice are now in the forefront of examination of our penal system. In this timely book the authors bring to bear their knowledge and experience of sentencing as Judges of the Crown Court and as former practitioners at the Bar. They analyse and comment helpfully and clearly on every stage in the proceedings governing the sentence of the Court from the initial plea to the passing of sentence.

In doing so they discuss with an abundance of authorities, which they analyse and relate effectively, the problems of sentencing from the point of view of both sentences and practitioners. I believe the book will provide helpful guidance to both. It is also written in a manner which will, I believe, make it of great interest to the general reader as well.

The book will also be valuable as a work of reference and guidance to legislators and administrators alike. Parliament itself does not emerge unscathed from the book. It states:

> "Sentencing legislation, as a glance at the various statutes will confirm, has been of a haphazard nature, with piecemeal attempts to improve the system. Whilst the Court of Appeal has in the past often said that it will not tinker with sentences, that is make minor alterations, the legislature happily tinkers away from time to time, with barely a glance at its earlier contributions."

The authors make it clear that few sentencing decisions are easy, save in relatively minor cases. They are inevitably complex, in particular those affecting the liberty of the subject. They point out that Parliament has rarely impinged on the discretion of the Courts to impose any sentence below the statutory minimum.

The decision whether a case calls for imprisonment and if so, for how long, or for one of the many alternatives now available to the sentencer in our penal system, is of crucial importance. This is not only because of its consequences to the man or woman in the dock, but because of its cumulative impact on our prison system. This was spelt out in the Report of the Chief Inspector of Prisons for 1985. He stated:

> "We were driven to the inescapable conclusion that parts of the system were wholly preoccupied with survival . . . . There is little new to say

about overcrowding except that it worsened considerably . . . the surging numbers were so rapid that an already overstretched system came perilously near to breaking point.

   . . . If this prison population is not reduced by the use of alternatives to custody and if drastic inroads cannot be made in the time defendants spend in custody awaiting trial, then new ways of coping with the prison population will have to be found."

As to this dire situation the authors quote with approval a statement of the Lord Chief Justice, Lord Lane:

"It is no good judges saying, as they sometimes do, that the fact that there are not enough places in the prisons is the Home Office's fault and they had better get on with it. We are all in the same boat, like it or not, and the prison service is part of the judicial system, just as the judges are."

There are no simple answers in this field.

As the Advisory Council on the Penal System stated in 1978:

"whether retribution, deterrence, prevention or rehabilitation (or any single one or more of them in combination) govern sentencing policy and practice, is the subject of constant controversy and debate."

Debates in Parliament in recent years on legislation affecting sentencing reveal this still to be the case. As the authors state:

"for the first three-quarters of the twentieth century, not only in England but in the Western world generally, the move was increasingly away from the purely retributive and deterrent approaches and towards an emphasis on the reformation of the offender."

The book illustrates how the idea of repairing the damage to the victim has also become an important consideration. The authors stress that "since the public, the police, the legal profession, the probation service and the reform lobbies have differing views about the appropriate measures to be used for different offenders, there should be ample time for consultation before any further legislation is passed . . . . In the meantime, the judiciary and the legal profession should give the important questions of sentencing the attention they deserve." This book can, I believe, help them greatly in that task.

Elwyn-Jones

Preface

In these days when working lawyers are bombarded with paper from all directions, they are entitled to some sort of explanation from authors producing yet another law book. This is especially so when other books on the subject are already available. By way of mitigation rather than defence we would like to point out that several of the recent books on sentencing were published only after we had been commissioned by Lord Silkin, Q.C., the Chairman of Waterlow Publishers, to write the present volume, and that they are mainly designed for students rather than the practitioner.

Before the appearance of those recent books there was comparatively little in print on the subject of sentencing that had not been written by Dr. David Thomas of the University of Cambridge Institute of Criminology. We would like to express our thanks to Dr. Thomas, not only for the help we have derived from his works, and particularly from the *Encyclopedia of Current Sentencing Practice* that he edits for Sweet & Maxwell, but also for his outstanding contribution over the years to the development of the law of sentencing. Although two generations of judges have by now benefited from Dr. Thomas's pioneering work, it has received little official recognition, so we are particularly happy to acknowledge our personal indebtedness to him.

We have attempted to write a book which will fill a different slot from that already filled so admirably by Dr. Thomas. We hope that the approach we have used, namely, that of discussing the various problems and pitfalls from the practising sentencer's or the practitioner's point of view, will prove helpful. The experienced sentencer and clerk to the justices will know everything that is to be found within the covers of this book, but we feel confident that the less experienced clerk or assistant recorder or even the occasional judge will find something that he did not know. So too, practitioners may well find some useful points not discussed elsewhere. Although we have inevitably discussed Crown Court problems more than those of the magistrates' court, we nevertheless feel sure that the magistrate keen to improve his or her skills will also be able to derive some assistance from the book. The University or Polytechnic student may also find it helpful; fortunately sentencing is being studied increasingly by students of law as well as of other subjects.

In order to keep the book within reasonable bounds we have had to curtail our discussion on many points. We have attempted to strike the correct balance between covering everything on a given topic and giving a very short summary only. In each section a particular reader may well find that he would like to know more. For example, the suspended sentence has led to a large number of decisions in the Court of Appeal, but we have deliberately confined our discussion to those cases which seem to us to be the most helpful ones. Similarly, we have kept our discussion of the fine fairly brief and have not dealt with enforcement – a topic of great importance, but well known to those who matter most in that field, the clerks to the justices.

We are happy to acknowledge with thanks the assistance we derived from the critical comments of our friends who read all or part of the manuscript, namely Judge Peter Goldstone, Dr. Silvia Casale, Kerry Barker and Tony Austin. Thanks are also due to Pamela Devlin for her assistance with typing.

We would like to pay tribute to Lord Justice Lawton, who has recently retired, and whose hard work was responsible for so many of the important sentencing decisions that we have cited. More than any other judge he has been responsible for the development of the important concept of the guideline judgment of the Court of Appeal. He will be missed.

Finally, our thanks are due to Lord Elwyn-Jones for writing the foreword.

Note

We had hoped to incorporate changes brought about by the enactment of the Criminal Justice Bill in 1987. The calling of a general election led to the abandonment of most proposals in that Bill. We have cut out all references to those proposed changes, but in the circumstances have considered it unprofitable to discuss in detail certain topics, such as criminal bankruptcy, which probably have a limited life. We have tried to state the law as it stood on 11 June 1987.

Contents

Table of Cases

Prosecutions brought by the Crown are listed under the name of the defendant. Cases reported only in the *Encyclopaedia of Current Sentencing Practice* are cited as C.S.P. This is a loose-leaf publication which is regularly supplemented with fresh pages. Sometimes a case is removed when the Editor considers it to have been superseded.

Table of Statutes

Table of Statutory Instruments

CHAPTER 1

The Inherent Difficulties

1.01 Some sentencing decisions are easy. Many of those easy decisions are made in relatively minor cases when the judge or magistrates speedily come to the conclusion that, say, probation or a fine is appropriate. Other relatively easy decisions are made in more serious cases. The armed bank robber does not as a rule present much of a sentencing problem; the murderer none at all. On the other hand, many sentencing problems are very difficult to resolve, and individual judges and magistrates have differing views on the appropriate sentence to be passed in many such cases. Members of the public are also often ready to disagree with a court's decision, though they will not be agreed amongst themselves as to what the correct sentence ought to have been. Sometimes a court may be criticised at the same time for being too harsh in a given case, and for being too lenient.

1.02 The explanation for the wide range of disagreement and uncertainty in sentencing matters is not hard to find. The courts are certain of their duty to try and reduce crime and to uphold the criminal law. They are certain that they have the right to punish by imprisonment or to use alternatives in different cases, because Parliament has told them so in statutory form. What they are less certain about is how they should distinguish between the occasions which call for imprisonment and those calling for a lesser penalty. Parliament has been extremely reluctant to give guidance to the courts by means of statutes dealing specifically with the day-to-day problems faced by the criminal courts. As a rule Parliament merely states, in effect, "The maximum penalty shall be ten years for this offence: now get on with it and pass the correct sentence – correct for *this* individual before you on the unique facts of *this* case."

1.03 The government, usually in the form of the Home Office or one of its advisory bodies, has from time to time given the courts information about penal institutions, but it is properly reticent about giving direct advice to the judiciary. If the Home Office feels strongly enough about a particular sentencing point, then it can always include an appropriate amendment in its quinquennial Criminal Justice Bill, or in some other criminal law bill. If the Home Office view should prevail in

1

Parliament, a statutory provision will follow. The courts will be obliged to implement the change in the law, even if Parliament has been vague about the purpose of the amendment. On occasion the Court of Appeal has been prepared to look at more than the statutory provision itself and to consider the legislative history. For example, in *Willis*,[1] a guideline case on sentences for buggery, the court considered the report of the Wolfenden Committee on Homosexual Offences and Prostitution.

1.04 The Court of Appeal, Criminal Division, is effectively the highest court for sentencing matters in England and Wales, for the House of Lords has hardly ever been troubled by such matters. In *Courtie*[2] Lord Diplock said of appeals against sentence:

> "This is a subject-matter which seldom involves a certifiable question of law of general importance such as would qualify it for the grant of leave to appeal to the House of Lords."

In theory the decisions of the Court of Appeal should make the decision-making process of the lower courts much simpler, but in practice this is not always so. One of the explanations for this state of affairs is that the Court of Appeal, Crown Court and magistrates' courts in practice work not only at three different levels, but at three levels which interlock only on comparatively rare occasions.

1.05 Another difficulty is created by the absence of any universal agreement about the causes of crime, or about what steps should be taken once the causes are thought to have been correctly identified in a given case. Leaving aside extreme cases, such as that of the dangerous defendant whose mental illness explains all, and who must be made the subject of a hospital order, finding the causes of crime and finding a solution to the sentencing problem do not necessarily go hand in hand. The court will still be left with the difficult question of whether one of the alternatives to a custodial sentence can be used, or whether custody is called for, and if so, for what length.

1.06 In considering the various alternatives the sentencer will be influenced by his conception of the various aims and theories of punishment. He will have to decide how important the question of retribution or of deterrence is in that particular case. In resolving questions of that kind he will have precisely no help from Parliament at all, and very little from the Court of Appeal. Hearing the opinions of his

1   (1974) 60 Cr.App.R. 146.
2   (1984) 78 Cr.App.R. 292.

colleagues at sentencing conferences or at other meetings may influence him little, or not at all. This is not all that surprising, as there is no universal agreement in the community about the appropriate way to tackle sentencing problems. It is the easiest thing in the world for the motorist stuck in the Clapham traffic jam, or for the journalist in his newsroom to criticise any sentence passed by a court on that day. It is far harder for him to discuss sentencing in a rational manner or for him to make constructive suggestions. Even if the Clapham motorist or the journalist were to become a magistrate, judge or legislator, he would not find the solution of sentencing problems easy, for nobody has yet devised a simple system acceptable to all.

1.07 The plight of the sentencer is not of recent origin, even though his options have become increasingly complex; nor is the carping journalist a new phenomenon:

> "In our attempts to award pain according to desert, we are fated to err either on the side of mercy or of severity. Hence, it has been a favourite habit with editors of newspapers to compare two discrepant sentences with a chuckle of triumph over the folly of one or other of the judges on whose proceedings they are animadverting, without a thought that the judges have neither weight nor scales."

So wrote the distinguished former Recorder of Birmingham, Matthew Davenport Hill, in 1870.[3] Hill shrewdly continued:

> "When the jury has convicted the prisoner, it remains to be considered whether the offence is mitigated or aggravated by its incidents; then must be considered the circumstances of the offender. Is he young, or of mature age? Has he had the advantages of education, or has he been left to the influences of ignorance, bad example and evil associations? Has he been previously convicted so frequently as to make it clear that he has adopted crime as his calling or profession; or is his deviation from honesty an exception, and not made in pursuance of his rule of life? All these, and many other points for consideration, will rise up in the mind of a thoughtful judge, but they assuredly will not be dealt with by any two minds so as to result in precisely the same infliction. And if we take into account the modifications of opinion which society undergoes from time to time, and observe its effect on the sentences pronounced at various periods for offences of similar magnitude, we shall, I think, all come to the conclusion that standards of punishment are much more easy to imagine than to realise."

1.08 In this chapter we shall briefly discuss the difficulties referred to above, none of which have become any easier since Hill's day. Our discussion will be undertaken under four headings:

3 In E. C. Wines (ed.), *Transactions of the National Congress on Penitentiary and Reformatory Discipline* (1871) Weed, Parsons, p. 107.

(1) The contribution of the legislature and the executive;
(2) The three sentencing systems;
(3) The causes of crime; and
(4) Theories of punishment.

THE CONTRIBUTION OF THE LEGISLATURE AND THE EXECUTIVE

"We have been struck by the fact that there has been no authoritative inquiry for a long time into such fundamental problems as the objects of punishment, the suitability of the existing methods of dealing with offenders, the desirability of introducing new ones, and the procedure for determining what is the appropriate method in a particular case."

1.09 This statement was made by the Home Office Advisory Council on the Treatment of Offenders in 1957, but it is still substantially correct.[4] The Royal Commission on the Penal System started its deliberations in 1964 and might have been able to provide at any rate some of the more important answers, but its members were unable to agree about essentials and were disbanded in 1966. The fact that this was the only Royal Commission ever that was unable to produce a report says something about the inherent complexity of the problems surrounding sentencing and allied topics. Lady Wootton, one of the Commissioners, later made the revealing comment:[5]

"Sixteen people cannot reform a system if they are not agreed about what the ultimate purpose of the system is."

1.10 The respective functions of the courts and Parliament, and the doctrine of the separation of powers were referred to by Sir John Donaldson, M.R. in the Civil Division of the Court of Appeal in *British Airways Board v. Laker Airways*:[6]

"It is a matter of considerable constitutional importance that the courts should be wholly independent of the executive, and they are. Thus, whilst the judges, as private citizens, will be aware of the 'policy' of the government of the day, in the sense of its political purpose, aspirations and programme, these are not matters which are in any way relevant to the courts' decisions and are wholly ignored. In matters of home policy, the courts have regard only to the will of Parliament as expressed in the statutes, in subordinate legislation and in executive acts authorised by Parliament."

---

4 *Alternatives to Short Terms of Imprisonment* (1957) H.M.S.O., para. 62.
5 Barbara Wootton, "Official Advisory Bodies" in N. Walker and E. Giller (eds.), *Penal Policy-Making in England* (1977) Cambridge Institute of Criminology, p. 16.
6 [1984] Q.B. 142.

1.11   The necessity for the judiciary to be independent of the will not only of the executive, but also of the legislature (save when formally expressed) is not always appreciated by individual Members of Parliament. From time to time a Member will express dissatisfaction with a particular sentence, and even go so far as to demand the dismissal of the judge in question. Lord Hailsham pointed out the dangers in a letter to *The Times* (26 June 1975):

> "My main object in writing, however, is to warn against the encroachment on the independence of the judiciary implicit in some actions by some Members of Parliament and some press comment. Modern practice does not inhibit, indeed encourages, criticism of individual sentences, and this is wholly healthy. But nearly four years as Lord Chancellor leads me to believe that it is seldom profitable to discuss sentences on the basis of press reports alone without, at least, a full transcript of the proceedings. When criticisms amount to demands for the removal of a Crown Court judge by political pressure brought on a Lord Chancellor, and are founded on the supposed inadequacy of a single sentence, they begin to constitute a serious danger to judicial independence."

1.12   Much of the criticism of individual sentences comes from politicians and others who appear to be unaware of the "inevitable complexity of sentencing", as a South Australian committee called it.[7] That committee observed,

> "It is too little realized that in a modern developed community it is impossible to have a simple sentencing system. Failure to appreciate this fact explains the sterility and over-simplification of much public discussion on sentencing."

1.13   There is less excuse for politicians to be unaware of the complexity of sentencing than there is for the ordinary layman, for it is the legislators who have contributed most to that complexity. They have done so by providing numerous new penalties and sentences for the courts to use, without any clear expression of what Parliament intended when introducing them. One example is the community service order: Parliament neither stated whether it was to be used only as an alternative to imprisonment, nor where on the penal "ladder" it was to be placed. So too, Parliament has never explained in statutory form how or when the suspended sentence is to be used. Courts may gather from legislation that they are required to rule out all non-custodial alternatives before arriving at the conclusion that a defendant must be sentenced to a term of imprisonment.[8] Having taken all the logical steps required and having arrived at the conclusion that prison cannot be

---

7   *First Report of the Criminal Law and Penal Methods Reform Committee* (1973).
8   See generally Chapter 9 *infra*.

avoided (much as a car driver goes through the gears from first to fourth in sequence) the court is then on occasion obliged to find a reason for going into reverse, and to suspend the whole or part of the sentence of imprisonment. Changing gear into reverse is not very satisfactory whilst a vehicle is in forward motion, yet this is the kind of action expected by Parliament in certain unspecified circumstances.

1.14 Whilst individual Members of Parliament have not been slow to make stern criticisms of individual sentences in cases which have reached, or are likely to reach the newspapers, Parliament as a body has been remarkably reluctant when it comes to passing laws which give helpful guidance to the courts on sentencing matters. Unlike the legislatures of some other jurisdictions, Parliament has never stated, other than in a piecemeal fashion, what the objects of its criminal legislation are and has never indicated how the courts are to carry out its expressed wishes. Occasionally the legislature has given a clue about its objective in a section of a Criminal Justice Act, but as a rule it has contented itself with providing a maximum penalty only. The Powers of Criminal Courts Act 1973 provided a rare exception, but even that cannot be considered a comprehensive sentencing statute. The provision of maximum penalties alone has been of relatively little value. Apart from anything else, as mentioned by the Advisory Council on the Penal System:[9]

> "The system of maximum penalties is not the product of a rational and consistent scheme, but rather the result of piecemeal legislation over more than a century in response to many different pressures such as, for example, transient Parliamentary concern with a specific crime."

1.15 More recently Ashworth has pointed out:[10]

> "There is no constitutional rule or convention which prevents the legislature from restricting or removing judicial discretion in sentencing: the simple fact is that Parliament has taken little interest in the matter and has rarely legislated so as to impinge on the discretion of the courts to impose any sentence beneath the statutory maximum."

1.16 A maximum sentence fixed by Parliament may have little relevance in a given case, either because it was fixed at a very high level in the last century when the particular offence was much more seriously regarded than it is now, or because it has more recently been set at a high catch-all level, as with the ten-year maximum for all thefts, even

---

9 *The Length of Prison Sentences, Interim Report* (1977) H.M.S.O., para. 2.
10 A. Ashworth, "Reducing the prison population in the 1980s: the need for sentencing reforms" in *A Prison System for the 80s and Beyond* (1983) NACRO, p. 10.

the most trivial. At other times the maximum may be highly relevant and sometimes may create real difficulties. If the maximum has been set by Parliament at a low level, say two years' imprisonment, the courts often find themselves "bumping" against it, as many individual offences would seem to call for a sentence at that sort of level. This point was one of the factors leading to the maximum for indecent assault on a female over 13 being raised from two to ten years, by the Sexual Offences Act 1985. Generally, if the maximum is, say, five years' imprisonment, the courts have to be careful to confine the use of that maximum to facts which show the case to be one of the worst of its kind.[11]

1.17 A change in a maximum sentence by Parliament will sometimes be helpful. Under the Street Offences Act 1959 the maximum for living on immoral earnings was increased from two years to seven, the two year maximum having been one of the low level ones referred to above. In *Farrugia*[12] Lawton, L. J. pointed out:

> "The Court can only speculate as to why it was so increased; but one reason may have been that cases did occur where girls and women were driven on to the streets either by threats of violence or, in some cases, by the use of violence. It may have been thought by Parliament that a maximum sentence of two years was inadequate to cover cases where there was an element of coercion."

The fact that the court was obliged to speculate shows that the legislature had not made its policy or its reasons clear, but the main message was obvious.

1.18 Parliament made its views on the seriousness of drug trafficking known to the courts when it increased the maximum penalty in relation to Class A drugs from 14 years to life imprisonment, by the Controlled Drugs (Penalties) Act 1985. Similarly, the reduction of the maximum penalty for simple possession of cannabis by the Misuse of Drugs Act 1971 gave the courts Parliament's altered views about the seriousness of that offence. An affirmation of an existing maximum by Parliament can also be helpful to the courts on occasion, as in the case of unlawful sexual intercourse: see the judgment of Lawton, L.J., in *Taylor and others*.[13] Where a maximum is increased after the commission of an offence by a defendant, but before he is sentenced, his sentence should be related to the earlier maximum.[14]

---

11 *Cade* (1984) 6 Cr.App.R.(S) 28.
12 (1979) 69 Cr.App.R. 108.
13 (1977) 64 Cr.App.R. 182.
14 *R. v. Penrith JJ. ex p. Hay* (1979) 1 Cr.App.R.(S) 265.

1.19 Reference has been made to the difficulty which is sometimes created for the Crown Court by a relatively low maximum penalty. This is particularly so when credit has to be given for a plea of guilty, so that a sentence less than the low maximum set by the statute will have to be passed, leaving some members of the public dissatisfied by the inevitable apparent leniency.

1.20 There are two occasions when similar difficulties can occur: both are brought about what may be called an overriding maximum that is quite separate from the statutory maximum for the offence itself. The most frequent occasion when this occurs is when a magistrates' court is dealing with an offence which in the Crown Court would carry a maximum of, say, five years' imprisonment. Clearly, if the lower courts deal with the matter the facts must be of the kind which would not justify anything like a five year sentence. However, because of the lower court's own normal limit of six months' imprisonment for a single offence, magistrates are constantly confronted with the question of how much discount should be given on a plea of guilty.[15] Some refuse to consider granting it despite the fact that the Court of Appeal pronouncements on the subject would appear to apply to all courts.

1.21 Similar problems are caused, albeit much less frequently, by the 15 and 16-year-old candidate for youth custody, since the overall maximum for that age group is twelve months.[16] Such an offender can plead guilty to any number of serious offences and can still argue that he ought to receive a sentence of less then the maximum of twelve months merely because of his plea. In some cases the pure chance of an appropriately high maximum for the offence (14 years or more for an adult) may make possible resort to detention under the Children and Young Persons Act 1933, Section 53(2).[17]

1.22 Hogarth[18] was writing about the Canadian scene, but what he had to say about the basic difficulties of sentencing applies equally to England:

"Failure of parliament to establish a criminal policy expressed in legislative criteria for the imposition of sentence is, perhaps, one of the main reasons for inconsistency in sentencing. It is not surprising, however, that our legislators have failed to address themselves seriously to this question as there are deep divisions in society as to what social purposes sentencing should serve. In the absence of legislative criteria and in an atmosphere of

---

15 See paras. 2.15ff *infra.*
16 Criminal Justice Act 1982 s. 7(8).
17 *Pilford* (1985) 7 Cr.App.R.(S) 23; *Reynolds* [1986] Crim.L.R. 125; paras. 2.23, 10.30ff *post.*
18 J. Hogarth, *Sentencing as a Human Process* (1971) U. of Toronto P., p. 5.

controversy about sentencing, it would not be surprising if the courts were inconsistent in the application of sentencing principles. This situation makes sentencing a lonely and onerous task for the courts."

1.23 In England the legislature's relative inactivity may have contributed to the decision of the executive to provide the courts at any rate with some information about criminal justice matters. One of the spurs was undoubtedly the recommendation of the committee chaired by Streatfeild, J. that such information should be provided to sentencers.[19] Since then the courts have been provided with a booklet *The Sentence of the Court*, currently in its fourth edition, and with other reports, such as the annual report of the Parole Board. Some judges have over the years been apprehensive about the propriety of the executive communicating with them at all, but the doctrine of the separation of powers was never intended by Montesquieu, or indeed anyone else, to prevent all communication between the executive, legislative and judicial branches. Quite apart from the fact that the Lord Chancellor, Montesquieu's nightmare, is a member of all three branches of government, we are quite happy to let our most senior judges sit as members of the House of Lords. The Home Office was surely correct when stating:[20]

> "Disposals in individual cases are for the courts but it is a proper part of the government's responsibility to seek to increase both the court's and the public's awareness of the purposes and limitations of the various penal sanctions, and of the constraints within which the penal system operates."

1.24 The House of Commons Expenditure Committee stated the constitutional position accurately when it reported in 1978:[21]

> "Perhaps we should begin by observing that there is no such thing as a sentencing policy in the sense of any nationally prescribed approach or prescription for sentencing other than the legal limits to their powers and the guidance laid down by appeal court decisions. The starting point of our discussion must be recognition of the constitutional position of the judiciary as independent of the executive arm of government and the legislature. This means that it would not be appropriate for the Home Office to tell the judges what to do, even if the result of judicial activity were to threaten the breakdown of the prison system, which is very nearly what has occurred."

The Committee went on to emphasise that Parliament can by legislation limit the powers of courts or require that certain powers should be used in certain ways or for certain cases.

19 *Report of the Interdepartmental Committee on the Business of the Criminal Courts* (1961) H.M.S.O. (Cmnd 1289), para. 299.
20 *A Review of Criminal Justice Policy* (1976) H.M.S.O., p. 7.
21 *Fifteenth Report from the Expenditure Committee: The Reduction of Pressure on the Prison System* (1978) H.M.S.O., para. 37.

1.25 In the Home Office Observations on that report, the government clearly acknowledged the accuracy of the committee's summary, stating:[22]

"Sentencing policy is the concern of the courts, not something laid down or even directly influenced by the Government. Nevertheless, the Government has a duty to ensure that the courts are fully aware of current pressures on the prison services and the consequences that these could have for the effectiveness of the criminal justice system as a whole."

1.26 Such attempts as the executive has made to influence the judiciary have usually been fairly innocuous, and may be said to belong in the category of the supply of information. Occasionally they have gone a little further. Although the interpretation of statutes and the unravelling of Parliament's intention is a matter for the courts, the Home Office distributed to all judges a guide on the young offender provisions in the Criminal Justice Act 1982, which included the following points:[23]

"It must be emphasised that Parliament has provided for short detention centre sentences in order to enable the court to keep the length of sentence to a minimum in cases where custody is unavoidable on the basis of the criteria specified in the Act. It is *not* the intention of Parliament that a short sentence of detention should be imposed on a young offender for whom custody would not otherwise be appropriate."

Copies of the Interim Report on *The Length of Prison Sentences* had been similarly supplied to the judiciary in 1977. The report was that of the Home Office Advisory Council on the Penal System (which later fell victim to the executive's wave of quangocide) and it included the suggestion that the courts should make their own contribution to an improvement of the prison overcrowding problem, posing "a few simple questions":

"Are there not cases of two years' imprisonment where 18 months, or even 15 or even less, might safely be passed, and sentences of twelve months when six months would do just as well? And for the offender going to prison for the first time, should not even a shorter sentence suffice? Are not many suspended sentences longer than the sentence would have been if it had been immediate, and, in many such cases, does not the eventual activation of the suspended sentence without reduction in its length create a situation where the total sentence is too long?"

1.27 Some judges have in the past undoubtedly resented any suggestion by the executive that there was something to be said for a little more parsimony in the use of custodial sentences, and have adopted the

---

22 *The Reduction of Pressure on the Prison System: Observations* (1980) H.M.S.O. (Cmnd 7948), para. 7.
23 *Criminal Justice Act 1982: Summary of Young Offender Powers* (1983) Home Office, para. 16.

stance that it is for the courts to pass the "correct" sentence and for the Home Secretary to execute it, no matter what difficulties he might have. The attitude, "That is his problem; let him build more prisons", is perhaps not fair at a time when everyone knows that the public purse is not bottomless and has other calls on it. It is about as helpful as Marie Antoinette's solution for the problem of her hungry subjects without bread: "Let them eat cake." Lord Lane, C.J. has taken what many regard as a more realistic and reasonable approach, and has indicated that the courts must have regard to the facts of life in the penal system. In *Bibi*[24] Lord Lane echoed the Advisory Council's words, pointing out:

"Many offenders can be dealt with equally justly and effectively by a sentence of six or nine months' imprisonment as by one of 18 months or three years."

In another judgment delivered on the same day,[25] Lord Lane stated:

"But the time has come to appreciate that non-violent petty offenders should not be allowed to take up what has become valuable space in prison. If there really is no alternative, as we believe to be the case here, to an immediate prison sentence, then it should be as short as possible. Sentencing judges should appreciate that over-crowding in many of the penal establishments in this country is such that a prison sentence, however short, is a very unpleasant experience indeed for the inmates."

1.28   In the following year, when addressing the Annual Meeting of the Central Council of Probation Committees, Lord Lane made the point more strongly:[26]

"It is no good judges saying, as they sometimes do, that the fact there are not enough places in prisons is the Home Office's fault and they had better get on with it. We are all in the same boat, like it or not, and the prison service is part of the judicial system just as the judges are. It may be a leaking boat, but we are all in it and we have all got to try and make it stay on the surface and not sink. If there is anything one can do to help the prison service within the proper confines of judicial function then we ought to do it."

1.29   In making the point that the legislature has not been of much help with the resolution of sentencing problems, the writers must not be thought to be suggesting that statutory provisions could resolve them all. Unless a sentencing statute removed judicial discretion altogether – in which case one could dispense with the judges at the sentencing stage – some element of discretion, and therefore of difficulty, must always

24   (1980) 2 Cr.App.R. (S) 177.
25   *Upton* (1980) 2 Cr.App.R.(S) 132.
26   Central Council of Probation Committees transcript.

remain. A high maximum sentence, coupled with the absence of a minimum, will of course provide the greatest scope for discretion.

1.30 A recent comprehensive sentencing statute was the United States Sentencing Reform Act 1984. One of the "factors to be considered in imposing a sentence", according to Section 212, is:

"The need for the sentence imposed –
  (a) to reflect the seriousness of the offense, to promote respect for the law, and to provide just punishment for the offense;
  (b) to afford adequate deterrence to criminal conduct;
  (c) to protect the public from further crimes of the defendant; and
  (d) to provide the defendant with needed educational or vocational training, medical care, or other correctional treatment in the most effective manner."

1.31 Without any statutory requirement to consider factors of this kind, the average English sentencer is likely to consider at any rate points (a), (b) and (c) when deciding on the appropriate sentence. For all the help of Congress the American Federal judge will to some extent – despite guidelines from a Sentencing Commission – still be left with much the same problems as his English counterpart, namely, the resolution of the question of the correct measure of "just punishment", "adequate deterrence" and of the extent of the protection which is both necessary and justified in all the circumstances. As Kittrie and Zenoff, two American law professors, have pointed out:[27]

"One avenue to reducing judicial power is for legislatures to specify the principal objectives of sentencing. However, this approach is not likely to reduce either discretion or disparity as long as judges remain free to select between several potentially conflicting objectives."

1.32 The truth is that neither the judiciary, nor the legislature, nor the executive can on their own resolve the various conflicting interests, objectives and ideas which raise their heads during the sentencing stage. Communication between the three branches of government can at any rate help with a reduction of some of the problems. It is essential that discussions take place between all interested parties if the proper balance is to be achieved, somewhere between unlimited judicial discretion at one end of the sentencing range, and a statutory strait-jacket at the other. In future we should all aim at finding solutions which avert the kind of disagreement between Parliament and the courts which followed on the passing of one of the first legislative attempts to restrict the use of imprisonment for young offenders by the Criminal Justice Act

27 N.N. Kittrie and E.H. Zenoff, *Sanctions, Sentencing and Corrections* (1981) Foundation Press, p. 56.

1961, Section 3(1). Many judges resented being prohibited from passing sentences of imprisonment between six months and three years (or sometimes 18 months) on such offenders. We should also be on guard against making alterations to the law which only make things worse. California's latest attempt to improve sentencing law veered towards the straitjacket end of the range, leading Norval Morris to recall the comment: "Reform, Sir, Reform. Don't talk to me of Reform. Things are bad enough as they are."[28]

THE THREE SENTENCING SYSTEMS

1.33 One of the facts that has to be faced is that there are in effect three sentencing systems in England and Wales. The magistrates' courts, mainly made up of laymen, make some 96 per cent of all the sentencing decisions every year. Although the suggestion has sometimes been made that consideration should be given to depriving them of their power to impose custodial sentences, as for example by Lord Scarman,[29] magistrates in practice impose many such sentences. In exercising their sentencing powers the magistrates are largely on their own, with little guidance from their legally qualified clerks except on essential points of law and practice.[30] The Justices' Clerks' Society in 1980 complained about "the emasculated role in sentencing of the magistrates' principal adviser, their clerk." The Society continued:[31]

"How else, except through their clerk, can the magistrates hear and be continually reminded of the statutory restrictions on their sentencing powers, the advice of the judges *ex cathedra* and the views of the Secretary of State? And yet, while the probation officer is encouraged to offer opinions on sentence, the clerk is effectively prevented from doing so."

1.34 In the circumstances it is not surprising that whilst magistrates achieve some degree of consistency within individual benches or counties, they do not manage to keep sentences in line with those of more distant colleagues.[32]

1.35 Appeals against sentence from magistrates' courts to the Crown Court are few in number, and it is virtually impossible for the magistrates, whose decision has been varied, to learn much about sentencing

---

28 N. Morris, *Madness and the Criminal Law* (1982) U. of Chicago P., p. 146. See also Judge R. Puglia, "Determinate Sentencing in California" in *The Future of Sentencing* (1982) U. of Cambridge Institute of Criminology.
29 L. Scarman, *Control of Sentencing* (1974) Howard League.
30 Practice Direction [1981] 2 All E.R. 831.
31 *Sentencing in the 1980s* (1980) Justices' Clerks' Society, para. 76.
32 R. Tarling, *Sentencing Practice in Magistrates' Courts* (1979) H.M.S.O., H.O.R.S. No. 56. For guidelines for magistrates, see para. 1.43 *post.*

principles from the short report (at best) that they may receive from the Crown Court about the appeal. They do not even receive a transcript of the presiding judge's short remarks on allowing an appeal – partly because the shorthand writer withdraws from the court when appeals are heard. A further learning difficulty is created by virtue of the fact that the case on appeal may be quite different from that in the court below, the Crown Court being entitled to hear fresh evidence in mitigation, whether or not such evidence was available on the first hearing. Magistrates do however have the advantage of being able to sit as judges of the Crown Court when appeals are heard, so that they may learn a little about the principles of sentencing there directly on such occasions, as well as on the other occasions when they sit there with a professional judge. It is only right to add that an experienced magistrate can contribute quite as much on occasion as his professional colleague.

1.36 One strange feature of the Crown Court as an appellate court is its wide power to increase a sentence on appeal;[33] it is strange, since such a power was taken away from the Court of Criminal Appeal by Parliament. There is no direct link between the Court of Appeal and the magistrates' courts, so there are relatively few occasions when that court is able to give guidance of use to the magistrates. It is most unusual for the court to have the opportunity to consider careless driving sentences, as happened in *Krawec*,[34] or small fines for shoplifting, as occurred in *Charalambous*.[35] The Divisional Court of the Queen's Bench Division has for years guided the magistrates on vital points of law, such as what is meant by indecent exposure of the "person", and whether a police officer has to wear a uniform cap or helmet when challenging a drunken motorist. However that court has rarely considered sentencing matters. Sentencing appeals as such go from the magistrates' court only to the Crown Court, but since the decision in *R. v. St. Albans Crown Court, ex parte Cinnamond*[36] it is clear that the Divisional Court will in exceptional circumstances also intervene in sentencing matters which started before the magistrates and were then appealed to the Crown Court.[37]

1.37 The circuit judges in the Crown Court between them exercise the most important sentencing function of all: the sentencing of the bulk of the defendants convicted of the more serious offences resulting in custodial disposals. Recorders and assistant recorders play their part

---

33 Supreme Court Act 1981 s. 48(4); *Dutta v. Westcott* [1986] 3 All E.R. 381.
34 (1984) 6 Cr.App.R.(S) 367.
35 (1984) 6 Cr.App.R.(S) 389.
36 [1981] Q.B. 480.
37 See N. Wasik, "Sentencing and the Divisional Court" [1984] Crim.L.R. 272; see also R. Henham, "The Influence of Sentencing Principles on Magistrates' Sentencing Practices" (1986) *Howard Journal* 25 p. 190.

also, having the same powers when sitting. Increasingly the High Court judges hear criminal cases in the Court of Appeal rather than at first instance. The High Court judges come to the Crown Court to hear only the most serious cases, such as murder, manslaughter and rape, and even some of those are now heard by nominated circuit judges. The circuit judges may be influenced by the magistrates who sit with them in the Crown Court, but they rarely see the High Court judge and, of course, never sit with him. The High Court judge, except when sitting as a member of the Court of Appeal, Criminal Division, will have a relatively easy sentencing task, as there is a mandatory sentence for murder, and as the other most serious crimes rarely present any great sentencing problem.

1.38 In theory, as we have a hierarchical system of courts, one need only look at the sentencing decisions of the Court of Appeal to discover what the inferior courts are likely to be deciding. Unfortunately the matter is not so simple, and this is only partly because the doctrine of precedent in the strict sense does not apply. The Court of Appeal, Criminal Division, presided over by the Lord Chief Justice, comprises distinguished Lords Justices and Justices of the High Court. As we have mentioned, none of them will as a rule any longer be trying the run-of-the-mill burglar or assaulter in the Crown Court. The appeals they will be hearing will largely tend to be those in which the sentence of the Crown Court was unusually high, for defendants do not appeal lightly and do not automatically get leave to appeal. The Court of Appeal will often reduce a sentence by a third or more, but the end result may still be higher than the usual sentence being passed routinely by a majority of circuit judges and recorders for that particular type of offence. One of the dangers is that the Court of Appeal may in such cases give a confusing impression to the bulk of sentencers – and especially to newly appointed ones – about the sort of sentence that is being passed by the majority of courts. It may be that the Court of Appeal considers a majority of sentences to be on the low side – but that is not likely, except in certain specific cases, such as rape.[38] As Hall Williams has pointed out:[39]

> "The decisions in the Court of Appeal concern only the extreme cases which are taken on appeal, and to judge current sentencing policy from such appeal decisions may be seriously misleading."

It is right that the sentencer should extract as much guidance as he can from Court of Appeal decisions, but as the court itself has been at pains

---

38 *Billam* (1986) 8 Cr.App.R.(S) 480
39 J.E. Hall Williams, "The contribution of the judiciary" in N. Walker and H. Giller (eds.) *op. cit.* (note 5 *supra*).

to point out more than once, even guideline decisions of that court are only to be used as guidelines, and not as holy writ.[40]

1.39 An additional problem for Crown Court judges is that the reported decisions of the Court of Appeal are not always consistent with one another. This is hardly surprising, in view of the complexity of sentencing problems and the fact that the Court of Appeal is forced by pressure of work to sit in many divisions, and with little time for the luxury of reserved judgments. As a result it is correct to say that disparity is not confined to the trial courts. The problem was foreseen by Lord Donovan's committee when it recommended the setting up of the Court of Appeal, Criminal Division.[41]

> "The opportunities for all those who may from time to time sit in the Court to get together and formulate consistent policies, for the lack of which separate divisions of the Court may go different ways, are few; for the pressure of work is heavy. On the same topic therefore different divisions of the Court may speak with different voices; and in the important matter of sentences, proceed on different lines."

The fact that the problem was foreseen (and illustrated with references to inconsistent decisions in the Court of Criminal Appeal) has not led to its being cured, although to minimise the problem short notes of recent appeals are now circulated to members of the Court of Appeal, and later published as the Criminal Appeal Office Index, in the form of a supplement to *Archbold*. One of the handicaps has been the massive upsurge in the amount of work; another has been the increase in the number of alternative sentences available, so that the courts are rapidly approaching saturation stage. As an editorial note in the *Criminal Law Review* pointed out:[42]

> "There may well be a point at which the proliferation of alternative sentences becomes so great that it is virtually impossible for a Crown Court judge or a bench of magistrates to choose rationally among the measures."

1.40 Thomas has most forcefully made the point about the Court of Appeal's inconsistent decisions:[43]

> "The difficulty is that the general body of the Court's decisions have become more erratic, more unpredictable and more inconsistent than they

---

40 See for example *Nicholas* (1986) *The Times* 23 April.
41 *Report of the Interdepartmental Committee on the Court of Criminal Appeal* (1965) H.M.S.O. (Cmnd 2755), para. 64.
42 [1984] Crim.L.R. 517.
43 D. Thomas, "Sentencing discretion and appellate review" in J. Shapland (ed.), *Decision-Making in the Legal System* (1983) British Psychological Society, p. 61; see also A. Ashworth, *Sentencing and Penal Policy* (1983) Weidenfeld & Nicolson, p. 41.

were throughout the 1960s and up to the mid to late 1970s, so that decisions which are carefully thought out in terms of principle are likely to be swamped by other decisions in which no principle is apparent, or a contradictory principle is adopted."

Thomas illustrated his criticism by referring, *inter alia*, to a number of appeals in which the sentence was reduced, even though the sentence had been correct at the time it was passed. The appeals had been allowed on the basis of subsequent events. He complained, "This is not the reasoning of an appellate court – it is the reasoning of a parole board", and added that such an approach was unfair to the defendants who had not appealed, but who might equally have been able to bring up post-sentence factors.

1.41 In giving weight to matters which have occured since the sentence was imposed by the Crown Court, the Court of Appeal is narrowing the gap between the two types of appeal: that from the magistrates to the Crown Court and that up to the Court of Appeal from the Crown Court. The appeal in the Crown Court is by way of a rehearing, so that it is perfectly proper for the appellate court to hear of factors arising since the magistrates passed sentence. Theoretically the appeal in the Court of Appeal is not a rehearing, although it should be added that the court, and its predecessor, has often on a compassionate basis been prepared to listen to people like Merfyn Turner,[44] when they have offered to give a place in a hostel to a particular appellant. Compassion in the Court of Appeal is no bad thing, but it can cause grievances on the part of other defendants. Also, decisions based on such considerations do not provide very helpful guidance to the lower courts, eagerly awaiting enlightenment by the Court of Appeal. There can be little doubt that the most helpful decisions for the Crown Court sentencers have been those in the various guidelines cases.

1.42 The guideline decisions have to date been of two kinds. The first has contained general guidance, for example, on the desirability of lower sentences, as in *Bibi*,[45] or on the proper use of deferment of sentence, as in *George*,[46] or of the partly suspended sentence, as in *Clarke*.[47] The second kind has set out the court's specific views about the proper range of sentence for a particular offence or type of offence.

---

44   Founder of the Norman House hostels and author of *Safe Lodging: The Road to Norman House* (1961) Hutchinson.
45   (1980) 2 Cr.App.R.(S) 177.
46   (1984) 79 Cr.App.R. 26.
47   (1982) 4 Cr.App.R.(S) 197.

Among these have been cases on rape,[48] robbery,[49] theft,[50] dangerous drug dealing,[51] unlawful sexual intercourse,[52] and death by reckless driving.[53] In view of what has been said about the Court of Appeal sometimes reducing a sentence to a point which is still above the norm in the Crown Court, it is perhaps desirable that in preparing guideline judgments the court should look not only at its own previous decisions, but also at what is happening throughout the country in the Crown Court, and also, where relevant, in the magistrates' courts.[54] If such research is too much to ask of the busy members of the Court of Appeal – and it probably is – then perhaps we ought to consider Thomas's suggestion that they be given some assistance.[55] At the moment even the Lord Chief Justice has no professional assistance with his heavy burdens.

1.43 If the guideline case practice were to be expanded and the exchange of ideas were to be encouraged to a far greater extent, then we might possibly achieve something approaching a unified sentencing system, in place of the tripartite one we have at present.[56] Fortunately, the Lord Chancellor has announced that in future the Judicial Studies Board will issue guidelines on sentencing to magistrates' courts. That should help.

THE CAUSES OF CRIME

1.44 The authors will not attempt to give an account of the massive amount of research that has been done on the causes of crime, partly because they agree with the conclusion of Morris and Hawkins:[57]

> "The search for *the causes* of crime is illusory, though recommended in some otherwise respectable criminological texts and pursued by many expensively outfitted criminological safaris."

48 *Roberts and Roberts* (1982) 4 Cr.App.R.(S) 8; *Billam* (1986) 8 Cr.App.R.(S) 48.
49 *Turner* (1975) 61 Cr.App.R. 67.
50 *Barrick* (1985) 81 Cr.App.R. 78.
51 *Aramah* (1982) 4 Cr.App.R.(S) 407.
52 *Taylor and others* (1977) 64 Cr.App.R. 182.
53 *Boswell* (1984) 79 Cr.App.R. 277.
54 See *McCann* (1980) 2 Cr.App.R.(S) 189 and Thomas's note thereon in [1980] Crim.L.R. 735. In *Billam* (*supra*) the court did look at the statistics.
55 *Op. cit.* (note 43 *supra*).
56 See also A. Ashworth, "Techniques of Guidance on Sentencing" [1984] Crim.L.R. 519.
57 N. Morris and G. Hawkins, *The Honest Politician's Guide to Crime Control* (1969) U. of Chicago P. p. 46.

Lord Scarman has made similar comments:[58]

"One of the most baffling features of the deep and wide-ranging research into the causes and cures of criminal behaviour that is the mark of modern penology has been its sterility. We know nothing fundamental of the causes of crime save that, given certain environmental circumstances, instincts such as acquisitiveness, display, aggression, and sexual passion, all of which have contributed to the dominance of the human species in the animal kingdom, stimulate conduct which society in self-defence condemns as criminal and treats accordingly; and nothing of the cure, save that imprisonment, which relieves us for a time of the distressing presence in our midst of offenders whom we fear, does little or nothing to reduce the volume of crime."

1.45 Despite these fundamental difficulties, the causes of crime are regularly discussed at the sentencing stage. The mitigation stage affords the defence an opportunity to put forward a number of possible causative factors to lessen the culpability of the defendant. The degree of weight to be attached to any given factor will depend on all the circumstances, including the sentencer's own individual response to each item of fact. A point which may carry considerable weight in the juvenile court may be of no assistance at all to the defendant when it is raised on his behalf in the Crown Court ten years later. The fact that the defendant was abandoned by his father when he was aged ten may have been one of the contributing causes of his subsequent delinquency, and on an appearance in the juvenile court it may well be considered a highly material mitigating factor. The same will not be true if he repeatedly appears in court, even though the original factor will not have disappeared.

1.46 The relevance of age to the court's consideration of causative factors has been seen by some to be of paramount importance. James, L.J. favoured the idea of exempting some young first offenders from the criminal process altogether, provided the cause of his offence could be "diagnosed" – a term disliked by many, as it suggests that crime is like an illness which may be diagnosed, treated and cured. The learned Lord Justice said:[59]

"This person offends because something has gone wrong. What it is may not be known to or understood by the person himself. It certainly will not be known to the court unless there has been a full investigation of the offender. My thinking is that, if the cause of offending for the first time

---

58 *Op. cit.* (note 29 *supra*).
59 A. James, *A New Approach to the Criminal Process*, The Riddell Lecture (1974) Institute of Legal Executives, p. 9; see also M. Zander, *Diversion from Criminal Justice in an English Context*, Report of a NACRO Working Party (1975) Barry Rose.

can be diagnosed, and that cause can be corrected by measures outside the criminal process, it is better to take such measures than to stamp the person with the imprint of a conviction."

The various police schemes for cautioning unsophisticated young and other offenders are, of course, based on a similar philosophy, as are the guidelines contained in the Code for Crown Prosecutors.[60]

1.47 The nature of the offence also has a bearing on the kinds of information, adduced by the defence or requested by the court, which is relevant to causative factors. Whatever the age of the defendant, offences such as those of a bizarre sexual nature or serious arson may lead to a psychiatric investigation. The probation officer or other social worker will probably include some discussion of the causes of the offence in question in a social inquiry report, whether or not the offender is young, and whatever the nature of the offence.[61]

1.48 After making the point that many theorists had placed undue emphasis on one particular event or factor, Professor Donald West added,[62]

"Our study, because it encompassed a wide range of items, was able to show that delinquency most often arises from an accumulation of different pressures rather than from any single salient cause."

The study to which West referred was the twenty-year project of a team from the Cambridge University Institute of Criminology, led by him, which followed up a cohort of London youngsters. The conclusion reached by West and his colleagues was that there were five main factors which had "a significant association with likelihood of delinquency". These were low family income, large family, parents with an unsatisfactory record as such, below-average intelligence, and having a parent with a criminal record. As could readily be guessed, many a young delinquent had the disadvantage of more than one factor applying in his case.

1.49 If a defendant with all or some of those five handicaps appears in court it is possible that not one of them will be mentioned by way of mitigation. Even the social inquiry report may not mention all the factors. Both the mitigating lawyer and the probation officer will be

---

60 (1986) H.M.S.O. New Guidelines on Cautioning were issued by the Home Office in February 1985 with H.O. Circular 14/1985.
61 For social inquiry and other reports see paras. 4.12ff *infra*.
62 D. West, *Delinquency: Its Roots, Careers and Prospects* (1972) Heinemann, p. 3; see also M. Rutter and H. Giller, *Juvenile Delinquency: Trends and Perspectives* (1983) Penguin.

likely to direct the court's attention to more immediate causes, or precipitating events, as West called them. The court may be told that the offence was committed because the defendant's girl-friend had left him because he got drunk and unpleasant after losing his job as a result of an argument with his foreman, which might not have occurred if he had not been unduly sensitive because he was illegitimate . . .. All these matters may be true. The difficulty for the court will be to allocate the appropriate weight to them, as we shall see when discussing the mitigation and decision stages.[63]

THEORIES OF PUNISHMENT

1.50 Over the years many different theories have been put forward to justify punishment or to explain the various aims of the courts when inflicting punishment. Apart from the fact that there has been much disagreement about the various components – often listed as retribution, deterrence (both specific and general), reformation, incapacitation and reparation – there has also been a lack of agreement about the relationship of one aim to any other. The Advisory Council on the Penal System pointed out in 1978:[64]

"Whether retribution, deterrence, prevention or rehabilitation (or any single one or more of them in combination) govern sentencing policy and practice is the subject of consistent controversy and debate. Attitudes change over the years."

1.51 Whilst questions relating to the aims of punishment have been discussed at length in academic circles and books, those questions must not be regarded as merely academic. They are important because different judges resolve them in different ways, thus contributing to the problem of disparity. As Hood and Sparks stated:[65]

"The information the judge regards as *relevant* will depend on which categories he uses. For example, the judge who is concerned with the inherent wickedness of the case may pay particular attention to public opinion, one who is concerned with its potential danger will look at the prevalence of the offence, and so on. The same is true for categorising the offender. The categories the judge will use will depend upon his general aims of punishment. Those aiming at retribution will be most concerned

---

63 See Chapters 5 and 6 *infra*. For a review of the main theories see A.K. Bottomley, *Criminology in Focus* (1979) Martin Robertson, Ch. 2, "The Search for Causes".
64 *Sentences of Imprisonment: A Review of Maximum Penalties* (1978) H.M.S.O., para. 73.
65 R. Hood and R. Sparks, *Key Issues in Criminology* (1970) Weidenfeld & Nicholson, p. 158.

with information about the offence; those who wish to rehabilitate will look mainly at the offender. But the retributionist is most likely to be concerned with categories such as degree of harm done, and inherent wickedness, whereas the judge aiming at generally deterring others from the offence will categorise seriousness by its potential danger. Thus views on the aims of punishment will control what information is thought relevant to the sentence."

Sentencing conferences may help to even out some disparities in sentencing, but they are unlikely to be able to change a judge's basic views about the aims of punishment, especially having regard to the fact that both the legislature and the Court of Appeal have been reluctant to say much on this difficult topic.

1.52 Even when a judge enunciates the principles applied by him, there is sometimes doubt about the respective proportions attributed to each heading. Lord Parker, C.J. sentenced the spy Blake in 1961 to three maximum terms of 14 years, each to run consecutively, for offences under the Official Secrets Act 1911. In dismissing Blake's appeal[66] Hilbery, J. said:

"The sentence had a threefold purpose. It was intended to be punitive, it was designed and calculated to deter others and it was meant to be a safeguard to this country."

Nobody would doubt that the sentence was punitive or retributive. It was also deterrent in that some state servants tempted to give away secrets of an important nature might well be restrained by the thought of a 42-year sentence. What is not clear is how much of the 42-year period was allocated to this aspect of the case. One might be forgiven for thinking that a mere 21-year sentence would deter all but the completely undeterrable, such as a dedicated enemy of the state prepared for martyrdom for his cause. So, too, it is not clear how much of the sentence was attributable to preventing Blake from giving useful information to an enemy. It is unlikely that after ten years in custody he would be able to reveal anything of value – a fact which may have occurred to those who helped him to escape before then. Professor Sprott commented on Blake's case and added,[67]

"One suspects that heavy sentences are imposed on retributive grounds and excused as deterrents."

Perhaps another way to look at the sentence on Blake is to say that the court considered the sentence justified on retributive grounds alone, but

66 (1961) 45 Cr.App.R. 292.
67 W.J.H. Sprott, "Sentencing Policy" in P. Halmos (ed.), *Sociological Studies in the British Penal Services* (1965) U. of Keele, p. 38.

that at the same time the aims of deterrence of others, if not of the defendant, and of safeguarding security were met. There was no attempt by anyone to apportion the various aims, and no need to do so.

1.53 One should add that even if two judges pass the same sentence on two defendants with similar facts in their cases and similar antecedents, it does not at all follow that both judges used the same route to arrive at their identical conclusions. As Sheriff Nicholson has pointed out:[68]

> "Equally, there are probably occasions when a false parity is achieved, that is to say when different judges make the same sentencing decision, but with quite different objectives in mind."

This phenomenon is also doubtless present at times when three lay magistrates agree on a sentence, but do so by using three different approaches.

We must now briefly consider each of the theories in turn.

Retribution

1.54 Retribution is the aim of punishment which has engendered the most heat and disagreement. In 1953 the Royal Commission on Capital Punishment pointed out one of the difficulties:[69]

> "Discussion of the principle of retribution is apt to be confused because the word is not always used in the same sense. Sometimes it is intended to mean vengeance, sometimes reprobation. In the first sense the idea is that of satisfaction by the State of a wronged individual's desire to be avenged; in the second it is that of the State's marking its disapproval of the breaking of its laws by a punishment proportionate to the gravity of the offence. Modern penological thought discounts retribution in the sense of vengeance."

1.55 There have been a number of critics of the theory of retribution. As long ago as 1937 Sir Leo Page stated:[70]

> "In my own opinion, the retributive theory of punishment is, in the state to which society has advanced today, no longer defensible."

In 1974 MacKenna, J. advocated the lowering of some sentences, adding:[71]

---

68 C.G.B. Nicholson, *The Law and Practice of Sentencing in Scotland* (1981) W. Green & Son, p. 201.
69 *Royal Commission on Capital Punishment: Report* (1953) H.M.S.O. (Cmnd 8932), para. 52.
70 L. Page, *Crime and the Community* (1937) Faber, p. 72.
71 B. MacKenna, "General Deterrence" in L. Blom-Cooper (ed.), *Progress in Penal Reform* (1974) Oxford U.P., p. 194.

"One obstacle is the belief, which dies hard, that the sentencer should have the retributive aim of punishing the offender, whatever may be the effects of the punishment. How is such a man to be persuaded to pass a lower sentence in the hope that that may be sufficient to deter, if he believes it is a good thing in itself to punish the offender and has an intuition that a heavier sentence is needed for this purpose? Perhaps our penal code, when it comes, will define the aims of criminal punishment and will exclude retribution once and for all."

1.56 The Advisory Council in 1978 (in the paragraph already cited at para. 1.50 *supra*) possibly put retribution into the proper context when drawing attention to the distinction between the old-fashioned retributive idea very close to collective vengeance, and the more modern view that it is appropriate and legitimate for the courts to punish in order to denounce certain conduct, thus educating the public as to what will and will not be tolerated. The Council stated:

"Retribution is now also questioned as a valid function of the sentencing process but may still retain its role under other guises, such as denunciation."

However, some would argue that denunciation is quite separate, and not disguised retribution.

1.57 Perhaps that most modern form of the retributive theory has been expressed by Norval Morris in his discussion of possible criteria for justifying a sentence of imprisonment:[72]

"The third criterion – that any punishment other than imprisonment would depreciate the seriousness of the defendant's crime (sometimes expressed, that imprisonment is necessary to deprecate the crime) – has received universal acceptance, and, currently at least, provides an unavoidable justification for imprisonment. It reflects the obverse of the argument of the maximum deserved punishment as a ceiling to punishment . . . . The criminal law has general behavioral standard-setting functions; it acts as a moral teacher; and consequently, requires a retributive floor to punishment as well as a retributive ceiling."

There is one other modern view of retribution, although it may be said that it is essentially a restatement of a part of the traditional approach. It is the just deserts approach, which is very close to the line taken by Morris. It will be considered further when we discuss rehabilitation and its decline as a principal objective of the sentencer.

1.58 In *Sargeant*,[73] a case concerning an offence of violence, Lawton, L.J., stated what he considered to be the modern version of retribution.

---

72 N. Morris, *The Future of Imprisonment* (1974) U. of Chicago P., p. 78.
73 (1974) 60 Cr.App.R. 74.

After pointing out that the old idea of an eye for an eye no longer played a part in the criminal law, he went on to say that another aspect of retribution was still relevant:

> "Society, through the courts, must show its abhorrence of particular types of crime, and the only way in which the courts can show this is by the sentences they pass. The courts do not have to reflect public opinion. On the other hand they must not disregard it. Perhaps the main duty of the court is to lead public opinion. Anyone who surveys the criminal scene at the present time must be alive to the appalling problem of violence. Society, we are satisfied, expects the courts to deal with violence . . .. Those who indulge in the kind of violence with which we are concerned in this case must expect custodial sentences."

1.59 Few would disagree with the principal sentiments expressed by the learned Lord Justice, but one or two points may perhaps be made about the passage quoted. The source of the right of the courts to lead public opinion is not easy to find. It is perhaps easier to accept the proposition that the courts have a right to state matters which have become apparent to them, for example, the fact that cases of senseless violence have been increasing. Public opinion can then be based on a number of factors, of which the experience of the courts would be but one. Another might well be the official statistics relating to such offences, so that the public might see whether the courts' statements were justified or, at the very least, might be able to place them in the proper context. Nigel Walker and Catherine Marsh made the comment,[74]

> "The belief of some judges that in sentencing 'the main duty of the courts is to lead public opinion' implies that the choice of sentence influences public approval or disapproval of law-breaking."

In order to test that belief they arranged for 1055 parents in three English towns to be questioned. The research showed fairly conclusively that the courts do not have much noticeable effect on the public's view of the gravity or otherwise of a particular offence. By and large people make up their own minds about the seriousness of an offence and the appropriate penalty. Walker and Marsh concluded:

> "The denunciatory theory has the attraction of appearing to justify a tough sentencing policy in a way which is independent of 'just deserts' or a belief in general deterrence, but the empirical facts make it most unlikely that the theory is realistic."

---

74 N. Walker and C. Marsh, "Do Sentences Affect Public Disapproval?" (1984) *British J. of Criminology 24* p. 27.

1.60 Lawton, L.J. in *Sargeant*[75] clearly considered that in certain circumstances there could be a low limit to the degree of toughness required. (The appeal in that case was against a two-year sentence.) He said:

> "But we are also satisfied that, although society expects the courts to impose punishment for violence which really hurts, it does not expect the courts to go on hurting for a long time, which is what this sentence is likely to do. We agree with the trial judge that the kind of violence which occurred in this case called for a custodial sentence. This young man has had a custodial sentence. Despite his good character, despite the excellent background from which he comes, very deservedly he has had the humiliation of hearing prison gates closing behind him. We take the view that for men of good character the very fact that prison gates have closed is the main punishment. It does not necessarily follow that they should remain closed for a long time."

The court reduced the sentence to one that permitted the immediate release of the defendant. Since that decision there have been a number of appeals in which "the clang of the prison gates" has been referred to in connection with a short sentence. It should be added that even before the Court of Appeal began to use this particular expression, or similar ones, courts up and down the country had for years been passing very short sentences in cases where it was felt that all that was necessary to mark the disapproval of society was a custodial sentence, which could be short.

1.61 In the same year that Sargeant's case was reported (1974), two judges made extra-judicial pronouncements which also showed an awareness of the fact that sentences of imprisonment might perhaps be made shorter than had been traditional in certain quarters — or avoided altogether. Lord Scarman stated:[76]

> "Certain conclusions can be drawn:
> (1) that no offender should be imprisoned, or subjected to custodial treatment, unless it can be shown to be essential in the interests of society,
> (2) that sentences of imprisonment should be as short as is consistent with the service of those interests of society that can be met only by the loss of his liberty."

MacKenna, J. went rather further:[77]

> "Do these exceptionally heavy sentences serve any useful purpose? A number of them have been passed from time to time. If they had been effective, our books should be full of instances of their being followed by a reduction in crime, even if only a temporary one. But there are very few

75 Note 73 *supra*.
76 *Op. cit.* (note 29 *supra*).
77 *Op. cit.* (note 71 *supra*) at p. 188 and footnote 12.

such instances. The Liverpool garrotters and the Notting Hill rioters do service suspiciously often to justify the heavy sentencer, and even these instances have been questioned. May there not be reason to suspect (as I do) that even the range of our normal sentences is unnecessarily high? Have we not experimented often enough by increasing our sentence? May there not be a case (as I believe there is) for experimenting in the other direction, moderately lowering the high level of punishment for serious crime?"

1.62 Leaving aside all questions of retribution, a long sentence may be justified in exceptional circumstances as a measure designed to protect the public by incapacitating the defendant. This separate aim of punishment will be considered in paras. 1.76ff below.

1.63 A case in 1981[78] demonstrated how the Court of Appeal, whilst reaffirming the denunicatory element in a sentence, was prepared by then to scale down the amount of imprisonment required to make the point. Some years earlier, in *Llewellyn-Jones*[79] a deputy County Court Registrar had been sentenced by Widgery, J. to four years' imprisonment for fraudulent conversion of money in court. On appeal it was argued that registrars did not require to be deterred. The Court of Appeal agreed, but added some remarks about retribution:

> "The Court is quite satisfied that this is not a deterrent sentence. It is a sentence which is fully merited, in the opinion of the Court, as punishment for very grave offences, and as expressing the revulsion of the public to the whole circumstances of the case."

It is interesting to compare that decision with that in *Jacob*. Jacob was also a solicitor who had been sentenced to four years' imprisonment: he had stolen over £40,000 from his clients and partners. Yet the Court of Appeal reduced the sentence to 18 months, O'Connor, L.J. observing that the climate was "very different from what it was several years ago". He added:

> "More and more the court now asks itself what is the least sentence that can properly be passed to mark the nature of the offence and public disapprobation of the conduct."

The principle of denunciation was applied as before, but the tariff had apparently been scaled down in the years following on *Llewellyn-Jones*.[80] The scaling-down of the tariff may also be assisted by the

---

78 *Jacob* (1981) 3 Cr.App.R.(S) 298.
79 (1966) 51 Cr.App.R. 204.
80 See also *Black* [1984] Crim.L.R. 694 and *Barrick* (1985) 81 Cr.App.R. 78, a guideline case in which Lord Lane, C.J. thought that two to three years' imprisonment would be appropriate for sums between £10,000 and £50,000. In making comparisons one should also try to make allowances for inflation.

introduction and use of a new non-custodial power, for example, by the community service order being used in cases of non-residential burglary.[81]

1.64 Perhaps in future the courts may take the comments of Professor Walker and his colleague to heart, and may realise that leading public opinion is not a role which is appropriate for them. "On the other hand," as Lawton, L.J. said in *Sargeant*, "they must not disregard it." The great difficulty is to ascertain what public opinion actually is about a given offence. As Stockdale put it:[82]

> "One of the major problems is that it is extremely difficult for the mere sentencer — never mind the social scientist — to ascertain what public opinion is. It is not difficult for the sentencer to gather that the public is basically against bank robbery and rape. It is not so easy to discover what the public at large, or even a majority of the public, feels is an appropriate sentence for a baby-snatcher. If the judge imprisons the disturbed female offender, he is liable to be called heartless and unnecessarily harsh by some. If he does not imprison her, he may well be attacked by others for 'putting all our babies at risk'."

1.65 The courts might perhaps also be well advised to note the Home Office research finding that the public is not so punitive as many people had assumed. The British Crime Survey stated:[83]

> "Criminal justice policy might also take account of the fact people are less punitive towards law-breakers than is usually imagined. Asked how 'their' offender should be treated, victims showed awareness of, and support for, court sentences involving community service and compensation, and frequently favoured informal warnings and reparation."

A later report came to similar conclusions, and added:[84]

> "These findings conflict with the widespread belief that the public are impatient with the leniency of the legal system."

It is only right to add that some commercial polls have found the public to be more punitive than the Home Office research; see, e.g. *The Times*, 31 July 1986.

---

81 *Lawrence* (1982) 4 Cr.App.R.(S) 69.
82 E. Stockdale, "The Courts as Sentencers" in H. Jones (ed.), *Society Against Crime* (1981) Penguin, p. 115. We are not suggesting that members of the public are agreed about the appropriate length of sentences for bank robbery or rape.
83 M. Hough and P. Mayhew, *British Crime Survey* (1983) H.M.S.O., H.O.R.S. No. 76, p. 36.
84 M. Hough and P. Mayhew, *Taking Account of Crime* (1985) H.M.S.O., H.O.R.S. No. 85, p. 50; see also the editorial note at [1983] Crim.L.R. 761, and M. Hough and H. Lewis, "Penal hawks and penal doves: attitudes to punishment in the British Crime Survey", Home Office Research and Planning Unit *Research Bulletin* (1986) No. 21, p. 5.

Deterrence

1.66 In *Sargeant*[85] Lawton, L.J. also pointed out that there were two aspects of deterrence: that relating to the defendant himself, and that relating to anyone else who might be tempted to commit an offence. (For a sentence aimed at schoolboys at large to deter them from setting fire to their schools, see *Storey and others*).[86] Lawton, L.J. continued:

> "Experience has shown over the years that deterrence of the offender is not a very useful approach, because those who have their wits about them usually find the closing of prison gates an experience which they do not want again. If they do not learn that lesson, there is likely to be a high degree of recidivism anyway. So far as deterrence of others is concerned, it is the experience of the courts that deterrent sentences are of little value in respect of offences which are committed on the spur of the moment, either in hot blood or in drink or both. Deterrent sentences may very well be of considerable value where crime is premeditated."

1.67 Similarly, the Advisory Council on the Penal System stated in 1978:[87]

> "While most commentators admit the role of deterrence in some disposals, such as the fine, criminological research has raised questions about the general effectiveness of deterrent sentencing and, in particular, the existence of any greater deterrent effect in longer sentences."

This was echoed in *The Sentence of the Court*, in the 4th edition, published by the Home Office in 1986:

> "The inference most commonly drawn from research studies is that the probability of arrest and conviction is likely to deter potential offenders, whereas the perceived severity of the ensuing penalties has little effect."

1.68 In one sense deterrence may be said to work best with those who do not need to be deterred, that is, those who would obey the law in any event. Packer put it as follows:[88]

> "It is clear that the deterrent role of the criminal law is effective mainly with those who are subject to the dominant socializing influences of the day. That it is effective with them is its strength. That it is not effective with others is its countervailing weakness. Deterrence does not threaten those whose lot in life is already miserable beyond the point of hope. It does not improve the morals of those whose value systems are closed to further modification, either psychologically (in the case of the disoriented or the conscienceless) or culturally (as in the case of the outsider or the member of a deviant subculture)."

---

85 (1974) 60 Cr.App.R. 74; paras. 1.58 and 1.60 *supra*.
86 (1984) 6 Cr.App.R.(S) 104.
87 *Op. cit.* (note 64 *supra*) at para. 73.
88 H.L. Packer, *The Limits of the Criminal Sanction* (1968) Stanford U.P., p. 45; see also F.E. Zimring and G.J. Hawkins, *Deterrence* (1973) U. of Chicago P.

1.69 One aspect of deterrence which has caused concern over the years is the propriety of an exceptionally heavy sentence intended to "stamp out" an offence which is considered by the court to be particularly rife in a given area. A number of objections have been raised, including the fact that the defendant in question had not been given notice of the risk he ran when committing the offence in question, so that the higher sentence could in a sense be said to be applying retrospective law to him. Another is that such a defendant is being punished twice over: once for his own offence, and once *pour encourager les autres*. The Court of Appeal has placed two brakes on this kind of deterrent approach. The first is by pointing out that the sentence must be kept within the conventional limits, save that the defendant may be deprived of some of the lowering effect of his mitigation, as in *Elvin*[89] and in *Storey and others*[90] (both cases of schoolboys setting fire to schools, apparently undeterred by previous stiff sentences on others). The second is by pointing out that there is a limit to how much judges should use their own knowledge of a given areas and its problems. Whilst it is appropriate to take into account the prevalence of a given kind of offence within the jurisdiction of a given court, it is not for local judges to lay down new principles in the same way as the Court of Appeal does. An illustration may make the point clearer.

1.70 It is permissible for a judge in the Crown Court to say that there is too much violence of a serious nature at the local football stadium, and that the court will as a rule consider a custodial sentence for such offences. So, also, if thefts are rife on the part of employees in the local docks, a custodial sentence on a local receiver of stolen property may well be justified, even if the amount involved is relatively small.[91] On the other hand it is not proper for a chairman of a magistrates' court to say that in future a certain rife petty offence in his area will be dealt with by imprisonment as a matter of course, if the Court of Appeal has indicated that custodial sentences for such an offence must be regarded as a last resort: compare *Lavin*[92] with *Motley*.[93] It certainly behoves the court to be very careful about a pronouncement that a given offence is rife and that it is being successfully curbed by the courts. Very often the decline and return to a more normal rate will have little or nothing to do with the sentences being passed in the local courts.[94] Furthermore as the committee chaired by Streatfeild, J. put it in 1961:[95]

89 [1976] Crim.L.R. 204.
90 (1984) 6 Cr.App.R.(S) 104.
91 *Bogle* [1975] Crim.L.R. 726.
92 (1967) 51 Cr.App.R. 378.
93 (1978) 66 Cr.App.R. 274.
94 See A. Ashworth, *op. cit.* (note 43 *supra*) at p. 345.
95 *Op. cit.* (note 19 *supra*) at para. 281.

"It is also desirable, in fairness to the offenders who are made an example of, that the courts should have reasonable grounds for the supposition that the example will have the result intended."

Rehabilitation

1.71 For the first three-quarters of the twentieth century, not only in England but in the western world generally, the move was increasingly away from the purely retributive and deterrent approaches, and towards an emphasis on the reformation of the offender. That emphasis was to be found increasingly both in the courts and in penal institutions. It goes almost without saying that it was a crucial part of the philosophy of probation services. Quite often, especially in the United States, long sentences coupled with the possibility of parole, led to extensive investigations as to whether a given defendant had been reformed, or had reached "a recognisable peak" on the road to reformation/recovery/ rehabilitation/salvation – for different people saw the goal in slightly different terms. In the United States disparity in sentences was aggravated by disparity in parole decisions. One bank robber might find himself serving five years only whilst another, who might have been less culpable, might end up spending 20 years in prison.[96] A part of the difference could be attributed to the fact that the first defendant had made a better impression on the parole authorities. The apocryphal stories of teetotal prisoners joining Alcoholics Anonymous and similar groups, merely to impress the authorities, had a sad background of truth. Cases of this kind led to an increasing disenchantment with parole, indeterminacy in sentencing and in pretences of reformation. By 1967, when the Criminal Justice Act introduced parole in England, the Americans were turning away from the idea. In England there has been no lack of criticism of our own parole scheme and of our rehabilitative ambitions.[97] Like the Americans, we are now seeing a retreat from the idea of reformation, whilst not abandoning the notion altogether, and a move "towards the rehabilitation of punishment", as Bottomley has called it.[98]

1.72 Another matter which has contributed to some disenchantment with the rehabilitative ideal, on both sides of the Atlantic, is the finding of researchers that there is little perceptible difference between defendants who have had retributive sentences and those who have been the beneficiaries of sentences with more of a rehabilitative or treatment

---

96 Judge Marvin Frankel, *Criminal Sentences: Law without Order* (1973) Hill & Wang.
97 See, *e.g.* R. Hood, *Tolerance and the Tariff* (1974) NACRO, and *Freedom on Licence*, Howard League Working Party Report (1981) Quartermaine House.
98 *Op. cit.* (note 63 *supra*) at p. 123.

aim. In the United States Martinson published an article entitled "What Works?"[99] In it he concluded that the 231 research studies into rehabilitation which he had evaluated demonstrated that no particular sentence worked markedly better than any other. Martinson was heavily criticised and later withdrew some of his stronger comments, but the message remained much the same: nothing works particularly well. Brody conducted similar research for the Home Office, looking at various English research projects.[100] He concluded that longer sentences were no more effective than shorter ones in preventing recidivism, that different types of institution worked equally well, that probationers did no better than if they had been imprisoned and:

> "that rehabilitative programmes – whether involving psychiatric treatment, counselling, casework or intensive contact and special attention, in custodial or non-custodial settings – have no predictably beneficial results."

1.73 All this research makes depressing reading for those working in the various services, and it is not exactly encouraging for judges striving hard to find what they consider to be the best available sentence in all the circumstances. To make it worse, as the committee chaired by May, J. pointed out:[101]

> "As confidence in the treatment model has waned in this way no alternative philosophy commanding wide public support has taken its place."

There are however some consequences which may be regarded as more encouraging. Brody pointed out that the apparent failure of research to prove the value of rehabilitation as a sentencing aim had led to an appreciation of the fact that reconviction alone was not a suitable single criterion for success or failure. A sentence may improve an offender to the extent of lengthening the gaps between offences, a matter the courts increasingly recognise as being relevant. Brody also concluded:

> "A noticeable trend has been a readiness to justify non-custodial or semi-custodial sentences in preference to imprisonment or incarceration, on the grounds that they cost very much less to implement, and decrease at the same time the risk of psychological and practical harm to the offender. As 'softer' sentences have apparently no worse effect on recidivism and still offer the chance of less tangible if as yet unknown advantages, they are seen as preferable by all schools of though except perhaps the retributivist."

99 R. Martinson, "What Works?" in *The Public Interest* (Spring 1974), p. 23.
100 S. Brody, *The Effectiveness of Sentencing* (1976) H.M.S.O., H.O.R.S. No. 35, p. 36; see also letter from I.J. Croft in (1985) *British J. of Criminology* 25, p. 320.
101 *Report of Committee of Inquiry into the U.K. Prison Services* (1979) H.M.S.O. (Cmnd 7673), p. 64.

1.74   The movement away from rehabilitation has led some people to espouse the more simple notion that a defendant should be punished sufficiently to get his just deserts and no more. Sometimes referred to as the justice model, it bears some resemblance to the retributive approach, and also in some measure to the deterrence approach favoured by Bentham and the Utilitarians, namely, that it is unjust to punish more than is necessary to deter. The judge who has confidently stuck to his retributive approach over the years may derive a certain amount of satisfaction from finding that he has in a sense been joined by some criminologists who have been on a rehabilitation tour, only to return to the idea of just deserts. Bean has made the comment:[102]

> "In Britain there is a growing interest in the 'justice model' aimed at reducing the arbitrariness of decision-making and directed towards the safeguard of procedural rules. Often, those supporting this model do so without realizing or acknowledging that they are moving towards a form of retribution."

1.75   It is of interest to note that some judges and magistrates preferring the rehabilitative or treatment approach may on occasion have been harsher, in practice, than their brethren who adopted a retributive line. This was found by Wheeler and others to be so in some juvenile cases in the United States, where some sentencers were keen to help defendants with lengthy treatment programmes which involved longer detention than that thought to be appropriate by colleagues with a traditional approach. Similar findings were made by Hogarth in Canada, and we shall discuss later some of the instances in which the Court of Appeal has commented on some "helpful" English sentences.[103]

Incapacitation

1.76   One of the aims of punishment which has been comparatively successfully carried into effect and with little dispute about its basic success, is that of incapacitation. When a court sentences a defendant to a term of imprisonment, which is not suspended, it is taking him off the streets for the term announced, less any period of remission for good conduct (or the absence of bad conduct, to be accurate) and less any period on parole. While he is in prison the defendant will either commit no offence at all, or his victim will be a fellow prisoner – who is himself entitled to the protection of the law. Less often the victim will be a prison officer, and occasionally, as when a prisoner dismantles a prison

---

102   P. Bean, *Punishment* (1981) Martin Robertson, p. 180.
103   S. Wheeler (ed.), *Controlling Delinquents* (1968) Wiley, p. 31; J. Hogarth, *op. cit.* (note 18 *supra*) at p. 159; and see paras. 6.29ff *post*.

roof, the public a large. (As loss of remission and additional consecutive sentences have not "stamped out" the latter offence, prisons have been modified so as to deny access to the roof.) Generally speaking, however, the members of the public are safe from the man in prison.

1.77 Despite the last conclusion there is no call for undue celebration over what is only the relative success of incapacitation. If all burglars were to serve an extra year in prison, that would not mean that the community would be spared from all, or even a large proportion of burglaries. Leaving aside the novice burglars starting out on their careers who had not yet been caught for the first time, many burglaries would be committed in the year by burglars currently operating in the community, who had never been caught, or had been caught and acquitted by a jury despite their guilt, or had been convicted and had either received a non-custodial sentence or completed a custodial one. Unfortunately the burglars in custody at any given time are responsible for only a small fraction of all burglaries, the clear-up rate for that particular offence being very low and disappointing.[104] If each burglar who was sentenced for that offence – let us say for residential burglary, which the courts regard as more serious than any other type – were to be given an extra year's imprisonment to incapacitate him and to reduce the level of crime, two consequences might follow.

1.78 The first is that the burglars in question might well complain that they were being sentenced twice over: once for their offence and once for some other reason. Their complaint would be similar to that of the man given an addition to the normal sentence because of the desire to deter others and "stamp out" a particular offence. Such an objection might be countered by the observation (which applies equally to the deterrent sentence recipients): "You have no cause to complain. Your sentence is less than the maximum, and nobody ever promised you a sentence shorter than that which was passed on you." The second consequence might be that, for the reasons already given, the public might complain that there was no marked reduction in the number of burglaries committed.

1.79 The courts have often tried to deal with defendants who were considered to be dangerous by imposing exceptionally heavy terms. The Court of Appeal has repeatedly pointed out that even in such cases a sense of proportion, or proportionality, has to be kept in mind. In *King and Simpkins*[105] the sentence passed on the two defendants was one of

---

104 S. Brody and R. Tarling, *Taking Offenders Out of Circulation* (1981) H.M.S.O., H.O.R.S. No. 64.
105 (1973) 57 Cr.App.R. 696.

14 years' imprisonment, because the court took the view that they were dangerous enemies of society – something they had in effect proudly proclaimed. The Court of Appeal reduced the sentences to ten and seven years respectively, Lawton, L.J. observing:

> "But the Court has to bear in mind that in our system of jurisprudence there is no offence known as being an enemy of society. The Court is concerned with the offences charged in the indictment. It may well be that at a trial the evidence establishes that those who have committed the offences charged are dangerous men. When the evidence establishes that the Court has no reason for mitigating the penalties in any way."

1.80 It is just as well that the Court of Appeal has warned the courts against unjustified additions to proper sentences in respect of the element of perceived dangerousness. Experience on both sides of the Atlantic has shown that courts are not very clever at getting their predictions right in this difficult area of future behaviour – particularly if the future being considered is the distant future, say, ten years or more. In the United States case of *Baxstrom v. Herold*[106] the Supreme Court compelled the early release of many so-called "dangerous" prisoners. Follow-up revealed that many of the men, some of whom had been detained for many years, were no more dangerous than other defendants who had not been dealt with under the same New York statute, declared to be unconstitutional.[107]

1.81 Parliament has now on three separate occasions attempted to legislate so as to enable the courts to deal satisfactorily with the protection of the public from the activities of persistent offenders. The first attempt was by the Prevention of Crime Act 1908, Section 10, which permitted "a further sentence" of between five and ten years if the jury found that the defendant qualified. The third attempt will be considered in some detail later when we discuss the extended sentence.[108] The immediately preceding attempt was contained in the Criminal Justice Act 1948, Section 21, which provided for a sentence of five to 14 years' preventive detention in certain specified circumstances, for offenders aged 30 and over who had had three convictions on indictment after attaining the age of 17, and who were once again before a higher court convicted of an offence punishable with a sentence of two years at least. The courts' experience with the sentence of preventive

---

106　(1966) 383 U.S. 107.
107　A.E. Bottoms, "Reflections on the Renaissance of Dangerousness" (1977) *Howard Journal 16*, p. 70; for the recommendations of the Floud Committee, see J. Floud and W. Young, *Dangerousness and Criminal Justice* (1981) Heinemann. See also the excerpts from *Fuat, Storey and Duignan* at para. 10.33 and from *Tunney* at para. 10.34 *post*.
108　Paras. 9.38ff *infra*.

detention was not a happy one. The Court of Criminal Appeal decided that the legislature's choice of five years' minimum for the new sentence was of little use, and stated that ordinarily the minimum sentence of preventive detention should be one of seven years.[109] The sentence could not be imposed unless in accordance with the statutory requirements the court was "satisfied that it is expedient for the protection of the public that he should be detained in custody for a substantial time."

1.82 The appeal of *Caine*[110] illustrates how unjustly the earlier incapacitation legislation could work out in practice. Caine was sentenced to five years' ordinary imprisonment for embezzling £21 at a time when two years would have been taken to be the normal maximum. The Court of Criminal Appeal at that time still had the power to increase sentences on appeal. The sentence of five years' imprisonment was quashed and a sentence of preventive detention, for which Caine qualified, was substituted. However, that replacement sentence was not for the five years minimum permitted by the statute, but for the seven years laid down as the ordinary minimum by the court itself. The appellant Caine might have been forgiven for thinking that the court had inadvertently added the two and five years together to arrive at seven years' incarceration for £21. The present slowness of the courts to use the extended sentence may be attributable in part to a reluctance of the judges to impose a "second" sentence for one offence, and in part on their recollection of distasteful decisions such as those in *Sedgwick* and *Caine*. Insofar as the extended sentence does appeal to the present-day courts, as we shall see later, it is more for the value of the licence provisions that go with such a sentence, rather than for the ability of the court to incapacitate the defendant for a longer period than the norm.

Reparation

1.83 A Canadian writer has observed:[111]

> "There has been a development, even if ever so slow, to shift from principles such as punishment, deterrence and rehabilitation to the principle of undoing the harm done by means such as restitution, compensation and community service."

This comment applies equally to England, where a growing concern about the victim has coincided with increasing disenchantment with the traditional theories of punishment, and more particularly, with a realisation that they have not decreased the volume of crime to any

---

109 *Sedgwick* (1950) 34 Cr.App.R. 156.
110 [1963] Crim.L.R. 63.
111 J.W. Mohr, in Brian A. Grosman (ed.), *New Directions in Sentencing* (1980) Butterworths, p. 26.

significant degree. Whatever doubts one may entertain about other aims of punishment, nobody doubts the justice of aiding the victim.

1.84 It is sometimes said that in the past (save in Saxon times, perhaps) the victim was too often overlooked by the criminal justice system. This was true, but he was never entirely forgotten. Wilcox, a former Chief Constable of Hertfordshire, pointed out in 1972:[112]

> "The views of the loser or the injured person are always taken into account; indeed the most common reason for not prosecuting is that the victim does not wish to give evidence."

Wilcox also drew attention to the fact that:

> "The Police in England are chary of agreeing to drop a prosecution for theft or fraud if the culprit offers to make restitution; a bargain of this kind comes uncomfortably close to paying for immunity."

The latter point illustrates the dilemma facing the courts: they are anxious to see victims compensated, but they are also reluctant to let defendants buy their way out of trouble. Apart from any other objection, there is always the danger that the court may be thought to be applying one law for the comparatively rich defendant who can pay (or borrow enough) and another for the poor who cannot. On the other hand Parliament in the Powers of Criminal Courts Act 1973, Section 1(1) specifically referred to reparation during a period of deferment.

1.85 It is probably true to say that the attitude of the victim towards the offender, both on the issue as to whether there should be a prosecution at all, and on the issue of punishment, has been allowed to influence decisions both in relatively minor offences, and in not-so-minor matters of a domestic character. It has not been accorded much weight where really serious offences of a non-domestic nature have been involved. In view of the increasing desire to respect the wishes of victims and to see them compensated, there may well be a drift towards taking the victim's view of the offence and its punishment more into account. The new Code for Crown Prosecutors[113] contains the following statement of principle on the question of the complainant's attitude:

> "In some cases it will be appropriate for the Crown Prosecutor to have regard to the attitude of a complainant who notified the police but later expresses a wish that no action be taken. It may be that in such circumstances proceedings need not be pursued unless there is suspicion that the change of heart was actuated by fear or the offence was of some gravity."

---

112 A.E. Wilcox, *The Decision to Prosecute* (1972) Butterworths, p. 80.
113 (1986) H.M.S.O.

The disadvantage of increasing the weight to be attached to the views of the victim is that one simultaneously aggravates the disparity problem.

1.86 Traditionally the courts have stated that certain matters are too important to be left to the decision of the victim, and the interests of criminal law enforcement must take priority.[114] In *Buchanan*[115] the Court of Appeal held that this principle applied equally to gross violence in a domestic context. In *Hampton*[116] the defendant had been convicted of raping his girl-friend and had been sentenced to three years' imprisonment. He applied for leave to appeal and the victim wrote to the Court of Criminal Appeal. She stated that although she had only met the defendant three weeks before the rape, she had "permitted him to indulge in a degree of sexual familiarity" before the date of the offence. The rape had been committed in the defendant's home, to which she had gone voluntarily. According to Ashworth, J.:

> "She had written to this court that she had been willing to have sexual intercourse but was afraid and had therefore struggled and did not give ready consent, and had not realized the outcome of her complaint. It might well be true that she had no idea of the serious view the courts took of the crime of rape on young girls; but her misgivings could not afford any justification for altering a sentence which was right in principle and in fact well deserved."

The court clearly did not regard the previous consensual "sexual familiarity" as having any relevance to the question of sentence either, but it is distinctly possible that the modern Court of Appeal would take a different view both of the victim's attitude and to the part she had played — even though nobody would refer to "contributory negligence".[117] Society's increasing concern for the victim ought perhaps to lead to an increased respect for his or her views. It is of interest to note that in the United States some state legislatures and judges are making a deliberate attempt to obtain "victim input", that is, the victim's views about the offence and the sentence.[118]

1.87 One of the first steps towards the improvement of the lot of the victim came with the introduction of the Criminal Injuries Compensation Scheme in 1964, albeit only for victims sustaining personal injuries from crimes of violence. That was followed in 1968 by the Civil Evidence Act, which enabled a victim to prove the crime in later civil

---

114 See *e.g. Attorney-General's Reference (No. 6 of 1980)* (1981) 73 Cr.App.R. 63.
115 (1980) 2 Cr.App.R.(S) 13.
116 (1965) The Times 16 July.
117 But see *Biggs* (1979) 1 Cr.App.R.(S) 30, a case with rather unusual aggravating features.
118 J.M. Burns and J.S. Mattina, *Sentencing* (1978) National Judicial College, p. 205.

proceedings against the offender by mere proof of the conviction. Whilst the compensation scheme has been a real boon, having enabled many victims to obtain some financial recompense from the State, the statutory change in the rules of evidence has helped victims scarcely at all. It is only rarely that the offender will be worth suing, as in *W. v. Meah*.[119] The understandable reluctance of victims to sue their attackers for damages which might never be recovered was one of the factors which led to the increase of the powers of the criminal courts to make and enforce compensation orders in favour of victims.

1.88   A significant event was the publication in 1970 of a report of the Home Office Advisory Council on *Reparation by the Offender*, a work substantially that of Widgery, L.J. and Hugh Griffiths, Q.C., as they then were. One of the principal recommendations was that there should be a single comprehensive provision for compensation to be paid by a defendant, instead of the piecemeal legislation going back to the Forfeiture Act 1870, Section 4. Parliament accepted the recommendation and introduced a wider power in the Criminal Justice Act 1972, which was soon replaced by the Powers of Criminal Courts Act 1973, Section 35. In an early appeal, the case of *Inwood* in 1974,[120] Scarman, L.J. made a comment similar to that of Wilcox:

> "Compensation orders were not introduced into our law to enable the convicted to buy themselves out of the penalties of crime."

1.89   The power to order compensation nevertheless enables the court to refrain from imprisoning in a number of cases which might otherwise have led to such a sentence.[121] Similar considerations apply to cases in which the defendant has made good the loss before his court appearance. Although he must not be permitted to buy himself out of prison, if a defendant can fully compensate the victim before the sentencing stage, his advocate may with justification point out both that the victim has in fact not suffered (or suffered relatively little) and that the defendant has done his best to make good. The extent of the victim's actual suffering is always highly material: this is one of the reasons why an attempt is in practice generally less seriously regarded than the completed offence, despite the same maximum sentence being available under the Criminal Attempts Act 1981, Section 4.

1.90   Whilst compensation orders could only be made in conjunction with other orders under the provisions of the 1972 and 1973 Acts, the

---

119   [1986] 1 All E.R. 935.
120   (1974) 60 Cr.App.R. 70.
121   For compensation orders, see paras. 13.32ff *post*.

Criminal Justice Act 1982, Section 67, amended Section 35 of the 1973 Act, so that a court may now make a compensation order on its own. At the same time Parliament changed the law so as to enable a compensation order to be made in respect of offences taken into consideration, and to be given preference over a fine.

1.91 The above schemes, together with various victim support schemes which have been set up in recent years by concerned members of the community, including police officers, have helped to ensure that the idea of repairing the damage done to the victim has become an important consideration. As we shall see later, community service orders provide another method of enabling an offender to make reparation, but to the community at large, rather than to any particular individual victim.[122]

---

122 See also M. Wright, *Making Good* (1982) Burnett Books.

CHAPTER 2

The Guilty Plea

2.01 The decision of a defendant to plead guilty to all or some of the charges laid against him is of crucial importance – principally to him, but also to the other participants in his trial: his own lawyers, the prosecuting lawyer and the judge or magistrates. Collectively the decisions to plead guilty are of great importance, since the current system could not cope if each defendant were to exercise his right to be tried on all charges. Each of the decisions to be made by all the participants should only be made after a realistic appraisal of the situation. One of the factors lurking in the foreground rather than in the background will be the well-established rule of practice in the English courts (unlike the Scottish courts) that a defendant should be given credit for pleading guilty.

2.02 In the present chapter we shall be considering, principally in the context of the Crown Court,
  (1) The duties of counsel and judge;
  (2) Plea bargaining;
  (3) The discount for the guilty plea;
  (4) The additional discount for informers; and
  (5) Some expressions of concern.

THE DUTIES OF COUNSEL AND JUDGE

2.03 Provided he is mentally fit, the defendant will know whether he committed the offence or offences charged, subject to some uncertainty where the law is not clear, or where the facts as he knows them could mean that he is guilty of either a more serious offence or of a less serious one. If, for example, the defendant hit his victim with an unbroken bottle or glass, at a time when he himself had been drinking heavily, he will not be clear whether he had the requisite intent for the offence of wounding with intent contrary to Section 18 of the Offences against the Person Act 1861, or whether he had merely committed the lesser offence of unlawful wounding, contrary to Section 20. He will rely on his lawyers not only for advice as to the differences between the two

41

offences, but also on the chances of the jury convicting or acquitting of the more serious offence. He will also depend on them for accurate advice about the court's attitude towards the discount for a plea of guilty. If he is properly defended, he will receive that accurate advice at a sufficiently early enough stage to be able to make up his own mind about his plea in an unhurried manner. Furthermore, he will not expect completely different advice on the morning of the trial from a barrister who has just taken over the brief for the defence as a late return from a colleague.

2.04 Guidelines exist for the conduct of prosecuting and defending counsel. As a general rule counsel for the prosecution should not accept a plea of guilty to the lesser offence if the depositions and statements show that the more serious one has been committed.[1] However, if he is told that the victim may decline to give evidence, or that he is likely to say that the defendant was acting in self-defence (although such was probably not the case) then he may properly accept a plea of guilty to the lesser offence. It is also proper for the prosecution to accept a plea of guilty to a lesser offence if a sensible assessment of all the circumstances suggests that a jury will most probably convict of that offence or acquit on both counts. Obviously the greater the danger of a defendant being wrongly acquitted on both counts, the greater the justification for accepting a plea to the lesser offence. An acceptance of the wrong plea, it must be remembered by counsel for the prosecution, apart from anything else can create sentencing problems for the court.[2]

2.05 In 1986 the Director of Public Prosecutions issued a Code for Crown Prosecutors which contained sensible suggestions for prosecutors to bear in mind when evaluating the strength of a case.[3] Among the matters prosecutors should have regard to are the following:

> "5. (iii) Does it appear that a witness is exaggerating, or that his memory is faulty, or that he is either hostile or friendly to the accused, or may be otherwise unreliable?
> (iv) Has the witness a motive for telling less than the whole truth?
> (v) Are there matters which might properly be put to a witness by the defence to attack his credibility?"

Thirteen separate points were listed, followed by the general advice:

> "6. This list is not of course exhaustive, and the factors to be considered will depend on the circumstances of each case, but it is introduced to indicate that, particularly in borderline cases, the Crown Prosecutor must

1 *Soanes* (1948) 32 Cr.App.R. 136.
2 *Booker* (1982) 4 Cr.App.R.(S) 53.
3 (1986) *Law Society's Gazette* p. 2308.

be prepared to look beneath the surface of the statements. He must also draw, so far as is possible, on his own experience of how evidence of the type under consideration is likely to 'stand up' in court before reaching a conclusion as to the likelihood of a conviction."

2.06 Defence counsel must consider the evidence in a similar manner – although with less inside information about his opponent's case – and he must advise his client on the various options open to him. He will have some idea of how his client and his version of the facts will fare in the witness box, and he may give the advice "in strong terms".[4] Clearly he must draw the line at bullying his client into making a decision he is unwilling or reluctant to make: the decision must always be that of the client and not that of his legal advisers.

2.07 When counsel for the defence has taken instructions on his client's wishes, there is no reason why he should not speak to his opponent about the possibility of the prosecution accepting, say, a plea to the lesser of two charges. Plea discussions are not improper; indeed one might say that it would be improper of defending counsel not to discuss the question of the acceptability of a particular plea with his opposite number. There is of course no objection to the discussion being initiated by the prosecution. What is objectionable is the plea bargain which puts improper pressure on an accused to plead guilty against his wishes, and we shall presently consider what the Court of Appeal has had to say about such matters.

2.08 If counsel for the prosecution agrees to accept a plea of guilty to the lesser offence, he is agreeing to drop the more serious charge by, in effect, offering no evidence on that count. The decision is his responsibility, as was recently confirmed by the Committee on the Role of Prosecution Counsel, chaired by Farquharson, J.[5] There has been over the years some doubt about the right of the judge to refuse to agree to the proposed pleas as accepted by the prosecution. The Committee made three recommendations on the point, and it is likely that they will in due course be universally accepted:

> "(i) If Prosecution Counsel invites the judge to approve the course he is proposing to take, then he must abide by the judge's decision.
> (j) If Prosecution Counsel does not invite the judge's approval of his decision, it is open to the judge to express his dissent with the course proposed and to invite Counsel to reconsider the matter with those instructing him, but, having done so, the final decision remains with Counsel.

4 *Turner* (1970) 54 Cr.App.R. 352.
5 See (1986) *Counsel 1*, p. 28.

(k) In the extreme case where the judge is of the opinion that the course proposed by Counsel would lead to serious injustice, he may decline to proceed with the case until Counsel has consulted either the Director of Public Prosecutions or the Attorney-General as may be appropriate."

The justification for leaving the final word with counsel for the prosecution is that he will know of the factors we have discussed above, such as the likely hostility or friendliness of the principal witness, whilst the judge cannot possibly be aware of them, unless the depositions and statements should make them apparent.

2.09 We make no apology for discussing what may at first sight seem to be matters of procedure only, since they are matters of great importance to the sentencing stage. Some of the cases show that unfair pressure on a defendant can lead to an inappropriate plea, and therefore to an unsatisfactory sentence.

PLEA BARGAINING

2.10 The question of unfair pressure was first considered in some detail by the Court of Appeal in the landmark case of *Turner*[6], where the Court of Appeal laid down some guidelines on plea discussions. Lord Parker, C.J. began by referring to counsel's duty:

"Counsel must be completely free to do what is his duty, namely to give the accused the best advice he can and if need be, advice in strong terms. This will often include advice that a plea of guilty, showing an element of remorse, is a mitigating factor which may well enable the court to give a lesser sentence than would otherwise be the case. Counsel, of course, will emphasise that the accused must not plead guilty unless he has committed the acts constituting the offence charged."

Lord Parker continued by stating that the accused had to have a complete freedom of choice between pleading guilty and and pleading not guilty. After stating that there must be freedom of access between counsel and judge, the Lord Chief Justice made the point,

"It is of course imperative that so far as possible justice must be administered in open court. Counsel should, therefore, only ask to see the judge when it is felt to be really necessary and the judge must be careful only to treat such communications as private where, in fairness to the accused, this is necessary."

Then followed the most important warning:

6 (1970) 54 Cr.App.R. 352.

"The judge should, subject to the one exception referred to hereafter, never indicate the sentence which he is minded to impose. A statement that on a plea of guilty he would impose one sentence but that on a conviction following a plea of not guilty he would impose a severer sentence is one which should never be made. This could be taken to be undue pressure on the accused, thus depriving him of that complete freedom of choice which is essential."

The exception that was referred to was the proper indication by a judge that in all of the circumstances of the case he considered, say, a probation order to be appropriate whether the accused pleaded guilty or were to be found guilty by the jury.

2.11 There have been a number of cases since *Turner* which make it clear that the guidelines of that decision have not always been followed. Perhaps the most serious failures to follow the guidelines were considered in *Inns*[7] and *Bird*[8]. Of counsel's right of access to the judge, Lawton, L.J., said in *Mainwood*,[9]

"It should not be used for the purpose of helping counsel to make decisions which are their own professional responsibility . . . We would point out the desirability of the experienced members of the Bar damping the propensity of the more junior members of the Bar to use this privilege."

2.12 With respect to the need for justice to be administered in open court, Roskill, L.J. said in *Winterflood*[10] that what had occurred in the judge's room in that case had been perfectly proper. He added that there had been no reason why the discussion should not have taken place in open court, in the presence of the public and shorthand writer, but after the jury had been asked to withdraw. Private discussions, he stressed, were undesirable unless absolutely necessary. In *Cullen*[11] the Court of Appeal stressed the need for a note to be taken of any discussion in chambers, and emphasised that the judge should not send for counsel to discuss sentence.

2.13 It is not enough for discussions to be in open court for them to be free from criticism. In *Atkinson*[12] the judge had told the defendant in open court that there would be a non-custodial sentence if there were a plea of guilty, but he sentenced him to a term of imprisonment after a

---

7   (1974) 60 Cr.App.R. 231.
8   (1977) 67 Cr.App.R. 203.
9   (1975) C.S.P. L1.1(b).
10   (1979) 68 Cr.App.R. 291.
11   (1985) 81 Cr.App.R. 17.
12   (1977) 67 Cr.App.R. 200.

trial by jury. An exceptionally strong Court of Appeal, Viscount Dilhorne, Lord Scarman and Cusack, J., reduced the sentence, Lord Scarman saying:

> "It is to be observed, greatly to his credit, that everything the judge did in the present case he did in open court in full view of the public. But unfortunately what he did could very well give the impression to this appellant, as well as to other defendants, that there was a bargain: if you plead guilty, one result; if you plead not guilty, another. Some, including the accused, might well think pressure was being exerted on him to plead guilty. It is that which is so damaging to the face of justice; it is that which leads this court to reach the conclusion that this sentence of six months, even if sustainable in other respects, must be quashed."

The last sentence of the judgment once again makes the point that the Court of Appeal will even quash a correct sentence if the circumstances surrounding the passing of that sentence leave the defendant with a legitimate grievance about a lack of fairness.

2.14 It should be borne in mind that none of the authorities have discouraged the sensible assessment of the case by all concerned, be they prosecuting or defence lawyers, police officers in charge of a particular case, or their superiors. There is no reason why discussions should not take place about the various pleas, as long as the guidelines of *Turner* are constantly borne in mind. Some confusion has been caused in the past by a failure to distinguish between proper discussions between the two sides which may be said to amount to legitimate negotiations, and such improper discussions in the presence of the judge as fall foul of the *Turner* principles. Sometimes the word "bargain" is loosely used in circumstances in which nothing improper has occurred. It is of interest to note that five years after *Turner* Lord Hailsham wrote of the complicated Rolls Razor case, which had been delayed for years:[13]

> "When the Rolls case came on it was virtually untriable and, not unnaturally, there was a sensible plea bargain which gave rise to criticism."

DISCOUNT FOR PLEA OF GUILTY

2.15 The fact that a defendant who pleads guilty may be given some discount from the otherwise appropriate sentence is well known to both branches of the legal profession. As we have seen, it is the duty of solicitors and counsel to advise their client to that effect if he is not

---

13 Lord Hailsham, *The Door Wherein I Went* (1975) Collins, p. 282.

already aware of it. The amount of the discount varies from very little to as much as a third in some instances. The Court of Appeal has not indicated that any particular proportion of discount is to be awarded, and has not suggested that there is any precise mathematical way of distinguishing between the defendant who has pleaded guilty after being caught red-handed, and the one who had surrendered himself to the police when they were unaware of his identity and who has made admissions and shown remorse throughout. However, the court has made helpful observations at different times, although Ashworth considers the decisions as a whole to be inconsistent and states that there is "a clear and urgent need for a declaration of principle".[14]

2.16 In *Davis and others*[15] the Court of Appeal was concerned with a gang of armed bank robbers who had been caught red-handed after a police tip-off. Despite this fact the court held that they were entitled to some credit for their plea. Although they might not have been successful in a trial, they could have invented a trumped-up defence. Lawton, L.J. pointed out:

> "The court bears in mind that these kinds of criminal will do anything at their trial to try and evade verdicts of guilty. They often do so by making attacks on police officers and by trying to beguile a jury into believing that in some way they have been treated unfairly. Fortunately they seldom succeed, but in the course of failing they waste much public time and money. They should be encouraged, as far as it is possible to encourage criminals, to stop these sort of tactics."

2.17 In view of these remarks of Lawton, L.J. it is not easy to understand the later comment of MacPherson, J. in *Stabler*:[16]

> "We can see no ground for giving any discount in the circumstances of this particular case. This man had no alternative but to plead guilty."

The alternative always exists.

2.18 It is probably as well for the sentencer always to refer to the fact that he is giving credit for the guilty plea, for Lawton, L.J. said later in the *Davis* judgment,

> "It is said on their behalf that no credit was given to them for pleading guilty. As far as we can see from the short transcript this point was never brought to the learned judge's attention. He certainly did not refer to it when sentencing the prisoners."

---

14 A. Ashworth, "Techniques of Guidance on Sentencing" [1984] Crim.L.R. 519, 526.
15 (1980) 2 Cr.App.R.(S) 168. See also the remarks of Wien, J. at para 3.08 *infra*.
16 (1984) 6 Cr.App.R.(S) 129.

It is nowadays considered to be good sentencing practice to give detailed reasons for a sentence, in fairness to the defendant, the public and the Court of Appeal, and a discount for the plea needs to be mentioned as part of the process by which that sentence was reached.

2.19 The courts regularly give credit to a defendant whose plea has saved the necessity of his victim having to undergo the harrowing experience of giving evidence at the trial. This is particularly the case with sex offences, and especially when the victim is young. Even if the defendant's conduct has been revolting he must as a general rule be given credit for the plea, as the extreme example of *Barnes*[17] demonstrates. Barnes had met his daughters and one of their young female friends at a station and had taken them to his home, instead of delivering the friend to her house. After sending his daughters to bed he attempted to rape their friend, squeezing her throat and threatening her with a knife. He was sentenced to seven years' imprisonment, then the maximum for attempted rape, the court having learned of his release a mere nine weeks before the offence from a prison sentence for rape and indecent assault. (The maximum sentence for attempted rape was only increased by Parliament to life imprisonment as recently as 1985, by the Sexual Offences Act, Section 3, a fact sometimes overlooked by some MPs.) In the Court of Appeal, after referring to the fact that Barnes had "saved the young girl the ordeal of going into the witness-box", Leonard, J. stated that he was entitled to a reduction for the plea, adding,

> "Clearly the reduction cannot be a substantial one, because the offence was itself very serious."

The Court of Appeal reduced the sentence from seven to six years.

2.20 If a defendant offers a plea of guilty to a lesser offence which is rejected by the prosecution, and the jury later convict of that lesser offence only, then the defendant should still be treated as though there had been no contested trial.[18] The trial will not have been his fault and so he should not be blamed for the fact that the victim had to give evidence.

2.21 There would seem to be one exception to the rule that even a "very serious" offence must be treated more leniently if admitted by the plea, and that is where the sentence is primarily intended to be one for the protection of the public, a sentence which Barnes had been lucky

---

17 (1983) 5 Cr.App.R.(S) 368.
18 (1984) 6 Cr.App.R.(S) 28.

enough to avoid in the Crown Court.[19] In *McLoughlin and Simpson*[20] the Court of Appeal declined to shorten a 15–year sentence passed on two defendants with very bad records who had forced their way into a woman's flat and raped her at knifepoint. After referring to the need to protect the public from the defendants, Lawton, L.J. added:

> "In the ordinary way, especially in cases of rape, when there is a plea of guilty, as there was in this case, that is a factor which the court should, and almost always does, take into account. But this is an unusual case; and in the circumstances, although there was a plea of guilty, it seems to us that it would not be right to interfere in any way on that ground with the sentences which were passed."

In the near future any appeal brought after the rape guideline case of *Billam* in 1986[21] will clearly be influenced more by that decision than by either of the two cases discussed here.

2.22 A danger about which lawyers should warn their clients where necessary is the risk that may be run where the plea of guilty is only entered at the very last minute, and where the plea has been one of not guilty until then for tactical reasons only. In *Hollington and Emmens*[22] a defendant pleaded not guilty, though intending to change his plea on the day of his trial. He made the decision because he preferred to spend his time awaiting trial in prison as a remand prisoner, rather than as a convicted prisoner with fewer privileges. In dismissing his appeal against a 14-year sentence for robbery and burglary Lawton, L.J. stated:

> "The idea seems to be getting around that if a defendant ultimately pleads guilty he is entitled to a very considerable discount on his sentence. The court has long said that discounts on sentences are appropriate but everything depends on the circumstances of each case. If a man is arrested and at once tells the police that he is guilty and co-operates with them in the recovery of property and the identification of others concerned in the offence, he can expect to get a substantial discount. But if the man is arrested in circumstances in which he cannot hope to put forward a defence of not guilty, he cannot expect much by way of discount. In between comes this kind of case, where the court has been put to considerable trouble as a result of a tactical plea. The sooner it is appreciated that defendants are not going to get full discount for pleas of guilty in these sort of circumstances the better."

2.23 It should be noted that the discount should not merely be taken off the maximum for the offence in question: sometimes it should be taken off the maximum which could be passed on that defendant at that

19   See *Hewson* [1987] Crim.L.R. 149.
20   (1979) 1 Cr.App.R.(S) 298.
21   (1986) 8 Cr.App.R.(S) 48.
22   (1986) 82 Cr.App.R. 281.

time. In *Pilford*[23] the 16-year-old defendant had pleaded guilty to four offences of burglary, with eleven further offences being taken into consideration. As he was under 17 the statutory maximum term of youth custody was twelve months: that term was clearly the operative maximum rather than the normal maximum for the offences themselves. The Court of Appeal stated that he ought not to have been sentenced to the maximum term of twelve months' youth custody in view of his plea, and reduced the sentence to one of nine months. However, if the sentencer has the option of using the court's power to order detention under the Children and Young Persons Act 1933, Section 53(2), then if he decides – partly because of the plea – that two years' detention would be too long, he may come down to youth custody and pass the full twelve months sentence on the offender under 17, even if he pleads guilty.[24] He would then already have given sufficient recognition to the plea.

2.24 Although it is both proper and customary for courts to give credit to a defendant for pleading guilty, it is improper for a sentencer to add to the appropriate sentence because a defendant has chosen to dispute his guilt and has exercised his right to be tried by a jury. So too, a defendant must not be given an addition to his sentence for lying to the jury, or for attacking prosecution witnesses, and any remarks suggesting that he has been punished for such conduct will lead to a reduction of sentence on appeal.[25] The sentencer should accordingly bear in mind that he must not add to the sentence for wholly extraneous matters. There is some artificiality in these rules, but that is inevitable as long as it is considered desirable to reward defendants for pleading guilty. A defendant is entitled to say to the courts: "If I am correctly advised that I am likely to be sentenced to the 'proper' term of four years' imprisonment after a trial by jury, but only to three years if I plead guilty, how can you say that I am not being punished for exercising my constitutional right to have the prosecution prove the case against me?" The only answer that the courts can give is, "You are not being punished for pleading not guilty; you are being rewarded for pleading guilty. We are using the carrot rather than the stick – and nobody can reasonably object to carrots being offered as rewards." The reward is based in part on the gratitude of the courts for the saving of time and money, partly on the sparing of the victim from the witness-box and partly because of the theory that a man who shows some contrition does not need to be punished so much as one who does not. Lawyers must not be too surprised if laymen regard this explanation as less than satisfactory. The

23 (1985) 7 Cr.App.R.(S) 23.
24 *Reynolds* [1986] Crim.L.R. 125.
25 *Harper* (1968) 52 Cr.App.R. 21; *Spinks* (1980) 2 Cr.App.R.(S) 335.

layman probably also has some difficulty in appreciating the rule that prohibits the Crown Court from punishing a defendant for exercising his right to be tried by a jury rather than by a magistrates' court, whilst making him pay the higher costs which have been incurred as a result of that choice.[26]

2.25 In 1985 Skinner, J., then Chairman of the Judicial Studies Board, told magistrates that they were also obliged to give discount for a plea of guilty, but many magistrates find it difficult to accept that advice in some of their more serious cases which are governed by their overall maximum of six months' imprisonment.[27] It would be helpful if the Court of Appeal or the Divisional Court could give some clear guidelines for cases of that sort. To be fair to the magistrates who decline to give a discount so as to reduce a sentence below six months, the Court of Appeal has on occasion refused to reduce a maximum sentence passed after a plea of guilty in the Crown Court.[28]

DISCOUNT FOR INFORMERS

2.26 The defendant who pleads guilty and in addition gives a great deal of useful information to the police is entitled to an appropriate amount of discount in respect of that additional consideration. It would obviously not be fair to give him only the normal discount for pleading guilty and no more. In deciding how much additional discount is justified, or how much in all is fair, the court must bear in mind all the relevant factors, such as the usefulness of the information, the degree to which the defendant is prepared to assist the prosecution, and the extent of the risk he runs for himself and his family in affording such help as in *King*.[29] Whilst the discount for a simple plea of guilty may be as much as a third, where in addition significant help is given to the police by a defendant a discount of a half or even more may be appropriate. In *King*, for example, the Court of Appeal thought that a scaling down from ten years' imprisonment to four-and-a-half was justified as the assistance given had been great. In a drugs importation case considerable assistance may be rewarded by "a substantial reduction".[30] Incidentally,

26 *Hayden* (1975) 60 Cr.App.R. 304.
27 (1985) *The Magistrate 41*, p. 146; see also R. Henham, "The Influence of Sentencing Principles on Magistrates' Sentencing Practices" (1986) *Howard Journal 25*, p. 190.
28 See *e.g. Pyne* [1984] Crim.L.R. 118, and *Coker* [1984] Crim.L.R. 184.
29 (1986) 82 Cr.App.R. 210.
30 *Aramah* (1982) 4 Cr.App.R.(S) 407.

where a defendant is offering to give evidence against a co-defendant, he should as a general rule not be sentenced until the end of the case.[31]

SOME EXPRESSIONS OF CONCERN

2.27 The response of many lawyers to the suggestion that some defendants may have pleaded guilty to offences they had not committed is: "They would not have pleaded guilty unless they were guilty in fact – and they knew best whether they were guilty or not." This response is based in part on the assumption that all innocent defendants have been able to withstand the pressure to plead guilty, brought about largely by the known existence of the discount system. However, when considering the choice of the defendant at the relevant time, it must be borne in mind that he will often have been advised that the evidence against him is very strong, and that a conviction is likely. He will also have been told that a failure to plead guilty can lead to a heavier sentence (although the Court of Appeal would put it somewhat differently). The defendant in such circumstances may well be tempted to avoid the strain involved in undergoing a trial and to opt for what he has been told will be the lesser of two alternative penalties, that is, the sentence following on a plea of guilty. Similar considerations will tempt him to plead guilty to the lesser of two alternative charges, both of which he would prefer to dispute.

2.28 A number of research projects have pointed out some of the dangers of the present system, and particularly of the discount for the plea of guilty. Inevitably the researchers have had to rely heavily on the accounts of admitted offenders, some of them with bad records. However, it would be a mistake to disregard all the evidence collected merely for that reason, especially in those instances when there is some support available from impeccable sources. The legal profession has generally speaking been cool in its response to some of the findings, and positively hostile to others. This is unfortunate, for the joint effect of the research findings is impressive, and ought not to be ignored by lawyers interested in the idea of criminal justice. It is some time since the various projects were undertaken, but nothing has happened to lessen the importance of their basic message, namely, that the whole area of the plea of guilty, and especially the discount, ought to be more critically examined by lawyers. The principal relevant research was that

31 *Weekes and others* (1982) 74 Cr.App.R. 161; and see *Sodhi* (1978) 66 Cr.App.R. 260.

undertaken by Dell, Bottoms and McClean, and Baldwin and McConville.[32]

2.29 Lest any lawyer be tempted to think that the concern expressed by those researchers (all of them with considerable academic reputations) is quite irrational and need not be considered further, he might like to ponder on the words of Sheriff Nicholson, the author of the Scottish book on sentencing.[33] After pointing out that the Scottish system does not have a system of a discount for a plea of guilty, he added:

> "– and, of course, it would be quite unacceptable that a person who was found guilty after trial should be punished more severely simply because he had not pled guilty."

Sheriff Nicholson made the following further points:

> "A more important reason, however, for not accepting a plea of guilty as being a mitigating circumstances in itself is that, if there were a regular practice to that effect, it might easily be seen as the court offering an inducement to accused persons to plead guilty rather than go to trial. It is one thing for a judge to take account – and to be known to be likely to take account – of certain factors which are properly mitigating in themselves. Whether such factors are present or not will depend on the whole circumstances of the case and, although they may influence the accused's plea, they will not be dependent on it. It is quite another thing for a judge to take account – or to be known to be likely to take account – of a plea of guilty simply for its own sake. Such an approach not only smacks of plea bargaining, which is wholly alien to the Scottish system, but is also one which could operate most harshly against those who exercise their entitlement to go to trial."

---

32 S. Dell, *Silent in Court* (1971) Bell; A.S. Bottoms and J.D. McClean, *Defendants in the Criminal Process* (1976) Routledge & Kegan Paul; J. Baldwin and N. McConville, *Negotiated Justice: Pressures to Plead Guilty* (1977) Martin Robertson. There is a great deal of U.S. literature on similar lines: see *e.g.* A. Rosett and D.R. Cressey, *Justice by Consent* (1976) Lippincott.
33 C.G.B. Nicholson, *The Law and Practice of Sentencing in Scotland* (1981) W. Green & Son, p. 219.

CHAPTER 3

The Relevant Facts of the Case

3.01 In one sense every single fact that is placed before the court during a trial and during the sentencing stage may be said to be relevant to the issue of sentence. The antecedents report and the social inquiry report will contain many relevant facts, but such reports will be considered separately later. The relevant facts that the present chapter will consider are of two kinds.

3.02 The first basic set of facts will depend on the charges which are before the court at the time the defendant comes to be sentenced. Charges which have never been brought against him; charges to which he pleaded not guilty in a case where the prosecution has accepted that plea; and charges of which the jury has acquitted the defendant, are all irrelevant at the sentencing stage. The sentencer must concentrate on the charges which remain live at the final stage, that of sentencing.

3.03 The second basic set of facts are those which make up the accurate picture of the offence or offences in question. In most cases in the Crown Court when there is a plea of guilty counsel for the prosecution will outline the facts as he has garnered them from the witness depositions and statements. He will try to be dispassionate while placing the relevant facts accurately before the court, so that the defence will not disagree with that outline, save on minor details. In his speech in mitigation counsel for the defence will on instructions explain the defendant's admitted actions so as to show them in the best possible light. If there appear to be minor differences between the version put forward by the defendant and his victim, nobody will object. If on the other hand there is a major dispute about one or more basic facts, that dispute will have to be resolved by the court in one way or another. We shall discuss the alternative solutions presently.

3.04 If counsel are aware that there is going to be a conflict about an important question of fact, then they should be prepared to deal with the matter in one of the appropriate ways. Once the prosecution knows that the defendant may be prepared to plead guilty to the lesser of two alternative charges, its representatives must consider whether an acceptance of the plea offered is justified in all the circumstances. Although counsel for the prosecution has a muted role to play in the sentencing stage, he nevertheless has a role, and it includes, as we have seen, the important question of the propriety of accepting the plea tendered. The alternative sentencing powers of the court should be borne in mind. Whilst the facts of the case may fit two alternative charges, they may be closer to the more serious offence than the lesser. In *Booker*[1] the defendant had thrown two petrol bombs at the public house from which he had been ejected. The indictment charged attempted arson with intent to endanger life, or with the requisite recklessness, and also the lesser offence of attempted arson with an intent to damage property. The prosecution accepted a plea of guilty to the lesser offence, and the judge passed a sentence of five years' imprisonment, referring to the risk of danger to the occupants. In the Court of Appeal Griffiths, L.J. said:

> "It appears to this Court that the judge was sentencing on the basis, correctly, that this man clearly was reckless as to whether or not human life was endangered. . . . As the court accepted the plea limited to an intent to damage property and not human life, the court considers the sentence of five years, when he pleaded guilty, to be excessive. Accordingly, with great reluctance because in truth he fully deserved the sentence of five years, this Court will reduce the sentence from five years to three years."

The Court of Appeal was clearly of the view that the prosecution ought not to have accepted the plea tendered. However, the decision to accept that plea could well have been based on a realistic appraisal of the likely verdict.

3.05 Counsel's duty at the second stage, that is after the pleas have been agreed but when it has become clear that there is a dispute about the facts of the admitted offence, was referred to in the Court of Appeal by Lawton, L.J. in *Miller, Vella and Walker*:[2]

> "We wish to call the attention of prosecuting counsel to the embarrassment which is created for judges when the Crown knows that a plea in mitigation is going to be put forward which is wholly inconsistent with the facts which the prosecution intend to rely upon in support of the indictment."

In that case the prosecution had not called any evidence to deal with the conflict of fact, and the learned Lord Justice was obviously indicating that its representatives should have directed their minds to that issue. It follows that the defence should help by notifying the prosecution if there is going to be a dispute about important facts on a plea of guilty.

1 (1982) 4 Cr.App.R.(S) 53.
2 C.A. 2 December 1974 (unreported).

3.06 Apart from the above matters we shall also be considering the sample or specimen count in this chapter. Accordingly we shall consider the topics under three headings:

(1) Sentence for offences proved only;

(2) Sentence for the offence as proved; and

(3) Sample counts.

SENTENCE FOR OFFENCES PROVED ONLY

3.07 The proposition that a sentence must only be passed on a defendant in respect of an offence proved against him, whether by his plea of guilty or evidence called at his trial, is so obvious that one might imagine that it scarcely needs to be stated. However, numerous cases in the Court of Appeal have shown the need for that proposition not only to be stated, but for it to be repeated with emphasis. A stranger to the law might find it hard to conceive how a professional lawyer sitting as a full-time, or even part-time judge could come to sentence a defendant for an offence not proved against him, but the cases show that it can happen because the judge falls into one or other of a number of similar traps. The cases can be divided into two categories: those in which the charge in question was never formally laid against that defendant in the sentencing court at all; and those in which it was so laid, but in which the charge has for one reason or another ceased to be relevant by the time of sentence.

3.08 A judge may, with carefully chosen words, say to a defendant that the offence is at the top end of the gravity scale, and that the facts came close to constituting a more serious offence. However, it is not permissible for him to sentence a defendant in respect of a more serious charge which *might have been* brought on the same facts as the instant charge. This is so whether he expresses the view that such a charge ought to have been brought, or whether refrains from making such a comment. In *Chadderton*[3] the defendant pleaded guilty to an offence of possessing a firearm as a person previously convicted of crime, contrary to the Firearms Act 1968, Section 21(1), which carried a maximum sentence of three years' imprisonment. The judge heard evidence about the defendant's reasons for being armed, and decided that he had really wanted to use the weapon. He added that the defendant ought to have been charged with the more serious offence under Section 18 of having the firearm with criminal intent, for which the maximum was fourteen

3 (1980) 2 Cr.App.R.(S) 272.

years. He passed a sentence of three years, the maximum for the offence actually charged, adding that he regarded that as insufficient. The Court of Appeal reduced the sentence, Wien, J. observing:

> "This Court takes the view that to sentence a man on the basis of an offence with which he is not charged is wrong, and moreover that some credit should have been given to the appellant for pleading guilty, however overwhelming the evidence was against him."

It seems likely that the sentence of three years would have been reduced even if it had followed a conviction by the jury of the lesser offence, for the Court of Appeal is constantly stressing that matters have to be approached on the basis of how the matter looks to the defendant. If the defendant is justified in having a grievance because, say, it looks as though he has been sentenced for a different offence or on the basis of facts not proved against him, then the court will often reduce a sentence on appeal, even if it might otherwise have been thought to be of the correct length.

3.09 In *Lawrence*[4] the defendant could have been charged with possession of a firearm with intent to endanger life, but was in fact only charged with, and pleaded guilty to the lesser offence of possessing a firearm within five years of release from prison. The defendant while drunk had threatened to assault a police officer, but after a while it was discovered he had had neither bolt nor ammunition for the weapon. The judge in passing sentence referred to the fact that the defendant "might well have done something dreadful with that shotgun". The Court of Appeal decided that the defendant had in effect been sentenced for the more serious offence which had not even been charged, Griffiths, L.J. stating firmly:

> "A man is entitled to be sentenced for the offence to which he pleads guilty, not for another offence which might well have been laid against him."

3.10 So too, in *Mitchell*,[5] where a defendant appeared in the Crown Court charged with two serious motoring offences, other offences having been left behind in the lower court to be dealt with there, the judge gave the appearance of sentencing for all the offences committed. The Court of Appeal pointed out that this was clearly incorrect.

3.11 Similar considerations have led to a successful appeal where a sentence appears to have been passed not only for the serious offence

---

4 (1983) 5 Cr.App.R.(S) 220.
5 (1982) 4 Cr.App.R.(S) 277.

actually charged, but also for minor offences not charged at all. In *Reeves*[6] the defendant was sentenced for receiving a valuable stolen item. In passing sentence the judge referred to his failure to keep proper records for tax purposes, and he seemed to add to the sentence for handling something in respect of the dishonesty neither proved nor even charged. Watkins, L.J. said:

> "Obviously we have to reiterate as firmly as we can that it is impermissible for irrelevant material of that kind, for which, it should be added, there was no confirmation, and in respect of which there was no charge, to be taken into account."

3.12 A judge may not sentence a defendant in respect of other offences which he suspects may have been committed. Even if it looks as though the offence was very likely one of a series, the sentence must relate only to the charge proved. If counsel in mitigation relies on the fact that the offence in question was an isolated one, he may receive an old-fashioned look from the judge, but the sentence must nevertheless be passed on the basis that one offence only is before the court.[7] However, if the defendant himself says that the offence is not an isolated one, the court may take that fact into account, whilst still sentencing for one offence only.[8] The problem of how the court should deal with offences which may or may not be regarded as sample ones will be discussed separately.

3.13 The principle discussed applies equally in cases in which the judge sentences a defendant in respect of an offence which was earlier before the court, but which is no longer a live matter. In *Johnson*[9] the defendant pleaded guilty to possessing cannabis with intent to supply, and the Crown accepted his plea of not guilty to a count of supplying cannabis. When arrested the defendant had had £509 on him. He was sentenced to nine months' youth custody and fined £400, the judge observing that some of the money found on him must have come from supplying cannabis. The Court of Appeal had "considerable sympathy with the learned judge in his approach to this problem and in his scepticism about the source of the £509". The court nevertheless quashed the fine, as the defendant had been given the impression that he was being punished for supplying. See also *Ayensu and Ayensu*.[10]

6 (1983) 5 Cr.App.R.(S) 188.
7 *Corby and Corby* (1974) C.S.P. L2.1(d)
8 *Russen* (1981) 3 Cr.App.R.(S) 134.
9 (1984) 6 Cr.App.R.(S) 227.
10 (1982) 4 Cr.App.R.(S) 248. See also para. 15.19 *infra*.

3.14 Similarly, if the jury acquits a defendant on the more serious of
two charges and convicts of the lesser only, the court must sentence for
the lesser offence on the basis of the facts as they must have been found
by the jury.[11] This is so even if the verdict of the jury is somewhat
strange: the court must loyally accept the jury's right to return any
verdict it chooses, and must sentence accordingly.[12] It was doubtless this
basic doctrine of fairness, that there should be no sentence in respect of
an offence that is no longer before the court, which prompted the
Queen's Bench Divisional Court to create new law in *R. v. St. Albans
Crown Court, ex parte Cinnamond.*[13] The Crown Court had on technical
grounds allowed a motorist's appeal against conviction for an offence of
driving with excess alcohol, for which he had been disqualified for 18
months, plus a further three months under the totting-up provisions. His
appeal against a second conviction for careless driving on the same
occasion was dismissed. For that lesser offence he had been disqualified
for a further three months under the totting-up provisions. Having
allowed his appeal in respect of the major offence, the Crown Court
then varied the sentence in respect of the careless driving, by increasing
it from three months' disqualification to 21 months in all (18 plus three).
Unlike the Court of Appeal the Crown Court retains its power to
increase a sentence on an appeal. The Divisional Court held that it had
the jurisdiction to vary the sentence using its *certiorari* powers. Donaldson, L.J. stated:

> "Disqualification was well merited, but 18 months' disqualification, par-
> ticularly in the circumstances in which he succeeded in obtaining the
> quashing of a conviction in respect of which that very period of disqualifi-
> cation had been imposed, and quite rightly imposed, seems to me to
> involve so great a disparity with the normal range as to constitute an error
> of law, if not an excess of jurisdiction."

3.15 A defendant must obviously be sentenced only once for any given
offence. He must not be sentenced for offences in respect of which he
has already served a sentence. It is not always easy for the court to
decide how to treat previous convictions, but in *Queen*[14] Kenneth Jones,
J. stated the basic proposition as follows:

> "Of course no prisoner is to be sentenced for the offences which he has
> committed in the past and for which he has already been punished. The
> proper way to look at the matter is to decide a sentence which is
> appropriate for the offence for which the prisoner is before the court."

11 *Hudson* (1979) 1 Cr.App.R.(S) 130.
12 *Singh* (1981) 3 Cr.App.R.(S) 180.
13 [1981] Q.B. 480.
14 (1981) 3 Cr.App.R.(S) 245.

In the passage immediately following, the learned judge made remarks which suggest that he was thinking of an appropriate bracket initially, rather than a specific sentence. He said:

> "Then in deciding whether that sentence should be imposed or whether the court can extend some leniency to the prisoner, the court must have regard to those matters which tell in his favour, and equally to those matters which tell against him; in particular his record of previous convictions. Then matters have to be balanced up to decide whether the appropriate sentence to pass is at the upper end of the bracket or somewhere lower down."

3.16 The previous convictions may properly "tell against him" if they indicate one of a number of relevant matters. If the defendant has on numerous occasions committed offences similar to the one for which he has to be sentenced, clearly he cannot be heard to say (at any rate, not with any prospect of success) that the instant offence was an isolated one. So, too the court will be entitled to come to the conclusion that past sentences failed to deter the defendant — although whether that will necessarily lead to a more severe sentence or to a more lenient alternative that has not been tried before, will depend on all the circumstances. Similarly, the repetition of a dangerous offence will be relevant because the court will then have to consider whether the protection of the public takes priority over any other aim of punishment. For example, in the rape guideline case of *Billam*[15] Lord Lane, C.J. said that a previous conviction for rape was relevant when a defendant was being sentenced for such an offence.

3.17 One of the matters that undoubtedly leads some defendants to feel that they have been sentenced for their past offences again, or largely on the basis of their record, is the habit of some sentencers of dwelling too much on previous convictions. It is appropriate to refer to relevant previous convictions which have influenced the sentence being passed and which help to explain the decision. It is, of course, not right to rub a defendant's nose in his list of previous convictions by referring to it in great detail when there is no occasion to do so.[16]

3.18 Finally, it need scarcely be said that a defendant must be sentenced for his own offences only, and not for those committed by his co-defendant. In *Wishart*[17] the judge in sentencing the defendant stated

---

15 (1986) 8 Cr.App.R.(S) 48.
16 For a further discussion of the problems of the persistent offender, see the section on extended sentences (paras. 9.38ff); see also A. Ashworth, *Sentencing and Penal Policy* (1983) Weidenfeld & Nicolson, Ch. 5.
17 (1979) 1 Cr.App.R.(S) 322.

that he was satisfied that he had been involved in his co-defendant's offence as well as his own. Defending counsel had protested when this was suggested by the judge, but to no avail: the judge insisted on taking the other offence into account. On the hearing of the appeal Lawton, L.J. stated (doubtless with some degree of satisfaction):

> "Indeed he went so far as to say that if he was wrong the Court of Appeal would put him right. That is what the Court of Appeal proposes to do."

The learned Lord Justice added that the judge's approach had been contrary to principle. He pointed out that ever since *Van Pelz* in 1943[18] it had been the law that the judge should disregard any information which might aggravate the sentence if the defendant did not accept that information, and if it was not proved. In any event, a man could only be sentenced for the offences of which he personally had been convicted.

SENTENCE FOR THE OFFENCE AS PROVED

3.19   Whether a defendant has pleaded guilty to an offence or been found guilty of it by a jury, there may still remain a dispute between him and the prosecution about the material facts of the offence, that is, facts which may affect the sentence one way or the other. There should be no problem where the sentencer is also the trier of the issue of guilt, whether a magistrates' court or the Crown Court on an appeal against conviction. Even in such a case, however, there is one trap to be avoided, namely, a pronouncement at the time of sentencing of an adverse finding of fact on a point which has not figured in the case, of which no notice was given to the defendant, and about which he has therefore had no opportunity to give evidence.[19] The problem of how to establish the facts on which to base a sentence will differ according to whether there was a plea of guilty or a conviction by the jury, and sometimes will differ according to whether the disputed facts could have been made the subject of a separate charge or not.

3.20   Although the Court of Appeal has discouraged special verdicts,[20] and questioning by the judge of a verdict which is unambiguous,[21] it is nevertheless proper to ask juries in advance to state which particular items they found to be stolen. This is so whether the theft is charged in a count on its own, or as part of a burglary count (where it does not offend against the duplicity rule). When a jury has determined a matter, either

---

18   (1943) 29 Cr.App.R. 10.
19   *Lester* (1975) 63 Cr.App.R. 144.
20   *Bourne* (1952) 36 Cr.App.R. 125.
21   *Larkin* (1944) 29 Cr.App.R. 18.

with a specific direction such as has been mentioned or without one, as in most cases, the judge must sentence in a manner which faithfully reflects the verdict, no matter how much he may disagree with it. Just as he must not sentence for an offence in respect of which the jury has acquitted,[22] so he must not sentence on a basis of facts inconsistent with the jury's verdict. In *Boyer*[23] the deceased had broken into the defendant's house. The defendant, who owned a collection of firearms, fired five shots at the intruder, killing him. The jury acquitted of murder and convicted of manslaughter. The Court of Appeal pointed out later that the jury must have found that neither an intention to kill nor an intention to cause really serious injury had been proved. The judge should accordingly have passed a sentence consistent with such a finding, that is, that the shots had been fired, as the defendant had claimed, in a panic and without any specific intent. The sentence of seven years' imprisonment was reduced, albeit by only two years.

3.21 There may be occasions when another offence is disclosed in addition to the one actually charged, but where the judge is nevertheless entitled to have regard to the full facts without any additional charge. However, the sort of situation which obtained in *Ribas*[24] is not likely to occur often. The defendant had pleaded guilty to importing 161 grammes of cocaine, at that time a rarely imported drug (sadly that is no longer the case). He claimed that the cocaine was for his personal use, and his counsel submitted that he was entitled to have a jury try the issue of whether that was true, or whether he had the drug for supplying to others. An additional count of possession with intent to supply was a possible way to get the question before the jury, but the judge rejected this suggestion. The Court of Appeal pointed out that the maximum penalty for both offences, importing and possessing with intent, was the same, then fourteen years' imprisonment. That being so, the seriousness of the offence of importing depended on the quantity imported: the specific intent with which the drug was imported was not material; and there was no obligation to add the count discussed. The defendant had not given evidence himself before the judge who had sentenced him, but medical evidence had been called on his behalf. The judge indicated that he did not believe the drug was all for his personal use, and the Court of Appeal held that he was entitled to come to that conclusion.

3.22 It is a matter of pure chance whether or not a given set of facts can give rise to one charge or two or more, as the important cases of

22 *Singh* (1981) 3 Cr.App.R.(S) 180.
23 (1981) 3 Cr.App.R.(S) 35.
24 (1976) 63 Cr.App.R. 147.

Newton[25] and *Courtie*[26] demonstrate. The distinction may be of importance at the sentencing stage, as we have seen. In *Newton* the defendant pleaded guilty to buggery with his wife, the offence being committed whether she had consented or not. Nevertheless absence of consent would clearly be material for the sentencer. As Lord Lane, C.J. observed, once the defendant had pleaded guilty, that "left the vital issue of consent unresolved and, on the count of buggery, unresolvable by a jury". Lord Lane pointed out that there were three alternative ways for a judge to resolve the difficulty where facts were disputed:

(1)   To use a jury – an alternative not open in *Newton*;

(2)   For the judge to hear evidence from both sides, and to arrive at his own conclusion, "acting so to speak as his own jury on the issue which is the root of the problem". Incidentally, it is for the judge, and not the defence, to decide whether a trial on the facts issue is necessary.[27]

(3)   To hear no evidence, but to come to a conclusion after hearing submissions from both sides.

In case of substantial conflict the judge must resolve the issue in the defendant's favour "so far as possible". The proviso contained in the last four words saves the judge from being obliged to accept any old cock-and-bull story which may be tendered.[28] In a borderline case it may be as well to invite the defendant to give evidence if he wishes.[29] It is clear that whilst a judge may resolve a conflict of facts on a given proven or admitted charge, he is not entitled to find further offences proved without a proper trial: he may not usurp the functions of a jury.[30]

3.23   In *Courtie* the charge was also one of buggery, but with a male aged 19, contrary to the Sexual Offences Act 1956, Section 12. The important difference from *Newton* was that in the case of males, unlike females, there are (for the present purposes) two separate offences: one of buggery with consent and another of buggery without. The indictment in *Courtie* had simply charged buggery with a male of 19 years, and had not stated that the offence had been committed without consent. When implementing some of the recommendations of the Wolfenden Committee's Report in the Sexual Offences Act 1967, Parliament provided that the offence when committed with a young man aged 16-20 should be punishable by a maximum of five years' imprisonment, but that the maximum should be ten years in the absence of consent.

25   (1982) 4 Cr.App.R.(S) 388.
26   (1984) 78 Cr.App.R. 292.
27   *Smith* (1986) 8 Cr.App.R.(S) 168.
28   *Connell* (1983) 5 Cr.App.R.(S) 360.
29   *MacKenzie* [1986] Crim.L.R. 346.
30   *Hutchison* (1972) 56 Cr.App.R. 307.

Buggery with a female was left as one offence with a maximum of life imprisonment.

3.24 Courtie pleaded guilty to the offence as charged. Counsel for the prosecution in his outline of the facts referred to the victim's lack of consent. This drew an understandable protest from the defence, and the very proper comment by the judge that he and the justices sitting with him would sentence on the basis that the offence in the case was the lesser one, that is, the consensual offence which carried a five year maximum. All would have been well had the matter ended there, but the prosecution then applied for leave to add a count charging buggery without consent. This application was turned down by the judge, who with his colleagues heard evidence and decided that the offence had indeed been committed without the consent of the youth. The sentence was passed on that basis, but was below the maximum for the lesser offence – the one actually charged and admitted. The House of Lords held that since 1967, by virtue of the different maximum sentences for different facts, there had been two separate offences, and that the defendant had been deprived of trial by jury in respect of the greater offence carrying the ten year maximum. The two offences ought to have been charged in separate counts, and then the jury could have decided the issue which really mattered.

3.25 We mentioned earlier that Parliament's changes of maximum sentences can sometimes be of help to the court in showing how the legislature feels about a given offence, and the same is true about Parliament's decision to leave a given maximum standing. This will not always be so, as a consideration of *Newton* and *Courtie* shows. It is inconceivable that the Court of Appeal would uphold a sentence of life imprisonment passed on a husband for consensual buggery of his wife, despite the legislature's confirmation of such a maximum only a few years ago; see *Dixon* (1982).[31]

3.26 Clearly the need to resolve a dispute about the facts only arises if the resolution of such a dispute is going to help. If the sentence is going to be the same either way, then there is no need to waste time resolving an academic point.[32] In one case a Recorder ordered the unnecessary trial of an issue in the following circumstances. The defendant had pleaded guilty to driving whilst disqualified and the prosecution alleged that someone had been killed by his car when he was driving it. There

---

31 (1982) 4 Cr.App.R.(S) 312.
32 See *Hall* (1984) 6 Cr.App.R.(S) 321.

was no charge relating to the death or to the manner of driving. Even if the disputed facts were resolved against the defendant, he could only be sentenced for driving whilst disqualified.[33]

3.27 Whenever a judge tries an issue of fact at the sentencing stage he must apply the criminal standard of proof to the prosecution's version. If he does so, and finds against the defendant, then it is most unlikely that the Court of Appeal will interfere with his finding, unless there were some exceptional circumstances.[34]

3.28 We have referred to the duty of the judge to sentence on the basis of the facts as they must have been found by the jury, but this will not always be possible. There will be some occasions where the judge is left in doubt about the jury's decisions on the facts. Sometimes, of course, jurors compromise in arriving at their verdict; it does not follow that all twelve or even ten are always agreed on all the facts. If there is doubt about the matter, the judge must give the benefit of that doubt to the defendant and only sentence him on the interpretation of the facts which is most favourable to him — subject to the proviso that the judge is not obliged, we suggest, to come to a conclusion which would be ridiculous. Nor is he obliged, if the jury's findings of facts — or apparent findings of facts — are equally consistent with more than one construction, to accept the view which is most favourable to the defendant.[35]

3.29 In *Stosiek*[36] the defendant was involved in a disturbance, during which a plain-clothes officer placed his hand on his arm and said that he was a police officer. The defendant did not calm down but injured the officer. The jury convicted of actual bodily harm, the only count. The verdict was simply one of guilty and therefore gave no clue as to whether the jury had found that the defendant knew that his victim was a police officer when he assaulted him. This was a matter of no consequence on the issue of whether the offence had been committed or not, but clearly relevant at the sentencing stage. As in the case of *Courtie*, it would have been possible for the prosecution to charge more than one offence arising out of the same offence: Stosiek could then have been charged also with assaulting an officer in the execution of his duty. The two verdicts would have resolved the sentencer's dilemma. As it was, the judge sentenced the defendant to a term of one year's imprisonment, a sentence inappropriate if the defendant did not know that the man

---

33 *Lawrence* (1983) 5 Cr.App.R.(S) 220.
34 *Ahmed* (1984) 6 Cr.App.R.(S) 391.
35 *Solomon and Triumph* (1984) 6 Cr.App.R.(S) 120.
36 (1982) 2 Cr.App.R.(S) 205.

intervening in his brawl was a police officer. In the Court of Appeal the sentence on Stosiek was reduced to a fine, Watkins, L.J. observing:

> "It is equally possible, so it seems from the papers, that the jury convicted him upon the basis that he had violently over-reacted to what could be said to have been a technical assault upon him by a person whom he did not know was a police officer. In those circumstances, the court has to be extremely astute to give the benefit of any doubt to a defendant about the basis on which a jury has convicted."

3.30 One matter creating difficulty from time to time is the proper allocation of responsibility between two or more co-defendants. Where a judge has presided at a trial and has heard all the evidence against and for each defendant in turn, he is in a good position to make a reasonable assessment of the varying degrees of culpability. In sentencing he will, of course, have to base himself on the verdicts returned by the jury and on the facts that must have been found by the jurors. Special difficulty may arise where one or more of the co-defendants have pleaded guilty. In such circumstances the judge will have to base himself on undisputed or proved facts before finding, say, that one defendant led the other into the crime. He must be particularly careful not to base himself solely on the statement of one defendant made to the police and implicating the other. If he forms a provisional view about the matter, he should consider giving the defence an opportunity of dealing with it: that can only be done, obviously, if the judge reveals what is in his mind as a provisional finding. Even more difficult is the situation which can arise when co-defendants have been tried separately, or when a given case is one of a series involving similar offences, such as separate thefts by a number of defendants from the same employer. The court should be careful to sentence each offender in respect of the offence and on the facts established against him. That may result in apparent disparity on occasion, but there can be no disparity in the strict sense if the *proven* basic facts are different in the cases of two or more defendants. Sometimes a defendant will be lucky in that a particularly damaging piece of evidence will be admissible only against some other defendant, but this sort of luck runs throughout the criminal justice process. Quite apart from the fact that some offenders get caught whilst others do not (the most serious disparity of all), one co-defendant may plead guilty only to find that his confederate is later acquitted despite overwhelming evidence. So it is with sentencing: some defendants may well come out of court with a lighter sentence than their colleagues — not because they were less blameworthy or had better records, but because the evidence available against them personally did not prove that they were as much to blame as those colleagues.

3.31   In *Bremner and Rawlings*[37] and *Cripps*[38] the Court of Appeal, whose members on each occasion included Roskill and Bridge, L.JJ., held that the sentencing judge ought not to have taken into account statements made by co-defendants. A similar line was taken by the Court of Appeal in *Michaels and Skoblo*.[39] Some decisions of the court have gone the other way, and somewhat surprisingly in *Depledge*[40] it was Bridge, L.J. who gave the judgment of the court, stating:

> "It is submitted that the learned judge was not entitled to take into account, in passing sentence on this appellant, anything which had come to his notice because he had tried the two co-accused upon whom he had passed lesser sentence. That, with respect, seems to us a wholly unrealistic argument . . . Any judge is bound, we think, to take an overall view and try to determine what are the appropriate sentences in the light of the view he takes of the totality of the evidence he has heard."

Thomas commented at the time:[41]

> "It is submitted that this ruling is inconsistent with principle and previous authority. It is surely wrong to sentence an offender on the basis of allegations or evidence which he has had no opportunity to challenge or refute."

The trend of the cases as a whole suggests that Thomas's comment is justified.

SAMPLE COUNTS

3.32   The difficult questions raised by the trial and sentencing of defendants in respect of sample or specimen counts have not yet been satisfactorily resolved. Let us assume that D1, D2 and D3 are managers of three different shops, who each steal £20,000 from their respective employer. D1 and D2 refuse to agree to the prosecution treating the twenty counts in their respective indictments as samples or specimens, and they also decline to have any other offence taken into consideration. Each of the three is of previous good character. Let us follow the three cases through separately, for the facts of each is different.

3.33   D1 stole £1 at a time from his employer's till, but each transaction can probably be proved separately against him. There is accordingly no

37   (1974) C.S.P. L2.2(b)
38   (1975) C.S.P. L2.2(h)
39   (1981) 3 Cr.App.R.(S) 188.
40   (1979) 1 Cr.App.R.(S) 183.
41   In [1979] Crim.L.R. 733.

justification for charging a general deficiency, and so any count referring to more than a single theft of £1 would be bad for duplicity.[42] The indictment contains twenty counts only to save it being overloaded, so that when convicted on all counts D1 will have to be sentenced for the theft of £20 only. A fine and compensation order would be a likely outcome, although a short sentence of imprisonment might conceivably be upheld, especially if suspicion had been cast on fellow employees.[43] The result would not be significantly different if the twenty counts had related to thefts of £10 at a time.

3.34 D2 stole £20,000 from his employer £100 at a time. When convicted on all twenty counts he will have to be sentenced for a theft of £2000 in all. He may well receive a short custodial sentence on the basis that whilst there was a breach of trust on twenty occasions, the "clang" principle makes a longer sentence unnecessary.[44] A community service order is another possibility for him.

3.35 D3 was less patient and stole £1000 on twenty separate occasions. When convicted on each of the twenty counts in his indictment he will be the only one of the three defendants actually convicted of stealing the whole amount he in fact stole. That also means that he will be the only one likely to be punished appropriately for stealing £20,000 possibly by a term of two years' imprisonment.[45]

3.36 As we shall see further in the next chapter, it would be wrong for the court to apply any pressure on D1 and D2 for them to apply to have their 19,980 and 180 other offences respectively taken into consideration.[46] The prosecution may indicate that another trial involving a further twenty counts is planned. Whilst that thought might trouble D2 a little, D1 would very likely point out that the prosecution might well get more stick from the court than him on a second trial! This bizarre situation would seem to be inevitable in view of the House of Lords decision in *Director of Public Prosecutions v. Anderson.*[47]

3.37 In that appeal Lord Diplock approved of the use of sample counts, but pointed out their limitations when he said:

> "Nothing that I have said should be understood as discouraging the practice of limiting the charges in an indictment to a limited number of

---

42 Archbold, 42nd ed., para. 1–61; *Cain and others* [1983] Crim.L.R. 802.
43 See *Upton* (1980) 2 Cr.App.R.(S) 132.
44 See *Gregson* (1980) 2 Cr.App.R.(S) 25.
45 See *Barrick* (1985) 81 Cr.App.R. 78.
46 *Nelson* (1967) 51 Cr.App.R. 98.
47 (1978) 67 Cr.App.R. 185.

"sample" counts in cases where, as in the instant case, the accused has adopted a systematic dishonest practice. Your Lordships were told that, where sample counts are used, it is customary to provide the defence with a list of all the similar offences of which it is alleged that those selected as the subject of the counts contained in the indictment are samples. In appropriate cases it may be that the evidence of all or some of these additional offences is led by the prosecution at the trial as evidence of 'system' – as was apparently done in the instant case . . . Where sample counts are used it is, in my view, essential that the ordinary procedure should be followed for taking other offences into consideration in determining sentence."

3.38 In *Singh and Singh*[48] Sheldon, J. suggested that if certain counts had been treated as sample ones only, with the knowledge of the defence, then it was legitimate for the court to sentence on the basis of the total criminality revealed. He said:

> "Where, to the knowledge of the defence, a count has been put forward by the prosecution as a sample or specimen count, and the trial has been conducted upon that basis, *a fortiori*, if no objection has been taken to that course, if the defendant is convicted the judge is entitled to deal with the reality of the situation and to sentence him in the light of the whole history of the matter as disclosed by the evidence, and to treat the individual offences charged as having been aggravated by what that history has revealed."

3.39 In the light of the House of Lords decision in *Anderson* it is difficult to see that the approach suggested by Sheldon, J. is any longer open. If a defendant is fully cooperative he will ask for other offences to be taken into consideration. If he does not, then the mere fact that he knew that the prosecution was suggesting at his trial that the indictment contained sample counts only can surely not justify his being sentenced in respect of offences which he has never admitted and in respect of which there has been no trial. It is submitted that the Court of Appeal's decision in *McKenzie*[49] accords more with the House of Lords decision. The defendant pleaded guilty to several counts involving a total of £640. The prosecution stated those counts were sample ones only and that the total amount involved was £11,000. The defendant was invited to ask the court to take 240 further offences into consideration, but declined the invitation. He was sentenced to four and a half years' imprisonment. Not surprisingly, he appealed. In reducing the sentence to one of 19 months in all, Mustill, J. said in the Court of Appeal:

> "the appellant should have been sentenced for the offences in respect of which he was convicted, leaving it to the authorities, if they thought fit, to

---

48   (1981) Crim.L.R. 509.
49   (1984) 6 Cr.App.R.(S) 99.

prosecute him on a subsequent occasion in respect of the outstanding matters, just as the learned Judge had himself told the appellant might happen."

3.40 In *Price*[50] the Court of Appeal sought to limit the application of *Anderson*, but it would seem that the House of Lords authority is of general application to cases involving sample counts. Legislation would appear to provide the only solution to the problems discussed, for merely altering the Indictment Rules or providing a Practice Direction could not adequately deal with the constitutional point involved, namely, that no defendant can be properly sentenced for an offence neither proved nor admitted.

50 (1978) 68 Cr.App.R. 154.

CHAPTER 4

Antecedents, Social Inquiry and Other Reports

4.01 On occasion the evidence called by the defence at the mitigation stage will prove very helpful, as we shall see when discussing that part of the trial in the next chapter. Generally, however, apart from the evidence relating to the facts of the case in question, the most fruitful assistance for the court in its difficult task of choosing the most appropriate sentence will come from various reports. Under the heading of reports we shall discuss:

(1) Police antecedents;
(2) Social inquiry reports;
(3) Medical reports;
(4) Reports from penal establishments; and
(5) Reports on juveniles.

4.02 One general difficulty should be mentioned at this stage, as it applies equally to the evidence of police officers and probation officers. The courts have over the years expressed the wish that the witnesses reporting on the defendant should have personal knowledge of the matters they are covering. At the same time everyone is anxious to save such witnesses from wasting time at court, and so the practice has developed of having court liaison officers to present reports of colleagues. This means that often neither the police officer nor the probation officer in the witness box has any personal knowledge of the case. It is obviously not desirable that cases should constantly be put back for the maker of the report to give evidence, but sometimes, where there is an important point of conflict, it cannot be avoided. At the very least, a police officer acting as a court liaison officer should arm himself with details of recent offences in the list of previous convictions, and must do so if there is any breach to be dealt with by the court, such as a breach of a suspended sentence.[1] It helps if the antecedents report contains the details of the last three convictions, as well as of any breach.

---

1 *Munday* (1971) 56 Cr.App.R. 220.

POLICE ANTECEDENTS

4.03 The police routinely supply the courts with reports or statements on the antecedents of the defendant. The main function of those reports is to provide the court, the prosecution and the defence with details of the previous convictions and findings of guilt of the defendant; also of any outstanding matters to be dealt with by the court, such as breach of probation, conditional discharge, community service order or suspended sentence. Reports on antecedents will also refer to any compensation claim put forward by any victim. A secondary function is to provide background information about the defendant's personal and family circumstances, including his employment record and his pay, a matter of some importance if a fine or compensation order is to be considered. Whilst the information relating to previous convictions is usually fairly accurate, that relating to employment is often out of date by the time the case reaches the Crown Court, though obviously it may still be correct if a case is dealt with fairly promptly in the magistrates' court. In the Crown Court the background information relating to the personal circumstances will often be superseded by the more detailed and later information provided in a social inquiry report. Of course, if the probation service has not provided such a report, the court may only have the incomplete information provided by the police, supplemented in due course by the mitigation speech and, less often, defence evidence.

4.04 In a Practice Direction[2] in 1966 Lord Parker, C.J. stated that the police must always provide the defence, on request, with details of previous convictions before the trial. Lord Parker gave as a reason the right of the defence to know whether it would be safe to put character in issue. It is also useful for defending lawyers to have an accurate account of those convictions when advising their client on the plea and when preparing the mitigation. Clearly it would be unreasonable to expect the preparation of the mitigation to be based solely on the defendant's faulty — and charitable — recollection of his own past, without any opportunity for his lawyers to see what had really happened. The Practice Direction also included the advice that:

> "It may also contain a short and concise statement as to the prisoner's domestic and family circumstances, his general reputation and associates."

The last five words quoted have occasionally led to difficulties. In *Wilkins*[3] the appellant had been convicted of living on immoral earnings.

2 (1966) 50 Cr.App.R. 271.
3 (1977) 66 Cr.App.R. 49.

As part of the antecedents a police officer gave evidence which linked the defendant with a large number of prostitutes not connected with any count in the indictment. Geoffrey Lane, L.J. said of this evidence when the defendant appealed:

> "That was on the face of it highly prejudicial evidence. The last passage which I have read went far beyond anything which had been proved at the trial itself."

4.05 The appeal court had earlier held in *Haighety* in 1965[4] that previous acquittals should not be referred to by the police. The Court of Appeal was clearly concerned in both cases with the same principle of fairness that has been discussed earlier in connection with the factual basis for sentencing. Just as a man must not be sentenced for an offence he did not commit, so it is quite wrong for the court to take into account any previous crimes, unless they led to a conviction or to a recent caution for an admitted offence. Even then there is a limit to how much effect previous convictions may have on the sentence there and then being imposed.[5]

4.06 The same principle applies to statements about the defendant not amounting to allegations of further offences, but intended to show that he has been up to no good. In *Sargeant*,[6] a case discussed earlier in connection with some of the principles of punishment,[7] the defendant took exception to a police officer's claim that he had been dismissed for drunkenness by his last employers. The officer's claim was mistaken. In the Court of Appeal Lawton, L.J. said:

> "The Court has no intention of trying to resolve the conflict of recollection, but what it does propose to do is to call attention once again to, and to underline, the need for great care in the giving of evidence of antecedents."

4.07 In order to help with the reduction of disparity, if any associate of the defendant has already been sentenced for his part in the offences committed jointly with the defendant, the officer should be prepared to give details of his antecedents also, as well as of the sentence passed on him. If such information is not available the court may decline to proceed with the sentencing of the defendant.[8]

4.08 When the Rehabilitation of Offenders Bill was in the House of Commons in 1974 the hope was expressed that a Practice Direction

---

4 (1965) C.S.P. L4.4(b).
5 See *Queen* (1981) 3 Cr.App.R.(S) 245, and *Cooper* (1983) 5 Cr.App.R.(S) 295.
6 (1974) 60 Cr.App.R. 74.
7 See paras. 1.58, 1.60 and 1.66 *supra*.
8 *McNally*, C.A. 15 April 1986 (unreported).

would be given to limit the extent to which certain old and relatively minor, or "spent" convictions were referred to in criminal courts, even though strictly admissible there. The Act of 1974 was followed by a Practice Direction by Lord Widgery, C.J. on 30 June 1975. Several of the directions given were relevant to the antecedents stage. It was directed that whilst all previous convictions should be listed in the report provided to the court, spent convictions should "so far as practicable, be marked as such". Counsel should not refer to such a conviction without the leave of the court, and even the judge should not refer to any, the Direction continued, "unless it is necessary to do so for the purpose of explaining the sentence to be passed". Whilst a spent conviction should not be referred to, its presence in the antecedents may well have some effect on the course of the proceedings, if only because counsel is not likely to say in mitigation that the defendant has never committed an offence of the instant kind before, if as a matter of record he has had one or more similar convictions that have become unmentionable only because of the passage of time.

4.09 It sometimes happens that the prosecution will not be aware of the fact that the defendant has previous convictions. This can happen where there has been a change of name or a communications breakdown, but is probably a fairly rare occurrence. What does happen rather more often is that the prosecution will not necessarily be aware of the defendant's most recent conviction. There is no duty on the defending advocate to reveal to the court that his client has convictions or additional convictions. Clearly he must not mislead the court by suggesting that a conviction, of which he is aware, does not exist. It is also wrong for him to ask one of the prosecution witnesses whether there are any recorded convictions, knowing that there are some, but hoping (because of an indication he has had earlier) that the answer will be in the negative.[9]

Offences to be taken into consideration

4.10 If the defendant has signed a form admitting other offences which he wishes the court to take into consideration when sentencing him, it is usual for that fact to be referred to either before or after the officer has dealt with all other matters. After the antecedents witness has produced a copy of the list of other offences which he has served on the defendant, and for which the latter has signed an acknowledgment, the court must ensure that each offence is clearly admitted and that there is a request

---

9 *Code of Conduct for the Bar* (1980) p. 155.

for each to be taken into consideration. If the defendant asks for any offence listed to be expunged, or if he shows any hesitation, other than momentary, about admitting the offences, then the court must not take them into account.[10] In *Urbas*[11] Salmon, J. stated:

> "The Court, in sentencing the prisoner, should take into account such offences, and only such offences, which the prisoner clearly admits, and if there is any doubt as to whether he is admitting an offence, it ought not to be taken into consideration."

It follows that an earlier request by a defendant for offences to be taken into consideration in the magistrates' court in no way binds him in the Crown Court should he subsequently be committed there for sentence.[12]

4.11 Although there may be no doubt about the defendant's wish to have an offence taken into consideration, the court may decline to do so if, for example, that offence is of a different nature or much more serious than the offence before the court. If the court does accede to the defendant's request, it may add to the sentence for the instant offence an additional amount for the offences considered. However, the maximum sentence is limited to the permissible maximum for the offence before the court. In the past it was sometimes necessary for a court to decline to take an offence into consideration because it could not then make an appropriate financial order with regard to that offence. However, the Theft Act 1968 and the Powers of Criminal Courts Act 1973 gave the courts certain powers with regard to restitution orders, compensation and other financial orders even where an offence is merely taken into consideration. Needless to say, the safeguards mentioned by Salmon, J., apply also in such circumstances.[13] One question which does not appear to have been considered authoritatively is the number of offences which the court can deal with in this manner. The largest number that the writers have come across is in a case cited by Thomas in his *Encylopedia of Current Sentencing Practice*,[14] in which the court agreed to take 738 other offences into consideration. (The case is discussed briefly in Chapter 11.) Presumably there is no limit. However many offences are considered, the court should in passing sentence always state the number that has been taken into consideration and then, as a matter of practice rather than strict law, the defendant will not be prosecuted further in respect of those matters.

10 *McKenzie* (1984) 6 Cr.App.R.(S) 99.
11 (1963) C.S.P. L3.3(b).
12 *Davies* (1980) 2 Cr.App.R.(S) 364.
13 *Anderson v. Director of Public Prosecutions* (1978) 67 Cr.App.R. 185.
14 *Smith* (1974) C.S.P. F2.4(b); para. 11.17 *infra*.

SOCIAL INQUIRY REPORTS

The requirement to obtain a report

4.12 Where no report is available it is up to the sentencing court to decide whether it wishes to incur the delay caused by asking for a social inquiry report, or whether to proceed to sentence without one. Whilst defence solicitors may suggest to the court that a report would be helpful, they cannot ask the probation service to prepare one.[15] There are certain statutory obligations that must be borne in mind, particularly in the magistrates' courts, where they are more onerous than in the Crown Court.

4.13 No court may pass a first sentence of imprisonment on a defendant over 21 unless that court is of the opinion that "no other method of dealing with him is appropriate": Powers of Criminal Courts Act, Section 20. For the purpose of determining that issue "the court shall in every case obtain a social inquiry report", unless the court is of the opinion that such a step is unnecessary (Section 20A). If a magistrates' court decides that a report is unnecessary it is required to state the reason for that conclusion in open court, and to record that reason both in the warrant of commitment and in the register. The Crown Court is not obliged to give or record any reason, but it would be as well for the judge to say why he finds it unnecessary to obtain a report, unless the case is of so grave a nature that it is clear that no sentence other than one of immediate custody is possible.

4.14 Section 20A also provides that no sentence is invalidated by a failure to obtain a report. If there is an appeal in such a case, the Crown Court or the Court of Appeal "shall obtain a social inquiry report". Once again the mandatory word "shall" is watered down by the exception that there is no obligation on an appellate court to obtain a report if it in turn considers such a step to be unnecesary. However, if a judge indicates that a report was really necessary, then his failure to obtain one may be regarded as a serious omission requiring a sentence to be varied.[16]

4.15 The other main statutory requirement for a social inquiry report is to be found in the provisions relating to defendants under 21. The

15 *Adams* (1970) Crim.L.R. 693.
16 *Massheder* (1983) 5 Cr.App.R.(S) 442.

Criminal Justice Act 1982, Section 2 states that with young offenders the court "shall in every case" obtain a report for the purpose of determining whether there is any appropriate non-custodial disposal available. ("Every case" does not include a case under the Children and Young Persons Act 1933, Section 53, for which see paras. 10.30ff *post.*) This requirement has been introduced because a youth custody or detention centre sentence may only be passed on the under 21-year-old defendant in limited circumstances. Once more Section 2 provides the exception that a court need not obtain a report if of the opinion that it is unnecessary, and that a magistrates' court must state and record the reason. The provisions in the section relating to reports at the appellate stage are similar to those relating to offenders over 21 facing their first sentence of imprisonment. Similarly the failure to obtain a report in the case of a defendant under 21 sentenced to custody does not invalidate the sentence.

4.16 There are occasions when the views of a probation officer or local authority social worker are particularly relevant for technical reasons, and so Parliament has insisted on reports or consultation in the following circumstances. The Powers of Criminal Courts Act 1973, Section 14 provides that a court shall not make a community service order until it has considered a report about the defendant and his circumstances and is satisfied that he is a suitable person to undertake the work under the terms of an order. Section 2(5) provides that before inserting a condition of residence in a probation order, "the court shall consider the home circumstances of the offencer". Whilst the statute does nor require it, the relevant inquiries will usually be undertaken by the author of the social inquiry report. Similarly Section 4A of the Act provides that certain conditions relating to reporting, and to participating or refraining from participating in certain activities, shall not be included in a probation order by the court unless it has first consulted a probation officer about the defendant's circumstances and the feasibility of the conditions. A magistrates' court may not imprison a fine defaulter who is subject to a money payment supervision order without first obtaining a report from the supervising officer on the defendant's conduct and means: Magistrates' Courts Act 1980, Section 88(6).

The time for preparation of reports

4.17 Unfortunately the courts, the probation service and the Home Office have not been able to arrive at a satisfactory solution of the problem of the correct timing for the preparation of a social inquiry report. The lack of agreement is brought about by the conflict between two important points of view, both concerned in part with wasting time. The last thing a sentencer wants after a defendant has been convicted, many weeks or months after the commission of an offence, is a further delay before sentence can be passed. Many defendants probably share such a view, and do not welcome the additional delay caused by the need for a report to be prepared at that stage. Incidentally, especially if a defendant is granted bail pending the preparation of a report, the court should make it absolutely clear in appropriate circumstances that custody has not been ruled out as a possible outcome.

4.18   On the other hand, many probation officers object to preparing reports before trial in cases in which the defendant has indicated that he will be disputing his guilt. A number of points are raised in this connection, some having more force than others. A valid point is that a great deal of time can be wasted in the preparation of reports on defendants who are eventually acquitted, or convicted of a trivial offence only or (conversely) of such a serious offence that the court is not concerned to see a report because prison is considered to be the only possible sentence. (The fact that such defendants may have received some assistance from the probation officer making his inquiries is neither here nor there for the purposes of the present argument.) Next it is said that there are ethical objections to preparing a report on a defendant who is proclaiming his innocence and who is in law innocent. On the other hand, arresting, charging and trying an innocent defendant is also an interference with his liberty. Unfortunately it is not possible to devise a criminal justice system which deals only with convicted or admitted criminals: each system is obliged to deal with defendants before their conviction. There would seem to be no ethical reason why the courts' own social workers should not also be obliged to deal with innocent people, if such a course is otherwise in the interests of justice. A better ethical point is that a defendant may be harmed if, say, his employer learns that he is awaiting trial from a probation officer making inquiries. (It should perhaps be added that not many defendants manage to get their trials fixed for their annual leave from work.) The technical objection is often raised that it is impossible to discuss a defendant's attitude towards the offence if he is denying it. That is true, and a report will have an important gap in it if it does not cover that point, or the defendant's explanation of how the offence came to be committed. Whilst the defendant's attitude towards the offence and offending can perhaps be best elicited by a probation officer, his explanation for the offence is something which he can often put forward by way of mitigation without any social work intervention.

4.19　The argument against pre-trial reports in not guilty plea cases is sometimes reinforced by the suggestion that the judge may misuse the contents of a report, that is, that he may use some information contained exclusively in the report to put a devastating question to the defendant during the trial. There is no reported case which supports this suggestion, but reliance is sometimes placed on the case of *Winter*,[17] in which the judge used the contents of a legal aid application form, supplied to the court by the defendant, as the basis for some questions when the defendant was in the witness box. The conviction was quashed for that reason. Finally it is right to add that the courts have no statutory power to order a report before conviction.

4.20　One of the dangers for a defendant is that a court may decline to adjourn his case for a report after conviction because of all the delay that has already occurred, and that a custodial sentence will be imposed which might not have been imposed if the court had been supplied with a report in advance. Such a point is justified, as it seems clear from various research projects that probation officers' recommendations influence the decision in a significant number of cases – and usually in the direction of a non-custodial disposal.[18] Another point that has to be borne in mind is that a probation officer's help during the preparation of his report can significantly improve the defendant's circumstances, and thus make him a better risk for a non-custodial sentence. The resolution of some of the defendant's problems, during what has been called a "mini-probation" period, might well not only afford him early relief, but also save him from custody. Such a man is unlikely to complain that he was helped whilst technically innocent.

4.21　One odd result of reports on first offenders in the juvenile courts has emerged. There is some support for the suggestion that juveniles may get a more lenient sentence if there is no report than if there is one. A report may make a court lean in favour of more drastic intervention than would be considered necessary or just without such a report.[19] This accounts for some of the reluctance on the part of officers to prepare reports at any early stage.

17　[1980] Crim.L.R. 659.
18　J. Thorpe, *Social Inquiry Reports: A Survey* (1978) H.M.S.O., H.O.R.S. No. 48; A. Ashworth *et al.*, *Sentencing in the Crown Court* (1984) Oxford Centre for Criminological Research Paper No. 10, p. 41.
19　N. Tutt and H. Giller, "Doing justice to great expectations", *Community Care*, 17 January 1985, p. 20; H. Kemshall, "The Justice Model in Warwicks" (1985) *Probation J. 33* p. 106.

4.22   At present the only legal obligation on a probation officer to produce a social inquiry report is that imposed by the Powers of Criminal Courts Act 1973, Schedule 3, para. 8, which provides:

> "It shall be the duty of probation officers to . . . inquire, in accordance with any directions of the court, into the circumstances or home surroundings of any person with a view to assisting the court in determining the most suitable method of dealing with his case."

As Charlotte Mitra has pointed out, an express direction by a court to prepare a report before trial is very rare. Such pre-trial preparation as has taken place has been as a result of Home Office circulars, or on the initiative of the service itself.[20] The National Association of Probation Officers has resolved that such reports should not be prepared unless the defendant intends to plead guilty, but some officers prefer to ignore the resolution. Home Office Circular 92 of 1986 suggests that reports should normally not be prepared before trial in the magistrates' court unless the defendant has indicated his intention to plead guilty. The circular also recommends that local arrangements should be made by Chief Probation Officers with the local Crown Court centres for the provision of reports, so as to take into account:

> "both the resource implications for the probation service and the importance to the Crown Court of ensuring that the case is dealt with on first hearing whenever possible, especially in cases involving visiting recorders and assistant recorders."

At some time the problems which have been discussed will have to be resolved on a national, rather than on a local basis. In the meantime it would be as well for sentencers to contain any irritation they may feel if there is no report available when they need one, and to make sure that they order one if there is the least chance that it may make a difference to the sentence.

Recommendations by probation officers

4.23   There has for some years now been fairly general agreement about the extent to which it is proper for the probation officer to make specific recommendations in his report. The difficulty, as so often with generally accepted rules, is in their application, and in that area there is still the occasional unfortunate disagreement. The word unfortunate is justified, as nobody benefits when a court rebukes a probation officer when he is doing his job conscientiously and in accordance with generally accepted practice. Home Office Circular 195 of 1974 stated:

---

20   C.L. Mitra, "The Pre-Trial Social Inquiry Report" (1984) 148 J.P. 22.

"The Secretary of State shares the view of the Lord Chief Justice that, if an experienced probation officer feels able to make a specific recommendation in favour of (or against) any particular form of decision being reached, he should state it clearly in his report. He also considers, and the Lord Chief Justice agrees, that probation officers, when offering advice in a report on the suitability of an offender for probation, should be encouraged to suggest the term of an order, taking into account their assessment of the offender's needs, his likely response to supervision, and any other relevant factors."

4.24 In *Blowers*[21] the defendant and another had attacked a man aged 65 and a woman of 55 with intent to rob them. The social inquiry report recommended that a community service order might be appropriate. In dismissing an appeal against the sentence of four years' imprisonment which had been passed, Lawton, L.J. observed,

"This kind of unrealistic recommendation creates difficulties for the trial courts and for this court."

A former probation officer, Helen Napier, pointed out that the court's strictures were themselves open to criticism on three grounds.[22]

"Firstly it invites probation officers to offer their own prejudgment of the sentence by considering the whole range of factors which are relevant to the court's decision . . . Secondly these comments suggest that probation officers should have in mind, at the time of writing their reports, what a court is likely to do and should keep their recommendations within a 'realistic' (*i.e.* acceptable to the court) amount of deviation from this . . . Thirdly it blurs the distinction between the role of the probation officer and that of the sentencer."

4.25 Speaking at the Annual Meeting of the Central Council of Probation Committees in May 1981, Lord Lane, C.J. commended Helen Napier's article and added the following suggestion:[23]

"The probation officer, if he is going to make what at first blush appears to be a somewhat startling proposition, can sit down and write it out very carefully. If he is suggesting in this particular case (if you like) a community service order then he can say that it may seem to the sentencer to be a rather extraordinary proposition but the reasons for it are (a), (b) and (c). It may be that having written those reasons down it will occur to the writer that what he is suggesting is nonsense, in which case he can tear it up and start again. But if, on the other hand, it is not nonsense, then the judge if he is worthy of his salt will read those reasons and he may very well be persuaded by them."

21 (1976) C.S.P. L5.3(a).
22 H. Napier, "Probation Officers and Sentencing" (1978) *Probation J. 25*, p. 122.
23 Central Council transcript.

4.26   In the circumstances it is not surprising that Home Office Circular 18 of 1983 repeated the 1974 view and stated:

> "A recommendation is likely to be more helpful, and carry more weight, if it is supported with reasons related to the consequence which the probation officer's experience indicates are likely to follow if the course recommended is – or is not – taken . . . If a report recommends a course of action to the court which may in the circumstances appear unusual, it is important that the reasons for that proposal should be carefully examined."

The notion that reasons should be given whenever a slightly unusual course is being recommended or taken is beginning to percolate through the whole sentencing stage. Home Office Circular 92 of 1986 repeated the advice that specific recommendations could be made and added much sensible advice, including the following:

> "A social inquiry report should provide the court with a clear indication of the sources on which the author has drawn. It is confusing to sentencers, and in the end self-defeating for the reporting officer, if there is no distinction between fact and opinion, or verified and unverified information."

4.27   There is one very good reason for the courts to be slow to rebuke a probation officer for making a suggestion which appears at first blush to be startling, and that is that the courts themselves are constantly changing their own position about the appropriateness or otherwise of a given sentence for a particular offence. A judge may well say in one case, "This type of case always merits immediate custody", only to find that a week later the Court of Appeal is suggesting that a non-custodial penalty may on occasion be appropriate, especially if Parliament has just introduced an additional rung into the penal ladder by providing a new type of sentence, such as the community service order or partly suspended sentence. It is in any event no part of the courts' function to continue to pass exactly the same sentences year after year without variation, whether in the interests of certainty or the avoidance of disparity. We can only improve the sentencing system if we continually try to use the various alternatives sensibly and with some imagination. It is not as though prison had been proved to be remarkably effective at preventing crime. Not only the probation officer, but the mitigating lawyer should be encouraged to make suggestions which will help the court to examine solutions other than the time-honoured ones – which were not necessarily all that wonderful and perhaps did not deserve to be honoured quite so much.

4.28   There are some recommendations in reports which are not so much unrealistic as foolish, as for example one for a sentence which is legally not available. Such a proposal can harm not only the credibility of the officer in question, but can also mislead the defendant into expecting a lenient sentence which cannot possibly be imposed. If his advocate wrongly adopts the mistake in the report, then the defendant may be doubly disappointed. There is another reason why a foolish recommendation can lead to unfortunate results. If the probation officer has made a statement or recommendation which approaches the nonsensical, there is a danger that the sentencer will ignore the whole report, even though the rest of it may be perfectly sound. Shapland reported the following views of lawyers she interviewed:[24]

> "Many legal representatives were worried that if a report made an unrealistic recommendation which could invite the derision of the judge then the rest of the content of the report would not be taken very seriously."

4.29 It is not only unrealistic comments which incur the risk of the total rejection of the report. Much the same can happen if, say, the writer of the report brushes aside the previous convictions, makes light of the instant serious offence, or gives the impression that he has adopted the defendant's rosy version of the facts without any attempt at objectivity.

4.30 A copy of the social inquiry report must be provided in good time to counsel or solicitor for the defence, or to the defendant himself if not represented. If he is under 17 and unrepresented, then the copy should be given to his parent or guardian: Powers of Criminal Courts Act 1973, Section 46. Particularly in the case of an unrepresented defendant, the judge in the Crown Court should ask whether the defendant has seen the report.[25] The contents of the report should not be read out, but it is sometimes useful if the judge refers to a particular passage by way of explanation of a sentence which might appear to some to be exceptionally lenient. The judge can say that he has been greatly influenced by certain facts which have been disclosed by the report, and he should then state in outline what they are, unless there are strong grounds for not making them public.[26] Very often counsel will have alluded to such mitigating facts in his mitigation speech, but this is not always so: it sometimes happens that counsel misses the best point in his client's favour.

---

24 J. Shapland, *Between Conviction and Sentence* (1981) Routledge & Kegan Paul, p. 132.
25 *Hughes* (1969) 53 Cr.App.R. 129.
26 For the giving of reasons generally, see paras. 7.11ff *infra*.

MEDICAL REPORTS

4.31 Medical and psychiatric reports may be particularly helpful at the sentencing stage, and on some occasions they are essential, as where a court wishes to make a hospital order or a probation order with a condition of treatment. Some of the most acceptable reports are those which come from medical advisers who were treating the defendant before he was apprehended. Any physical or mental illness existing at the time of the commission of the offence may be a mitigating factor, but the court may be a little sceptical if the doctor in question was only consulted for the first time after the arrest of the patient. On occasion the actual commission of the offence may provide the first clue to the existence of a genuine medical or mental condition, and the defence will then be able to point out that there is nothing sinister in the fact that the defendant had not attended for treatment on any occasion before his arrest.

4.32 The need for a report will usually be suggested by the defence solicitor or by the probation officer charged with the preparation of the social inquiry report. If the defendant is on bail, the probation officer may arrange for a medical examination with the consent both of the defendant and of the court. If a defendant is in custody, the prison medical officer may decide that a report would be helpful to the sentencing court, and he may then provide one. The court itself may ask for a report, whether the defendant has been on bail or in custody, and may adjourn the case for a report to be prepared. A defendant may then be remanded in custody or on bail, but the court should always bear in mind the general principles relating to bail, and should not remand in custody for a report unless driven to the conclusion that such a course is unavoidable.

4.33 Medical reports are mandatory only in limited circumstances, and we shall discuss the relevant provisions of the Mental Health Act 1983 and those relating to probation orders with a treatment condition later. As a general rule a court considering a life sentence should also obtain a report.[27] A new power was given to both the Crown Court and the magistrates' court by Section 35 of the 1983 Act: a defendant may in certain circumstances be remanded to a named hospital for a report on his mental condition. Such a remand may only be ordered after the court has received the appropriate evidence from a registered medical practitioner, and after it has ruled out the possibility of bail. Section 35

---

27 *De Havilland* (1983) 5 Cr.App.R.(S) 109.

contains many other detailed provisions which must be carefully followed before such a remand is ordered.

4.34 The magistrates' court has a rather unusual power under the Magistrates' Courts Act 1980, Section 30 to ask for an inquiry into the defendant's physical or mental condition once the court is satisfied that "he did the act or made the omission charged", but before convicting him. This applies only where the trial is of an offence punishable on summary conviction with imprisonment, and when the court is of the opinion that the inquiry should be made "before the method of dealing with him is determined". The court must supply the institution or person who is to make the enquiry with a statement of the reasons why the court has come to its conclusion: Magistrates' Courts Rules 1981, rule 24. Prison medical officers have sometimes complained that they are not helped very much by reasons which simply read, "Demeanour in court" or "Nature of offence", so courts should ensure that reasons for the inquiry are adequately stated. It can be helpful if courts bear in mind what was said by the Butler Committee on Mentally Abnormal Offenders.[28]

"Due explanation of these reasons will enable the doctor to relate his report to the points in which the court is interested. It is also important for the doctor that the court should always provide adequate particulars of the circumstances of the offence, especially where its nature suggests that the offender may be dangerous or violent. It would be helpful if the courts could make available to reporting doctors copies of any medical, probation or other reports in their possession."

4.35 Recent research supports the writers' impression that most specific recommendations contained in psychiatric reports are followed by the Crown Court, unless the case is so serious that imprisonment cannot be avoided.[29]

REPORTS FROM PENAL ESTABLISHMENTS

4.36 Reports from penal establishments used to be received by the courts quite often in the past, for example, when the court was considering the passing of a sentence of corrective training or borstal training, both now defunct. Such reports are rarely supplied to the trial courts nowadays. In the Court of Appeal on the other hand the use of

---

28 *Report of the Committee on Mentally Abnormal Offenders* (1975) H.M.S.O. (Cmnd 6244), para. 11.8.
29 R.D. MacKay, "Psychiatric Reports in the Crown Court" [1986] Crim.L.R. 217.

such reports has continued to play an important, if somewhat haphazard role. At times the effect of a report can be neutral: it may merely confirm that the court is correct in its assessment of the case on appeal, as in *Smedley*[30]. In *Meade*[31] the court reduced a sentence from six years to four "despite the adverse prison report". At other times a report can alter the outcome of a case significantly. Thomas has drawn attention to the unfortunate effects that can result from the use of such reports after conviction and commencement of an appeal hearing. In *Roe*[32] the appellant, a youth of 18 or 19, had pleaded guilty to an assault with intent to rob. He and another youth had attempted to grab takings of about £500 from a bookmaker. His resistance made them run off but, probably to deter pursuit, the appellant had thrown a stone at the bookmaker, bruising his head. He had two previous findings of guilt and one previous conviction for theft recorded against him and had been sentenced to three years' imprisonment. After stating that the sentence was right in principle, the Court of Appeal added that it had received a very favourable report on the appellant from the governor of his prison. The sentence was thought to have taught him a lesson, and an order for 120 hours community service was substituted. As we commented earlier when touching on this topic, compassion in the Court of Appeal is not undesirable. Whilst many people would be pleased about the outcome of Roe's case, the fact that his appeal was allowed on the strength of a report from the prison where he was serving his sentence is not a very helpful indication to sentencers striving hard to apply the messages descending from on high.

4.37   Thomas asked the following questions in his note on *Roe*:

"What interpretation should a judge of the Crown Court place upon a decision such as this? Is the Court to be taken to indicate that a community service order would be an appropriate sentence in the first instance for what appears to have been a premeditated street robbery? . . . The Court however states that the original sentence was undoubtedly right in principle; presumably therefore a judge in the Crown Court should continue to pass sentences of the kind appealed against in similar cases, and leave it to the Court of Appeal to vary them in the light of the appellant's behaviour in prison."

At a later stage he added the comment,[33]

"This is not the reasoning of an appellate court – it is the reasoning of a parole board."

30 (1981) 3 Cr.App.R.(S) 87.
31 (1982) 4 Cr.App.R.(S) 193.
32 [1982] Crim.L.R. 57.
33 D.A. Thomas, "Sentencing Discretion and Appellate Review" in J. Shapland (ed.), *Decision-Making in the Legal System* (1983) British Psychological Society, p. 64.

He might have added that it is also the method of the Parole Board, for that body quite properly considers various reports on the post-sentence behaviour of the defendant.

4.38   It should also be noted that a favourable report from a prison governor is not necessarily always helpful to an appellant. The defendant in *Graham*[34] was a young prostitute who was sentenced to borstal training for soliciting, an offence for which three months' imprisonment was the maximum for adults. In view of the girl's wild past the Court of Appeal felt that borstal was in her best interests, having regard, *inter alia*, to the favourable reports from the institution in which she was undergoing her training. It is ironic that unfavourable reports might have led to her appeal succeeding and to a shorter period in custody resulting. This appeal is yet another illustration of the point made by Stanton Wheeler and others that a desire on the part of a court to treat or help a young defendant can lead to a sentence which is longer than one based solely on retribution or just deserts. We shall consider further later the dangers inherent in some of the attempts by courts to help unfortunate defendants.[35]

REPORTS ON JUVENILES

4.39   Where a court is dealing with a juvenile, the social inquiry report may be prepared by a social worker from the Social Services Department of the appropriate local authority. Such social workers are often required to give evidence, but they do not as a rule have the same degree of experience of appearing in court as the average probation officer. They will certainly have less experience of dealing with sentencers than a court liaison probation officer. As Carlen and Powell have pointed out,[36]

> "Anecdotes abound about social workers' maladroitness in court. Specific criticisms concern the inappropriateness of their reports and their demeanour. More generally, their attitude to the judicial process is seen to be cavalier and lacking in judicial finesse."

4.40   With sufficient training, and some sympathetic assistance both from the courts and the probation service, social workers should be able to learn that certain ground rules apply in the courts, and that a failure

---

34   (1975) unreported; D.A. Thomas, *Principles of Sentencing* (2nd ed. 1979) Heinemann, p. 13.
35   S. Wheeler, *Controlling Delinquents* (1968) Wiley; see also paras. 6.29ff *post*.
36   P. Carlen and M. Powell, "Professionals in the Magistrates' Court", in H. Parker (ed.), *Social Work and the Courts* (1979) E. Arnold, p. 109.

to comply with them may get everyone off on the wrong foot. If one wishes one's report to be taken seriously, then it should be presented in a style and manner that the resident social workers, that is, the probation officers, have found to be the most acceptable from a professional point of view. Sentencers can help by not being overly concerned about relatively minor matters, such as the mode of dress of the witness, or the precise way in which he may refer to the subject of the report.

4.41 Whenever a child or young person is found guilty of an offence, the question of reports is covered by rule:[37]

> "The court shall take into consideration such information as to the general conduct, home surroundings, school record and medical history of the child or young person as may be necessary."

What is different here from the case of the adult is principally the requirement relating to school reports. If any of the reports obtained, whether from the school or otherwise, have not been read out, the court must, subject to minor exceptions, inform the juvenile, or if appropriate his parents, of the substance of the information considered to be material.[38]

4.42 About the provision of reports by probation officers and local authority social workers nothing need be added to what has already been stated in connection with adult offenders. However a word of warning is necessary in respect of school reports, which are often prepared without regard to the fact that the report may be used against a child in court without the writer of the report attending to be cross-examined. Furthermore, matters are made worse in some juvenile courts by the failure of the court to inform the juvenile or the parents of the substance of the adverse information contained in the school report. A Clerk to the Justices told a recent inquiry:[39]

> "Many justices are unwilling to comply with rule 10(2) by revealing the substance of any part of the information in a school report which the court considers material to the manner in which the case is to be dealt with, and they hide behind the fiction that statements critical of the parents have not influenced them in determining sentence."

37 Magistrates' Courts (Children and Young Persons) Rules 1970 (S.I. no. 1972), r. 10(1).
38 *Ibid*. r. 10(2).
39 *Social Reports in the Juvenile Court*, Report of a NACRO Working Group (1984) NACRO, p. 8.

4.43   Courts should be particularly astute to express adequate indignation about school reports containing statements such as those of which the same inquiry was told, and which were taken from actual reports to juvenile courts:

> "This boy is big, black and smelly", and
>
> "Jimmy is a cancer to the student body – if he didn't commit this offence, then someone else in his family did."

The writers of those reports would not have dared to make such comments in the witness-box. They are equally outrageous in a written report.

CHAPTER 5

Mitigation

PREPARATION BY THE DEFENCE

5.01 Aggravating features will appear quite often from the statements of witnesses, and particularly that of the victim. The statements will show that as well as committing the offence in question, the defendant used unnecessary violence or did an excessive amount of damage, or that he humiliated his victim. Counsel for the prosecution may put such facts before the court dispassionately, but he "should not attempt by advocacy to influence the court in regard to sentence".[1] Obviously, aggravating features may affect the sentence, and in the guideline case on rape, *Roberts and Roberts*,[2] Lord Lane, C.J. listed some of the factors in such cases which could affect the length of the sentence. He similarly listed some of the aggravating features which are to be found in cases of reckless driving in *Boswell*.[3] If the defendant disputes any important allegation of fact, then, as we have seen in Chapter 3, there must be a resolution of the facts issue before sentence. If on the other hand the defendant accepts that he did the acts complained of, but insists that they were not quite so serious as might at first sight appear, then that is a matter which can be dealt with by his advocate by way of mitigation. For example, if the damage done by the young defendant's arson was far greater than intended by him, as was the case in *Storey and others*,[4] that point should be made in his favour, for the court should take it into account.

5.02 The prosecution cannot add anything to the facts of the case by way of aggravation (leaving aside the production of the list of previous convictions) but the defence may always add to the facts by way of mitigation. The past difficulty that the defence never knew the full facts to be relied on by the prosecution before a trial in the magistrates' court is fortunately diminishing with the serving of advance notice. Whilst the prosecution can do no more than rely on the witness statements, the

1 *Code of Conduct for the Bar* (1980) p. 163.
2 (1982) 4 Cr.App.R.(S) 8.
3 (1984) 79 Cr.App.R. 277.
4 (1984) 6 Cr.App.R.(S) 104. See para. 10.37 *infra*.

defence lawyers can and should take positive steps to prepare the mitigation. There are minor exceptions to the general rule that the prosecution cannot make things worse (or "put the boot in", as it is known to some lawyers and police officers). The officer presenting the antecedents may in response to a question from the bench, sometimes of a leading nature, state that the offence has become or is becoming very rife in the area. One of the writers recalls another exception from his days at the Bar. When a certain police officer gave antecedents evidence he would often add, "*In fairness to the defendant* I should add that . . ." and then followed a bit of aggravation! The writer was driven to requesting the officer to stop being fair to his clients.

5.03   It is difficult to exaggerate the importance of a proper preparation of the mitigation by defence solicitor and counsel. Obviously counsel for the defence, like his opponent, has a duty to acquaint himself as a first step with the maximum penalty,[5] and as a second step, we suggest, with the real alternatives before the court. These should always be borne in mind from the first. There are two overlapping parts to the preparation of the mitigation. The first is concerned with showing both the facts of the case and the defendant in the best possible light. The second is concerned with the most appropriate but also relatively lenient disposal possible. All too often the defendant's explanation for the offence is not adequately sought at an early enough stage. Defence solicitors should find out from their client in good time, well before the hearing, what the excuses or explanations for the offence are. It is not enough to send a dim clerk to interview an even dimmer client. It is difficult to extract even favourable facts from some defendants, and an experienced solicitor or clerk should undertake the work (even if – dare one say it – it is not adequately remunerated). If the solicitor feels he cannot do a proper job for the current rates of pay, he should decline to take the case on rather than conducting it in a half-hearted manner. The importance of getting the facts out of the defendant as soon as possible is twofold. First, it may be necessary to seek witnesses to confirm his account of, say, provocation by the victim. Provocation in assault cases often leads to a large, and sometimes a surprisingly large, reduction from the sentence which might otherwise have been expected, so it is certainly worth following up such a point. It may also be necessary to seek medical evidence to confirm his account, for example, of being desperately ill and seeking treatment shortly before the time of the offence. Secondly, it is only when one has the basic facts that one can begin to prepare proposals for the sentence.

5   See *Clarke* (1974) 59 Cr.App.R. 278.

5.04 On some occasions the fact that the defendant has been in custody for some weeks before the hearing may turn out to be to his advantage, although one can never be sure about the matter – and there may ultimately be parole disadvantages.[6] If the offence is one which might well have attracted a sentence of six months' imprisonment and the defendant has already been in custody for six or eight weeks, the court may well feel able to pass a non-custodial sentence by virtue of the fact that he has already seen the inside of a prison. Such a decision would be analagous to a decision to impose a short sentence on the "clang" principle. It is of course quite wrong for any court to remand a defendant in custody merely to give him a taste of prison, when the intention has already been formed to pass a non-custodial sentence in any event.

5.05 Despite these occasional advantages to be derived from pre-trial custody, it is nevertheless generally the duty of defence lawyers to try for bail for a number of reasons, not least the fact that pre-trial imprisonment can worsen both the defendant's chances of acquittal, and his personal position by the time the mitigation stage is reached. Research has revealed that pre-trial custody may more readily lead to a custodial sentence.[7] It is obviously easier to mitigate successfully for a defendant who is still in good regular employment and who has a home to go to, than for one who has lost both his job and his home because of his remand in custody. It is also much easier for a defendant who is on bail to instruct his solicitor and to seek out mitigating witnesses.

5.06 The defendant's solicitor should discuss with his client the best way in which to present him in a good light at court. If repayment or reparation in some other form can be undertaken, then that should be done. If there are difficulties about repaying the victim before the trial, the money for such repayment should be put to one side and out of reach of the defendant. It is true that the court will always be on guard to ensure that a defendant does not buy his way out of prison, and that one co-defendant does not escape with a lighter sentence than another merely because he has money available whilst another does not. Having said that, the courts are as a general rule happy to see victims compensated.

5.07 Similarly, if the defendant can do something else to show his remorse, then he should be encouraged to do so. Again, the court may

6 See paras. 6.44ff *infra*.
7 M. King, *Bail or Custody* (1971) Cobden Trust, p. 74.

well decide that the contrition has only followed on solicitor's advice, but it may nevertheless find it to be genuine. Some contrition likely to be more helpful than none.

5.08 A checklist of points to be covered, such as suggested by Joanna Shapland, can be helpful.[8] In going through such a list the solicitor should bear in mind that the period before sentence has sometimes been called a "mini-probation" period. The defendant should be helped to show the sentencing court that since his arrest he has been a model citizen: not only has he not offended, but he has held down a job, supported his family, put aside money for his victim and co-operated with the police and the probation officer preparing the social inquiry report. Mitigating witnesses should be approached for a proof of evidence in good time, and not merely asked to attend court at 10.29 on the morning of the hearing. In a borderline case an employer can make all the difference if he gives evidence for the defendant. If the defendant could be helped by a member of the community acting either as a known personal friend or as a volunteer with the probation service, then all the options should be explored in advance, if possible with the probation officer. Honest members of the community can often help to avert a custodial sentence by offering practical help to reduce the risk of re-offending. Furthermore, as Stockdale put it:[9]

> "If the judge can be told that, say, a retired bank manager is prepared to help the accused with his financial problems, and that a student teacher or housewife is available to help the accused's wife with her manifold problems, it might go some way towards persuading him that honest citizens would not be outraged by a probation order."

If the defendant is a member of a black or other ethnic group, one of the appropriate organisations should be approached and asked to find a volunteer or volunteers to assist the defendant.[10]

5.09 If the defendant has a physical, psychological or addiction problem, then it is clearly the duty of the solicitor to follow up every possible alternative. Bail is highly desirable at this stage for, apart from other considerations, the overworked prison medical officers are not renowned for their optimism about treatment. Once again, there is a possibility that the court will reject the suggested non-custodial sentence, such as probation with a condition of treatment, but if the groundwork has not been done by the defence, the defendant's only

8　J. Shapland, *Between Conviction and Sentence* (1981) Routledge & Kegan Paul, p. 148.
9　E. Stockdale, *The Probation Volunteer* (1985) The Volunteer Centre, p. 81.
10　See *Black People and the Criminal Justice System* (1986) NACRO, p. 29.

hope for such an order is that the social inquiry report may persuade the court to follow up a medical problem discussed in it.

MITIGATION IN COURT

5.10 An enthusiastic professional approach to the problems of the sentencer on the part of defence lawyers can on occasion make a significant difference to their client's future. A distinguished American Federal judge made the following comments about the mitigation stage:[11]

> "The usual defense lawyer's statement pleads for compassion, stressing the defendant's virtues, if any; family ties; the good opinions of clerics, employers, teachers, and the like. Such things are relevant, to be sure. They appear, however, to be neither novel nor wholly accurate to the judge who has read the presentence report. They are, at any rate, the best most defense attorneys can muster. Again, as in the case of prosecutors, there are exceptions. An occasional lawyer for the defense has made the sentencing problem a subject of genuine study; has managed effectively to size up the judge and his concerns; and succeeds in proposing an appropriate, imaginative, and sensible sentence that appears genuinely to serve both the client's and the public's interests."

Most sentencers welcome really helpful submissions from the defence. Fortunately, the universities and polytechnics are more and more interesting their law students in sentencing, and the profession is becoming increasingly aware of the need to regard the mitigation stage as more than the time when the advocate merely mumbles a plea "for the most lenient sentence that is open to the court in all the circumstances".

5.11 It is clearly the advocate's duty when mitigating to deal realistically with the facts as they are, and not with the facts as he or the defendant would like them to have been. With equal realism he must consider the alternatives in practice open to the sentencer. As a rule a properly prepared advocate will go all out for one or two of the alternatives available. If the preparation discussed has been done, then the court can be urged to make a probation order on the specific grounds put forward, such as that the defendant has a job, home, family and the ability to pay compensation, and that the probation officer has shown why and how he can benefit from supervision. A compensation order may properly be made in respect of the same offence with a probation order, unlike a fine, and the combination of supervision plus a

---

11 Judge M.E. Frankel, *Criminal Sentences: Law without Order* (1973) Hill & Wang, p. 37.

reimbursement of the victim is often an attractive solution for a court considering a custodial disposal. If the defendant has no family, or only a fairly light job, the advocate may prefer to concentrate on putting over the idea of a community service order as an alternative to custody. To some extent the advocate must be guided by what the usual range of sentences is for offences of that sort (a matter not always easy to determine); to some extent he may adjust his speech to fit in with what he knows about the sentencer; and to a large extent, especially if he does not know the sentencer at all, he must listen and look out for clues from the bench. If the sentencer makes it clear that he is thinking of a custodial disposal because of the nature of the offence, then the advocate may well be advised to consider switching his efforts, either proposing a suspension of the sentence (if the defendant is an adult) or pointing out that a community service order is an alternative which will incorporate punishment as well as discipline and reparation to the community.

5.12 It might be thought that an advocate should always stick to his guns, come what may: that if he is sure that probation is the right disposal, he should go on trying for probation. Such an attitude, whilst commendable, may in fact harm the client, for a sentencer who finds the defence proposals "unrealistic", or worse still "ridiculous", may just switch off and not pay full attention to the advocate thereafter. The sentencing stage of the trial, like every other, is one during which the advocate must keep wide awake and think on his feet. Another reason why the advocate must be prepared to change tack is that a number of matters can be looked at in two ways, and it is as well for the advocate to note which view the tribunal is taking. For example, the Court of Appeal has often accepted the defendant's retarded mental state or low intelligence as a mitigating factor, even in cases of rape or buggery of a boy.[12] On the other hand, an offender with mental problems may well be regarded as dangerous by the court, particularly if there are a number of offences of a similar nature to be considered, and stressing the low intellect could result in a long sentence designed to protect the public. As Norval Morris observed:[13]

> "Mental illness at the time of the crime is properly taken into account to *reduce* the severity or duration of punishment; mental illness continuing or likely to recur is also properly taken into account to *increase* the severity or prolong the duration of punishment."

12   *Taylor* (1983) 5 Cr.App.R.(S) 241; *Harvey* (1984) 6 Cr.App.R.(S) 184.
13   N. Morris, *Madness and the Criminal Law* (1982) U. of Chicago P., p. 129; see also A. Ashworth and L. Gostin, "Mentally Disordered Offenders and the Sentencing Process" [1984] Crim.L.R. 209.

5.13 The mitigation stage of a trial is often the most important of all, so it should be accorded the time and attention it deserves. As it was once put:[14]

> "The mitigation speech must be recognised as being one of the most important functions of the advocate, and should not be regarded as something which prevents the court from getting on with its 'real' work, namely the trial of pleas of not guilty. The advocate should equip himself properly for his double task of representing his client, and of helping the court to come to the correct conclusion, and the court should listen with patience even if the plea does take longer than the previous 'bogey' time for that court. There is no merit in speed if the offender is made to feel that his future does not matter either to the court or to his lawyer; nor if the speedy sentence is wrong."

5.14 Every defendant, whether he has pleaded guilty or been found guilty after putting up a defence, whether scurrilous or otherwise, is entitled to have his say in mitigation, or to have his representative speak up for him. No court may deprive any defendant of his right to be heard in mitigation. Counsel mitigating for the defendant has the widest discretion to use whatever matters he thinks may help. Shapland has demonstrated that there is no limit to the variety of points that can be found for mitigation purposes.[15] However, counsel must in this context, as in all others, be careful not to abuse his privileged position in the courtroom. For example, he must be extremely careful about making allegations against third parties who have no opportunity to rebut what has been said against them in their absence. The Magistrates' Association, as well as some judges, has expressed some concern about what has aptly been called "malicious mitigation". Obviously there is a limit to the extent to which counsel and solicitor can check on the truth of their client's mitigating facts. If the defendant says that all his troubles stemmed from the time when his unnamed landlord wrongly evicted him a year before the trial, there is no obligation to take statements from the landlord and co-tenants to check the story. However, counsel should be careful before putting forward wild allegations discrediting third parties who are then named in court. He should also decline to air the defendant's political views.[16] It is no good putting wild allegations forward with the lame excuse, "Those are my instructions". Counsel has full authority and the right to decide what to use and what not to use: the client cannot insist on the wording of counsel's speech. There may come a time when a defendant insists that a particularly outrageous and unsupported point be used in mitigation, and when he rejects all advice

---

14 E. Stockdale, *The Court and the Offender* (1967) Gollancz, p. 202.
15 *Op. cit.* (note 8 *supra*).
16 *King and Simpkins* (1973) 57 Cr.App.R. 696.

against its use. If he persists, then counsel may have to withdraw from the case with the leave of the court, if he is not dismissed by the defendant. One way to deal with the problem of mentioning the name of a third party is to write it down and hand it to the court.[17]

5.15　Whilst counsel in mitigating for his client has great latitude — and certain far more than counsel for the prosecution — he should not allow himself to be carried away. He must not say, "He asks me to tender his apologies to the victim and to the court", when there has been no such request by the defendant. He should remember the general rule that counsel personally should not figure in the case. Assertions such as the following should be avoided: "I have seen him in the cells and it is plain to me that he has learned his lesson", or, "I feel sure that he bitterly regrets what he has done, and that he is most unlikely to repeat this kind of offence". On the other hand, there is no harm in making submissions to the like effect in proper form: "In the circumstances in my submission he is most unlikely to offend again". The circumstances referred to will not include evidence given by counsel about what he has observed, or any personal opinion of his.

5.16　It sometimes pays the advocate to "take the wind out of the sails" of the court by facing up to a difficult point. It is often a sound idea to say something on the lines of, "Clearly the fact that my client failed to surrender to his bail" or "was in a position of trust (or whatever) makes the matter worse". Concessions of this kind can sometimes reduce the number of barbed comments in similar vein from the bench. Once again, counsel should be careful not to go over the top with his concessions, for he may give his client the impression that he is trying to get him the maximum sentence permitted by the law.

5.17　We have already pointed out that one of the difficulties which accounts for sentencing disparity is the fact that there is no universal agreement amongst sentencers as to which class of offence is more serious than another, nor how one offence compares in gravity with another in a different class. There are certain general propositions which would be accepted by all sentencers, for example, that crimes of violence are to be discouraged, and that such crimes committed against the very young or the old are more serious than others. There would also be general acceptance of the proposition, supported by decisions of the Court of Appeal, that an offence committed by someone in a position of trust is more serious than one committed by someone who is

---

17　*Code of Conduct for the Bar* (1980) p. 157.

not in a special relationship with the victim. That proposition applies with equal force whether the offence is one of tampering with funds or pupils; it applies to property offences and sex offences alike.[18]

5.18 The fact that sentencers have differing perceptions applies also to aggravating and mitigating factors. A mitigation speech may include a number of matters which will appeal to one sentencer as reducing the sentence *prima facie* appropriate, and which may seem to another to have no effect whatsoever, or even to make matters worse, such as the frequently heard plea, "Since being committed for trial, he has got his 16-year-old girlfriend pregnant;" or for the confidence trickster, "He now has a steady job making antiques." The reader might like to try himself out by answering the following questions. Would you consider any of the following to be mitigating factors in, say, a case of dishonesty or of indecent assault? If not, would you regard them as mitigation for any other offence?

(a) The defendant served for twelve years in the Army, including the Falklands campaign, and was discharged with a very good character.

(b) The defendant saved a child from drowning two years ago.

(c) The defendant was unemployed for a year before the offence.

(d) The defendant lost his job two weeks before the offence.

(e) The defendant is a man of low intelligence.

(f) The defendant shortly before the offence had, characteristically, been drinking to excess.

(g) The defendant shortly before the offence had, uncharacteristically, been drinking to excess.

(h) Shortly before the offence the defendant's wife had left him.

5.19 Each of the foregoing points has been put forward in mitigation many times. Sometimes they have succeeded; at others they have failed. On occasion they have appealed to the Court of Appeal though not to the trial judge. Sometimes the sentencer has merely rejected them as irrelevant; at others he has made a comment to the effect that he could not possibly regard the particular point as helping the defendant. Sentencers should be very careful in the way in which they reject the proffered mitigation points. It is often possible to say of each one: "That is no excuse. What would happen if every unemployed man (or whatever) were to . . .?" It is easy to give the defendant the impression that nothing is going to affect the sentencer's mind in his favour.

5.20 On the issue of drink, which figures particularly in cases of violence, it is not without interest that the question of whether it

---

18 *Barrick* (1985) 81 Cr.App.R. 78; *Taylor and others* (1977) 64 Cr.App.R. 182.

mitigates or not has always caused trouble. A well-known Bow Street magistrate made the following comment on the topic in 1749:[19]

> "To say the truth, in a court of justice, drunkenness must not be an excuse, yet in a court of conscience it is greatly so; and therefore Aristotle, who commends the laws of Pittacus, by which drunken men receive double punishment for their crimes, allows there is more of policy than justice in that law."

5.21 There will be some occasions when the court accepts that there are one or more factors which would normally be accepted as mitigating the penalty, but which must be rejected nevertheless. An illustration of such an instance is to be found in the appeal of *Inwood*,[20] in which Scarman, L.J. said:

> "But in the balance that the Court has to make between the mitigating factors and society's interest in marking its disapproval for this type of conduct, we come to the irresistible though unpalatable conclusion that we must not yield to the mitigating factors. The sentence was correct in principle when measured against the gravity of the offence."

5.22 One of the matters which the court should always consider taking into account is the total effect on the defendant of having been caught. In *Rolt*[21] Lord Lane, C.J. made a number of useful comments in the nature of guidelines for cases of importation of pornographic items. After remarking that "the balance which the Court has to try and strike is never easily achieved", he listed a number of factors which should be borne in mind, including the value and nature of the pornographic items, the defendant's rank in the organisation and the profit he stood to gain. However, his loss was also relevant. The Court of Appeal reduced Rolt's sentence because the recorder who had sentenced him had not been aware of the fact that the customs authorities had forfeited his tractor unit, which he had used for carrying the items, with resultant heavy financial loss.

5.23 Accordingly it is always worth the defence pointing out the total loss to the defendant, such as loss of profession or job, pension, or accommodation, even though there is a risk that the court may retort, "He should have thought of that before he committed the offence" or, "He has only himself to blame for that". Sometimes the court will feel able to take the matter into account in the defendant's favour, as Lord Lane did in *Rolt* and in *Richards*.[22] Lord Lane gave another example in

19 In Henry Fielding, *The History of Tom Jones*, p. 240 in 1966 Penguin edn.
20 (1974) 60 Cr.App.R. 70.
21 (1984) 6 Cr.App.R.(S) 129.
22 (1980) 2 Cr.App.R.(S) 119.

the case of *Barrick*,[23] in which he gave guidelines on theft by persons in a position of trust. One of the examples of a matter which could properly be taken into account in the defendant's favour, he said, was long delay, perhaps for two years, between the defendant's first being questioned about his defalcations and the trial, provided, obviously, that he was not responsible for the delay himself. This was an acknowledgment of the fact that some, though not all, defendants suffer considerably as a result of the waiting period. The advocate should also point any other "cost" to the defendant, so as to prevent double punishment. If, say, the defendant is to be sentenced for breach of a community service order, he is entitled to credit for any substantial numbers of hours completed, as he will have paid for his offence in part already.[24]

5.24 As a general rule, it may fairly safely be stated, advocates prefer judges and chairmen of benches to remain silent when they are addressing them. During the sentencing stage complete silence is not always thought to be quite so desirable. It can be very disconcerting for an advocate who makes a lengthy mitigation speech about the two alternatives of a fine or a probation order, without any word from the bench, to find when the sentence is passed that the sentencer had only been concerned about whether to suspend a term of imprisonment or not. It is even more disconcerting if the social inquiry report has recommended a fine or probation, and if the judge, without any explanation for his decision, merely announces a sentence of immediate custody "in a somewhat laconic fashion" (to quote the expression used by Shaw, L.J. in *Newman*.)[25]

5.25 If an advocate is not facing up to the problems which require addressing, then it may assist if the judge or chairman intervenes with a comment, such as, "It would be helpful if you could address the court on the issue of custody", or "Would it be open to the court to take such a course, having regard to . . .?" The courts are increasingly developing the natural justice principle that parties ought to be given an opportunity to deal with a specific point before it is found against them.[26] Although a court has the power to pass any lawful sentence, even though the defending advocate has not dealt with the alternative eventually chosen, it is safer for the court to ask him to deal specifically

23 (1985) 81 Cr.App.R. 78.
24 *Whittingham* [1986] Crim.L.R. 572.
25 (1979) 1 Cr.App.R.(S) 252.
26 *Page* (1980) 2 Cr.App.R.(S) 247; *Mahon v. Air New Zealand* [1984] 3 All E.R. 201; *R. v. Mental Health Review Tribunal ex p. Clatworthy* [1985] 3 All E.R. 699.

with a particular order it may have in mind – especially if an unusual or drastic one – or with a particular interpretation of the facts which has not been canvassed, but which the sentencer is disposed to accept.[27]

27 *Powell and Carvell* (1984) 6 Cr.App.R.(S) 354; *Lester* (1975) 63 Cr.App.R. 144; *Antypas* (1972) 57 Cr.App.R. 207; *Lake and others* (1986) 8 Cr.App.R.(S) 69.

CHAPTER 6

The Consideration Stage

6.01 At the consideration stage the sentencer must have regard to all the matters that we have discussed so far. After making some general comments about this crucial stage of the sentencing process, we shall discuss certain points in more detail, and under the following headings:

(1) Avoiding unjust disparity;
(2) Avoiding bad combinations of orders;
(3) A sense of proportion;
(4) Resisting the temptation to help;
(5) Improper considerations;
(6) Parole; and
(7) Revocation of parole licence.

GENERAL COMMENTS

6.02 Most sentencers would agree that choosing the most appropriate, or least inappropriate sentence is as a rule the most difficult task they have to perform in the criminal court. That being so, it is as well for all sentencers to bear in mind the need to give adequate time to the consideration stage. Although full lists create great pressure on judges to get through their work as rapidly as possible, there is no disgrace attached to retiring to consider the effect of the mitigation speech on the alternatives one had provisionally placed on the short-list. Retiring is usually essential when there is more than one sentencer, as the facts in *Newby*[1] demonstrate. At the end of the mitigation speech the recorder presiding at the trial passed sentence without apparently consulting the magistrates who were sitting with him. It transpired later, when the Court of Appeal asked for an explanation, that the recorder and justices had come to a provisional conclusion before the case began, and that he had passed a note to his colleagues in court shortly before announcing the sentence of the whole court.

6.03 Retiring is often desirable when a single sentencer is sitting, when there are a number of defendants or a number of charges of different

1 (1984) 6 Cr.App.R.(S) 148.

kinds. Time is also needed to ensure that all the appropriate orders are made in relation to offences connected with motor vehicles. We shall discuss in Chapter 8 the powers of the courts to correct their errors, but must point out now that many of the errors considered in the reported cases could have been avoided if a little more time had been devoted to the crucial consideration stage.

6.04 At this stage the sentencer will have to make up his mind about the facts that have been properly established. He will have to decide how serious those facts make the instant offence. The answer to that important question can only be arrived at by an assessment of the facts established by the prosecution, as explained by any defence evidence and submissions. We have seen that the Court of Appeal has laid down guidelines on the gravity of various forms of rape, but even with such a serious charge, or perhaps one should say especially with such a serious charge, it is necessary to take into account the defence explanations. For example, even the most serious assaults involving grievous bodily harm can be mitigated by the defence satisfying the court that there had been, or may well have been a significant degree of provocation on the part of the victim. Despite the limited, albeit increasing, amount of help available from the Court of Appeal guideline cases, essentially gravity is in the eye of the beholder. Research has shown over the years that different judges have differing ideas about the gravity of one kind of offence as opposed to another: some regard property offences as extremely serious, even if the attacked premises are non-residential, whilst others are much more offended by sexual offences.[2] Within the latter category some judges are more concerned about homosexual offences or offences involving animals than about heterosexual assaults. The point was demonstrated most recently in *Higson*,[3] in which the defendant successfully appealed against a sentence of two years' imprisonment for attempted buggery with a bitch. In the Court of Appeal Leggatt, J. made the pointed comment:

> "When all is said and done, it is the appellant and indeed his wife, and not the dog, who need help. That is best afforded by making a probation order."

6.05 Each sentencer should be aware of the fact that different people have different prejudices – as well as divergent ideas about the objects of punishment – and should try to be aware of his own and not let them

---

2 J. Hogarth, *Sentencing as a Human Process* (1971) U. of Toronto P.; R. Hood and R. Sparks, *Key Issues in Criminology* (1970) Weidenfeld & Nicholson, Ch. 5.
3 (1984) 6 Cr.App.R.(S) 20.

get out of control: he should try and overcome them, or at the very least make allowances for them. As Ashworth has pointed out:[4]

> "The purpose of discretion is certainly to allow the sentencer to select the sentence which he believes to be the most appropriate in the individual case, considering both the facts of the case and any reports on the offender's character. The purpose of discretion is surely not to enable individual judges and magistrates to pursue purely personal sentencing preferences."

6.06 The sentencer must always be aware of the maximum sentence and of the other powers of the court. Magistrates should if necessary ask their clerk for advice on the subject, and they may send for him for such advice after retiring.[5] Counsel has a duty to be aware of the maximum sentence in any given case and in the Crown Court should, like the judge, always be on the lookout for those cases in which the powers of the court may be limited to those of the lower court only, as in some circumstances where there has been a committal for sentence, or an appeal.[6]

6.07 The next stage for most sentencers will be a first tentative fixing of the case on the seriousness scale. Even if the experienced sentencer does not consciously go through the exercise, he will still make a decision of this kind. He will decide, taking account of all he has heard from both sides, whether the case is one of the most serious of its kind, one of the least serious, or somewhere in between.

6.08 The next step will normally be the tackling of the vital question, simply put by some American writers as the IN/OUT decision, that is, custody or non-custodial sentence. Others prefer to say that the dichotomy is between punishment and non-punishment, the principal difference being that in this division a fine and a community service order are classed with prison as a first alternative, the second comprising discharges, probation and all other non-custodial solutions to the problem of sentencing. There are further ways of dividing up the alternatives, but most helpful is the statement on the court's decision-making process by Lord Lane, C. J. in *Clarke*,[7] the guideline case on the partly suspended sentence:

> "First of all, is this a case where a custodial sentence is really necessary? If it is not, it should pass a non-custodial sentence. But if it is necessary then the court should ask itself secondly this: can we make a community service

---

4 A. Ashworth, "Judicial Independence and Sentencing Reform" in *The Future of Sentencing* (1982) Cambridge U. Institute of Criminology, p. 50.
5 Practice Direction [1981] 1 W.L.R. 1163.
6 *Arthur v. Stringer* (1986) The Times 11 October. See paras. 9.51ff *infra*.
7 (1982) 4 Cr.App.R.(S) 197.

order as an equivalent to imprisonment, or can we suspend the whole sentence? . . . If it is possible to make a community service order or to suspend the whole of the sentence, then of course that should be done. If not, then the third point arises: what is the shortest sentence the court can properly impose? . . . Sometimes 14 or 28 days may suffice, which is shorter than the shortest term which is at present available under section 47, which of course is one quarter of six months, that is one and a half months . . . If imprisonment is necessary, and if a very short sentence is not enough, and if it is not appropriate to suspend the sentence altogether, then partial suspension should be considered."

6.09 It will have been noted that the Lord Chief Justice did not advocate a direct progression from the fully suspended sentence to the partly suspended one, since that might lead to a longer term than necessary of custody actually served. This is because Parliament in providing for the partly suspended sentence exceptionally used its powers to specify a minimum period as well as a maximum.[8]

6.10 In cases at either end of the gravity scale the court will have little difficulty. The rapist and the armed bank robber do not present much difficulty as far as the first question is concerned: as a general rule custody must follow. At the other end of the scale most minor offences of dishonesty can be resolved in a non-custodial way. It is always in the middle, or at the edges of the various bands of cases that difficulty can occur. Once again, the sentencer should take his time over the decision, considering carefully what he ought to try and achieve by way of deterrence, retribution and so on. There is no harm in trying out the various alternatives in one's own mind if sitting alone, and there is certainly a great deal to be gained from discussing those alternatives with colleagues if one with sitting with others. Junior magistrates should not be afraid to bring forward their own ideas merely because the chairman has already indicated what he considers to be the appropriate outcome. The same applies in the Crown Court. If a magistrate is sitting there with a judge or a recorder, he has an equal say on the sentence and must not be afraid to speak out.[9] Fortunately, research at the Institute of Judicial Administration at Birmingham University demonstrated that magistrates do in fact influence the outcome of the case, outvoting the judge on occasion if they think that is the right course.[10] The professional judge in the Crown Court must clearly consult the magistrates sitting with him, and make it clear in passing sentence – if there has been

---

8 It should be noted that the Criminal Justice Act 1982, s. 30, shortly after *Clarke*, reduced the minimum qualifying term from six to three months, and the minimum part to be served to 28 days.
9 Supreme Court Act 1981, ss. 8, 73.
10 G. Hawker, *Magistrates in the Crown Court* (1984) Institute of Judicial Administration, U. of Birmingham.

any cause for doubt – that the sentence is indeed one of the whole court and not just that of the presiding judge.[11]

6.11 The American author Daniel Glaser was undoubtedly correct when he wrote:[12]

> "In a society that values freedom the decision to imprison a man is one of the heaviest responsibilities anyone can assume."

If a sentencer is certain, because of the facts of the case and the rest of the information placed before him, that a sentence of imprisonment is necessary and cannot be avoided, then he must fearlessly pass such a sentence, even if he has doubts about the ability of the prison system to rehabilitate the defendant: there are after all other reasons for resorting to the use of custody. If on the other hand he is in doubt about the matter, then he ought to resolve the question by passing a non-custodial sentence. As Lord Lane pointed out in *Clarke*,[13] if the custodial sentence is really not necessary, the court should use a non-custodial disposal. Imprisonment should be used as a last resort. This should be regarded as a fundamental rule of sentencing.

6.12 Once the decision has been made on the IN/OUT issue, the court has to decide how much custody is necessary and on what basis, in accordance with the decision in *Clarke*, or which non-custodial alternative is the most apt. Further information may well be required from the probation service or other sources, and an adjournment may be inevitable. The question of bail must always be considered for the interim period and, as we have pointed out, the defendant should never be remanded in custody just to show him the inside of a prison before he gets the benefit of a non-custodial sentence.

6.13 When the length of the term of imprisonment is being selected, the sentencer would do well to bear in mind the "few simple questions" of the Advisory Council on the Penal System, including the following:[14]

> "Are there not cases of two years' imprisonment where 18 months, or even 15 or even less, might safely be passed, and sentences of twelve months when six months would do just as well?"

---

11 *Newby* (1984) 6 Cr.App.R.(S) 148.
12 D. Glaser, *The Effectiveness of a Prison and Parole System* (1969 abridged edn.) Bobbs-Merrill, p. 197.
13 (1982) 4 Cr.App.R.(S) 197; para. 6.08 *supra*.
14 Advisory Council on the Penal System, *The Length of Prison Sentences: Interim Report* (1977) H.M.S.O., para. 14.

Very similar words were used by Lord Lane, C.J., in connection with certain offences in the case of *Bibi*.[15]

6.14 The maximum sentence should be reserved for the most serious cases of the offence in question,[16] and the need to give a discount for a plea of guilty, which we discussed at length in Chapter 2, should always be borne in mind by the sentencer.

AVOIDING UNJUST DISPARITY

6.15 Disparity of sentence as between two or more defendants has often been a ground for a reduction of sentence by the Court of Appeal. What is objectionable is unjustified disparity, that is, disparity which is justified neither by the facts of the case nor by the differing circumstances of the defendants.[17] If D1, D2 and D3 plead guilty to the same offence committed jointly, then there is nothing wrong in the court passing different sentences on all three if such a course is justified. D1 may properly be sentenced to twelve months' imprisonment if he is an adult with a number of previous convictions; D2 to six months' imprisonment suspended for two years if he has fewer previous convictions and/or played a minor part in the offence only; and D3 may properly be placed on probation at the same time if he is under 21 and recommended for it in the social inquiry report. What would be objectionable would be a similar range of sentences passed on three defendants jointly charged who had similar records, ages, degrees of culpability and similar mitigation, or lack of it. Such a range would be considered as unjustly disparate by the Court of Appeal, which might well reduce the two longer sentences, being unable to increase the shorter ones.

6.16 In the past there were some cases involving a number of defendants jointly convicted of a very serious offence, such as armed robbery, in which the appeal court declined to differentiate between them despite their different antecedents. For example, in *Curbishley and others* in 1964[18] the whole gang had received sentences of 15 years and the court declined to reduce any of them, although the criminal record of the least serious offender was not nearly as bad as that of the worst one, saying that there was no point in distinguishing between

---

15 (1980) 2 Cr.App.R.(S) 177.
16 *Cade* (1984) 6 Cr.App.R.(S) 28.
17 *Church* (1985) 7 Cr.App.R.(S) 370.
18 [1964] Crim.L.R. 555.

them in that type of case where deterrence was the principal aim of the sentence. Similar comments were made in the robbery guideline case of *Turner* in 1975.[19] Since that time the Court of Appeal has regularly allowed appeals in that kind of case, reducing the sentence on some individual offenders to take account of their individual histories, as well as their respective roles in the joint offence. It would be as well for the sentencer to be extremely careful before passing identical sentences on a number of joint defendants, unless he is satisfied that each individual sentence is justified. One fairly new manifestation in the courts is the man of good character, or lightly convicted defendant who jumps from a petty theft right up to participation in an armed robbery. He will not be able to escape a heavy sentence merely because of the absence of previous convictions, but he should as a rule not be treated in the same way as his confederates who have graduated in the more traditional manner to armed robbery.[20]

6.17 Anyone who has ever had to sentence a trio of defendants at the same time will be aware of the difficulty involved in selecting three sentences which are appropriate and which cannot reasonably be complained of by any defendant. The fact that one of the defendants may be in work and able to pay a fine and compensation will often be coupled with the fact that his two co-defendants are unemployed and heavily in debt. It is clearly wrong to imprison a defendant because he cannot afford to pay a fine, if a non-custodial disposal is regarded as suitable.[21] In such a case, if there is no recommendation for a community service or probation order, a conditional discharge may have to be used, even though almost everyone but the defendant may regard that as too lenient. (The conditional discharge, incidentally, has some of the advantages of a suspended sentence without its disadvantages.) If a sentencer has considered a particular order to be suitable, but is forced to reject it on technical grounds, then as a general rule he should come down the penal ladder by one rung rather than going up it to a more severe alternative. It is different where a sentencer has tentatively decided that prison is probably unavoidable, and where he had been urged to explore the possibility of, say, a community service order. If the social inquiry report thereafter shows that the defendant is unsuitable for community service, there is no reason why the sentence of imprisonment should not be passed. This would be a case of the sentencer staying on the original rung of the ladder rather than of his moving up it. Whenever there is an adjournment in such circumstances,

19 (1975) 61 Cr.App.R. 67.
20 *Gould and others* (1983) 5 Cr.App.R.(S) 72.
21 *Reeves* (1972) 56 Cr.App.R. 366.

the sentencer should make it clear when putting the case over to another day, that imprisonment has not been ruled out as an alternative.

6.18 Another difficulty, albeit a minor one, is caused by virtue of the fact that different people have differing views about the relative severity of various disposals.[22] It is possible that a trio of defendants may leave the court with a fine, probation and a short suspended sentence respectively, and that each one will regard himself as having been more severely dealt with than his confederates. It is not clear whether the really perceptive sentencer is the one who can pass three such different sentences and leave all three defendants convinced that they have been more harshly dealt with than the other two, or the one who leaves all three happy that they have got away with it more lightly than the others!

6.19 Whenever a sentencer or panel of sentencers is faced with three or more defendants, it is as well for extreme care to be taken over the choice of the various alternatives. Such a selection can sometimes only be done properly in the retiring room with adequate time, although there may be occasions when a single sentencer feels he has had enough time to consider the alternatives before and during the mitigation stage. Obviously the greater the number of defendants and of charges, the greater the need for care.

AVOIDING BAD COMBINATIONS OF ORDERS

6.20 Clearly a court must not use combinations of orders prohibited by statute. In addition the sentencer should try to avoid marrying up two different orders in respect of the same defendant which may lawfully be made at the same time, but which cannot co-exist very well. The clearest example is that of a sentence of custody for one offence, coupled with a probation order "instead of sentencing" in respect of another. As long ago as 1959 Lord Parker, C.J. stated in *Evans*:[23]

> "There are no express words which prevent these two orders being made at one and the same time. But although that may well be so, the court is clearly of opinion that the making of a probation order in such circumstances is contrary to the spirit and intention of the Act."

6.21 Similar considerations apply to custodial sentences with community service orders,[24] and to sentences of immediate custody coupled

---

22 N. Walker, *Sentencing: Theory, Law and Practice* (1985) Butterworths, para. 5.33.
23 (1959) 43 Cr.App.R. 66.
24 *Starie* (1979) 1 Cr.App.R.(S) 172.

with a suspended sentence:[25] they just cannot work together. On the other hand, there is no reason why in a proper case a sentence of imprisonment (whether suspended or immediate) should not be coupled with a fine. So too, there is statutory provision for coupling a suspended sentence with a supervision order on appropriate occasions. However, when a sentencer adds a fine to a sentence of imprisonment, whether suspended or not, he should bear in mind the need to avoid punishing the defendant twice over, and also the need to avoid giving the impression that the fine has bought some exemption from prison.[26]

6.22 Whenever a sentencer is contemplating the simultaneous use of two different disposals for the same defendant, whether for the same offence or for different ones, he should ask himself a number of questions about the intended combination:

(1) Is such a combination lawful?

(2) Is each part of the combination available?[27]

(3) Even if lawful, is such a combination contrary to the spirit of one or other of the orders?

(4) Can the defendant comply with both orders? For example, has he the means to pay a fine if imprisoned?

(5) Is it fair to impose the two different orders at the same time?

The last question is a basic one which runs throughout the sentencing stage, but it is relevant here because a sense of proportion may make the sentencer come to the conclusion that a double penalty would be oppressive in the circumstances of the case. Proportionality is a matter which deserves further consideration.

A SENSE OF PROPORTION

6.23 It is obviously necessary for the sentencer to keep a sense of proportion when deciding on the total sentence. It is sometimes said that the totality of the offences or of the criminality must be borne in mind, more often that the totality of the orders of the court must be appropriate. The point arises in practice in different ways.

6.24 One common way is in the case of a defendant who has committed a number of offences on different occasions, so that consecutive sentences are justified. The individual offences may well justify consecutive sentences of four, three and two years' imprisonment. No

---

25 *Sapiano* (1968) 52 Cr.App.R. 674.
26 See letter from M. Wasik in [1982] Crim.L.R. 66.
27 See *Genese* (1976) 63 Cr.App.R. 152.

criticism of the three individual sentences may be possible, yet the total of nine years' imprisonment for that defendant at that stage of his career might nevertheless be found by the Court of Appeal to be excessive, as in *Hunter*.[28] The same is true when the total sentence for various offences short of murder exceeds that which a murderer might be expected to serve.[29] Lawton, L. J. warned in *Holderness*:[30]

> "Only too frequently courts which impose these consecutive sentences do not take the step which this Court on numerous occasions has said should be taken, namely, of standing back and looking at the overall effect of the sentences which have been passed."

6.25 Sometimes the point arises when a defendant appears for sentence in two courts within a short space of time. The second court should not merely consider whether a concurrent sentence rather than a consecutive one would be more appropriate. If deciding in favour of a consecutive sentence, the sentencer should look at the total of the two sentences, and should scale down his own sentence if the total would be excessive. The second sentencer cannot scale down the first sentence, but he can reduce his own so as to arrive at a fair combined sentence.[31] Incidentally, the extent of this problem should be lessened now that Crown Court staff have directions to try to ensure that all outstanding matters against a defendant come on before the same court at the same time. The Court of Appeal has stressed the importance of avoiding sentencing by two different judges if at all possible.[32]

6.26 The suspended sentence has also thrown the problem up on occasion. After a breach a sentencer may decide that he must "order that the suspended sentence shall take effect with the original term unaltered" under the Powers of Criminal Courts Act 1973, Section 23, as amended by the Criminal Justice Act 1982, Section 31. Normally that would lead to the original term being ordered to take effect consecutively to the fresh sentence for the later offence.[33] However, once again the sentencer may feel that the sum total of two such sentences would be longer than desirable in all the circumstances. If he does conclude that the overall effect would be too drastic, he can either scale down his own sentence for the fresh offence, or implement a part of the suspended sentence only.[34] In the latter case he would be required to give reasons

---

28 (1979) 1 Cr.App.R.(S) 7.
29 *Turner* (1975) 61 Cr.App.R. 67. See Chapter 9 for concurrent and consecutive sentences (paras. 9.18ff) and also for suspended sentences (paras. 9.23ff).
30 (1974) C.S.P. A5.3(b).
31 *Millen* (1980) 2 Cr.App.R.(S) 357.
32 *Bennett* (1980) 2 Cr.App.R.(S) 96.
33 *Ithell* (1969) 53 Cr.App.R. 310.
34 *Bocskei* (1970) 54 Cr.App.R. 519.

for his opinion that it would be unjust to order the original term to take effect unaltered.

6.27 The totality principle applies equally to non-custodial penalties. It is tempting sometimes for the sentencer to order the defendant with some means to pay compensation as well as a fine, and both prosecution and defence legal aid costs. The temptation to try and ensure that no-one is the loser as a result of the defendant's activities is understandable, but it should be resisted if it results in a defendant having to pay three or four times over – unless "the overall effect" is justified. The court must in any event be satisfied about the ability of the defendant to pay, and should bear in mind that he cannot appeal against any order relating to his contribution towards his legal aid costs.

6.28 The principle of proportionality also applies to youth custody. In the past the now defunct sentence of Borstal training was often passed despite the fact that the period in custody could be longer than the offence merited. The justification was often the desire to help the youth in question with what the court optimistically thought might be helpful training. Now that youth custody has replaced Borstal, a sentence must be of a fair length and no longer.[35] Any sentencer wishing to help a defendant by getting him "training" in custody should restrain himself.

RESISTING THE TEMPTATION TO HELP

6.29 Helping a defendant, for example, by placing him on probation despite a long record of offending, is often quite proper. If the offence is not too serious the court may properly help the defendant by giving him a last chance. There will be occasions when the sentencer is confronted by a situation in which he is tempted to step outside the normal sentencing role, and when he feels the urge to assist the defendant in some other way, or to try and help the local mental health authorities. He may feel that a longer sentence of imprisonment than is strictly justified ought to be used to assist the defendant with his problem of accommodation, drink, drugs or whatever, or to help the community by providing an unsatisfactory solution to a difficult problem. The temptation to help should be resisted if the proposed remedy involves either going up the penal ladder by resorting to a harsher disposal than would otherwise be used, or by sentencing to a longer term of imprisonment than would be used were it not for the desire to help. In Chapter 4 we

---

35 *Hart and Hart* (1983) 5 Cr.App.R.(S) 385. See para. 10.24 *infra*.

referred to the "help" rendered in *Graham*[36] by the Court of Appeal, and some further illustrations may make the point clearer.

6.30 In *Coombes*[37] a strong court (Lord Lane, C.J., Lord Roskill and Skinner, J.) was concerned with a man with a long record who had broken a shop window and had taken a pair of boots. He had given himself up at the police station. In the past he had had spells in mental hospitals and had been subject both to hospital orders and probation orders with conditions of treatment. No place could be found for him in any hospital. He was sentenced to two years' imprisonment and appealed. Delivering the judgment of the court, Skinner, J. pointed out that the defendant had committed the offence in order to obtain refuge, and added:

> "It is important to bear in mind what Lawton, L.J., emphasised in the case of *Clarke*,[38] that the courts should not use prisons as a dustbin for social misfits for whom other social agencies can do nothing. It is very important in cases of this sort that the court should sentence specifically for the offence and no more."

The two-year sentence was reduced to one of seven days. The problem of mentally disturbed persons in court could well increase significantly as a result of increasing social pressures and the policy of dealing with them in the community rather than in mental hospitals. The warning of the Court of Appeal remains of crucial importance: the mental health open-door policy must not be replaced by a closed cell-door policy for mentally disturbed nuisance cases.

6.31 The Court of Appeal pointed out in *Cooper*[39] that the fact that the defendant liked being in prison could not possibly justify a disproportionately long sentence. The road to the Court of Appeal is paved with good intentions. The court has quite often been obliged to reduce sentences in cases in which the judge was trying to help the defendant, and seeking to obtain treatment, hostel or probation assistance for him, so as to give him a better chance of avoiding crime in future. In *Gisbourne*[40], for example, the judge thought that two years' imprisonment would have been appropriate, but he was anxious to assist the defendant by making it possible for him to have parole with probation service help, and possibly a hostel placement. He accordingly passed a three-and-a-half year sentence. The Court of Appeal pointed out that it

---

36 Para. 4.38 *supra*.
37 (1981) 3 Cr.App.R.(S) 300.
38 (1975) 61 Cr.App.R. 320. See para. 11.25 *infra*.
39 (1983) 5 Cr.App.R.(S) 295.
40 (1977) C.S.P. A3.2(a).

was wrong to take the possibility of parole into account, and reduced the sentence to that originally thought to be appropriate, namely two years.

6.32 In *Roote*[41] a woman offender had been sentenced to five years' imprisonment in respect of hard drugs offences, instead of to the period of three years which the Court of Appeal later thought appropriate. Drake, J. delivering the judgment of the court, pointed out forcefully:

> "This Court is firmly of the view that, save in exceptional circumstances, the court should not pass a sentence of imprisonment outside the range appropriate for the offence and for the particular offender on the grounds that the additional term of imprisonment will be of benefit to the offender in society helping overcome some addiction to alcohol or drugs . . .. The extra term of imprisonment should not have been added to the one appropriate for these offences, given the antecedent history of this offender, merely in order to assist her."

6.33 The judge or magistrate tempted to assist a young offender by passing an unusually long sentence in order to get him training and education, should bear in mind the above observations of the Court of Appeal, and also the research findings both in the United States and Canada, referred to earlier.[42] Those showed that courts wishing, with the best of intentions, to help young offenders, often passed more severe sentences than those wishing merely to punish them. The same applies to some attempts to stop young, and sometimes other offenders, "in their tracks", by means of a sentence longer than justified.

6.34 A sentencer may on occasion be tempted to pass a sentence of imprisonment and then suspend it, rather than make a probation order or impose a conditional discharge, on the basis that such a course will provide a heavier or more pointed sword of Damocles to hang over the defendant – a course thought to be in his interests. Such temptation should also be resisted. If a probation order or conditional discharge is appropriate, then it is wrong to pass a sentence of imprisonment, even if it is suspended.[43] By the same token it is also wrong to increase the length of a suspended term just to help the defendant to keep out of trouble. There is little doubt about the fact that some terms of suspended sentences have been longer than they would have been had the sentence been an immediate sentence of custody.[44]

41 (1980) 2 Cr.App.R.(S) 368.
42 Para. 1.75 and note 103 *supra*.
43 *English* (1984) 6 Cr.App.R.(S) 60.
44 A.E. Bottoms, "The Advisory Council and the Suspended Sentence" [1979] Crim.L.R. 437.

6.35 As we shall discuss further in the next chapter, it is also important that sentencers should refrain from promising defendants that they will be helped by treatment in prison.

IMPROPER CONSIDERATIONS

6.36 It is improper to add to a sentence because a defendant has pleaded not guilty, has perjured himself or has attacked the evidence of the police officers in the case. So too, if the defendant is guilty of contempt of court, he should be separately dealt with for that, rather than having his sentence increased.[45] Not only should the sentencer rigorously guard against any improper addition to the correct sentence, but in due course he should be careful when pronouncing the sentence to avoid giving the impression that he has made such an addition. It would be as well for the sentencer to avoid expressions such as the following:

> "He saw fit to contest this case, put up a lying defence and attacked the police into the bargain. It was not surprising at the end of the case, particularly as this was a second offence of the same character within a short period of time, that the learned Deputy Chairman took a serious view of the matter."[46]

> "He put up a wholly lying defence at the trial, which was rebutted at every point. Criminals who do that can hardly expect, when they are finally brought to book, either the trial judge or this Court to extend leniency to them."[47]

As the context reveals, both these observations were made in the Court of Appeal (and both by Roskill, L.J.) but if they had been made by the sentencer in the court of trial, both defendants could have complained on appeal.

6.37 A court must not punish a defendant for exercising his right to be tried by jury. However, if it is proper in such a case to make him pay the costs of the prosecution, it is also proper to make the costs order the appropriate one for the more expensive court of trial chosen by the defendant himself.[48]

6.38 When fixing the appropriate length of a custodial sentence it is improper for the sentencer to include an additional amount to

---

45   *Powell* [1985] Crim.L.R. 802.
46   *Playfair* (1972) C.S.P. C2.2(h).
47   *Sharp* (1972) C.S.P. C2.2(g).
48   *Hayden* (1975) 60 Cr.App.R. 304.

compensate for the fact that the defendant may be released on parole after serving one-third of the term,[49] or after serving two-thirds with the benefit of full remission for good conduct,[50] or at any time, theoretically, if a juvenile sentenced to detention under Section 53, Children and Young Persons Act 1933.[51] In *Findlay v. Secretary of State*,[52] a case brought by four defendants caught by the Home Secretary's decision in November 1983 to restrict parole for many prisoners serving sentences of over five years' imprisonment, Sir John Donaldson, M.R. reaffirmed the basic rule as follows:

> "Save where a sentencing judge is considering a suspended or partly suspended sentence of imprisonment, he is not concerned with periods of incarceration. He is concerned with the length of a sentence of imprisonment."

It is because of this rule, and the knowledge that no defendant serves the full term of imprisonment passed on him, that many judges prefer to say to a defendant: "The sentence of the court is one of three years' imprisonment", rather than, "You will go to prison for three years."

6.39 It is very important that at the consideration stage the sentencer should obey the spirit of the rule, as otherwise he may be denying the defendant his constitutional right to be properly sentenced and then considered for parole at the proper time. The danger inherent in a judge trying to defeat Parliament's parole scheme was pointed out when parole was being introduced:[53]

> "A harsh judge might pass a sentence of nine years merely to ensure that the prisoner served the three years which he intended him to spend in prison. The authorities might well find the man embittered by his harsh sentence and quite unsuitable for release before six years had elapsed. The result would then be that the man would have spent twice as long in prison as the maximum time intended by a harsh judge."

6.40 There are nevertheless a few occasions when the Court of Appeal has sanctioned a look at the implications of remission or parole. We shall discuss the extended sentence in Chapter 9 but it is appropriate to point out now that a consideration of that sentence does require the court to have some regard to the question of remission. The Court of Appeal has pointed out that it is permissible to use the extended sentence where it is thought desirable to ensure that the defendant, if he is a persistent offender who meets the statutory criteria, should be either

49 *Gisbourne* (1977) C.S.P. A3.2(a).
50 *Maguire* (1957) 40 Cr.App.R. 92; Criminal Justice Act 1967, s. 61(1).
51 *Burrowes* (1985) 7 Cr.App.R.(S) 106.
52 [1984] 3 All E.R. 201.
53 E. Stockdale, *The Court and the Offender* (1967) Gollancz, p. 29.

in custody or on licence for the whole period of his sentence. In the case of ordinary imprisonment, assuming no loss of remission and no revocation of the licence, a parole licence will last only from the date of release on licence to the two-thirds stage of the sentence (known as the earliest date of release, or E.D.R.). The last third will be free of any supervision. If the court wishes to ensure that a persistent offender will be on licence for the final third of the sentence, an extended sentence may in certain circumstances be imposed.[54]

6.41 Similarly, the Court of Appeal has on occasion had to consider the question of the powers of the Home Secretary and the Parole Board when testing whether the flexibility of a life sentence has been unduly impaired by concurrent sentences of imprisonment for determinate periods.[55]

6.42 Where a court passes a sentence of imprisonment and fines the defendant as well for the same offence, care should be taken that the maximum sentence of imprisonment is not imposed, as the non-payment of the fine might lead to a consecutive term being served in default.[56] Not only would the defendant then serve longer than the maximum permitted for the offence itself, but the sentencer should bear in mind that a sentence in default has to be served up to the two-thirds date, as parole does not apply. (Of course, payment of a part or all of the fine can reduce or stop the imprisonment in default altogether.)

6.43 There is one other reason why the sentencer should be aware of the basic rules of remission and parole, and that is that such knowledge can help him to avoid making unfortunate remarks about the length of incarceration. A judge will sometimes express surprise in open court when he sees a defendant back in the Crown Court "shortly" after sentencing him to prison for an earlier offence. It should be borne in mind that the defendant may well have served more than six months in custody while waiting for his first trial, and that that period may have been credited towards the time of the sentence under the Criminal Justice Act 1967, Section 67.

PAROLE

6.44 The main rule is that each defendant sentenced to a term of immediate imprisonment, to youth custody or to a detention centre (but

---

54   *Cain* (1983) 5 Cr.App.R.(S) 272.
55   *Middleton* (1981) 3 Cr.App.R.(S) 273; *Daniels* (1984) 6 Cr.App.R.(S) 8.
56   *Michel and others* (1984) 6 Cr.App.R.(S) 379.

not detention under the Children and Young Persons Act 1933, Section 53) is entitled to one-third remission for good conduct. If serving a sentence of imprisonment or youth custody, he is additionally entitled to be considered for parole after serving one-third of his sentence or six months, whichever period expires later. In other words, parole may be considered for the middle third of the sentence. As we have seen, the parole licence will come to an end at the two-thirds date, or E.D.R.[57]

6.45 A defendant sentenced to life imprisonment may be released on licence at any time, subject to very stringent safeguards. Unless his licence is revoked, whether for a further offence or for some other reason, he will remain subject to the licence for life: Criminal Justice Act 1967, Section 61.

6.46 For the prisoner with a term of years, time served before sentence counts towards the minimum of one-third which must be served, as long as the time in custody was attributable to the instant offence and not to some other reason (Section 67). However, time served before the sentence does not count towards the statutory minimum of six months, which must be served after sentence. The defendant must satisfy two tests: he must serve at least one-third of the sentence and he must serve the minimum period of six months after sentence has been passed.

6.47 Inevitably any rule may lead to boundaries and thus to disparities. An illustration may make the point clear. Two co-defendants are each sentenced to 18 months' imprisonment at the same time because the judge considers them to be equally to blame and to have similar antecedents. D1 was lucky enough to get bail pending trial but D2 spent six months in a remand prison awaiting trial. After serving only six months D1 will be eligible for parole consideration because he will by then have satisfied the double test of having served both one-third of the sentence and the minimum specified period of six months in custody after being sentenced. D2's six months in custody before sentence will count towards, and indeed equal, one-third of his sentence, but he will also be obliged to satisfy the minimum period to be served after sentence, that is, another six months. He will be obliged to serve twelve months in all, or two-thirds of his sentence and so will have no opportunity to qualify for parole. D2 might argue, not unreasonably, that he had served, or was obliged to serve, twice as long as his co-defendant, and that the sentences were accordingly disparate. The

---

57 Criminal Justice Act 1967, s. 60 (as amended); the minimum specified period to be served was reduced from twelve to six months by the Eligibility for Release on Licence Order 1983 (S.I. no. 1959).

answer of the Court of Appeal would be that there was no disparity as each sentence had been identical. Any blame for disparities of this kind could only be blamed on the legislation which created the scope for the anomalies to exist. Defending lawyers and magistrates dealing with bail applications might bear in mind the fact that time spent in custody awaiting trial does not always redound to the credit of the defendant, as D2's case shows.

6.48 The partly suspended sentence will attract both remission and parole in appropriate circumstances, but as Walker has rightly observed:[58]

> "The three-legged race run by remission, partial suspension and parole demands abstruse calculations."

We shall spare the reader an explanation of those calculations.

6.49 The youth detained under the Children and Young Persons Act 1933, Section 53(2), for a determinate period may be released on licence at any time during the sentence. As a matter of practice the Home Secretary seeks the advice of the Parole Board at the one-third stage, so that such defendants are treated in a similar manner to those qualifying for ordinary parole consideration. Furthermore, although not entitled to remission, it is rare for such a Section 53 defendant to be detained without a further review should he still be in custody when the two-thirds stage has been reached. The Court of Appeal has stated that it is wrong for the sentencer to take these licence provisions into account when fixing the term.[59]

6.50 Thomas has pointed out that the extension of the parole scheme by the 1983 Order in Council has had a great effect on the practical results of most Crown Court sentences, many of which have turned out to be similar in terms of the time served in prison, that is six months or thereabouts. He has criticised the change in the law in the strongest terms, writing:[60]

> "The extension of the parole scheme . . . has, in my view, reduced the process of custodial sentencing in the Crown Court to a complete farce . . . The relationship between the sentence pronounced in court, and the sentence as served, is now, at least so far as the majority of custodial sentences imposed by the Crown Court is concerned, so tenuous that debating ways and means of harmonizing the nominal sentences pronounced by the Court has by comparison been rendered irrelevant."

58 *Op. cit.* (note 22 *supra*), para. 23.15.
59 *Burrowes* (1985) 7 Cr.App.R.(S) 106; for the relatively unimportant supervision provisions following on detention centre and youth custody, see Criminal Justice Act 1982, s. 15.
60 D.A. Thomas, "Parole and the Crown Court" (1985) 149 J.P. 344.

6.51 Thomas's views are undoubtedly shared by some members of the judiciary, but all sentencers are still obliged to disregard the possibility of parole when fixing the sentence. It might be said that the change in the law, and the strongly held views about it on the part of some judges, makes it more imperative than ever that the possibility of parole, and of remission, is consciously excluded. It also follows that no sentencer should ever tell a defendant that he will in due course benefit from parole or remission. At the moment the courts appear to be obeying the injunction to disregard parole when fixing sentences, but two academics, Worrall and Pease, have given the warning:[61]

> "However there may come a point at which the effective sentence diverges so dramatically from the pronounced sentence that courts will increase sentence lengths in retaliation."

It is devoutly to be hoped that we never reach such a stage.

Revocation of parole licence

6.52 It is entirely proper for a Crown Court dealing with a defendant who has committed a fresh offence whilst on parole to consider the question of the revocation of his licence. Indeed, a Practice Direction[62] states that the court should consider in each case whether to revoke the licence or to leave the decision to the Parole Board. Either way, any pertinent remarks by the judge will be carefully noted by the Parole Board. If the court decides that in all the circumstances the defendant should be returned to custody to complete his original sentence, it should revoke the licence. The sentencer must then, as always, make it clear whether the fresh sentence is to run consecutively to the original one – which in most cases will be the appropriate decision – or concurrently. The Practice Direction points out that if the Crown Court does not revoke the licence, any later revocation by the Board under the provisions of the Criminal Justice Act 1967, Section 62 cannot provide for the fresh sentence to run consecutively. Quite often there is no problem left for the court to solve, for either the defendant's licence period will have run out by the time he reaches the Crown Court, or he will have already been recalled by the Board.

6.53 Section 62(10) provides that where a court has revoked the licence, the defendant must not be released on parole again until the expiry of one year after the revocation or after the expiration of a third of the balance of the licence period, if that is later.

---

61 A. Worrall and K. Pease, "The Prison Population in 1985" (1986) *Br. J. Criminology* 26, p. 184.
62 (1976) 62 Cr.App.R. 130.

CHAPTER 7

Passing Sentence

7.01 In the present chapter we shall consider the climax of the sentencing stage: the time when the court comes to pass the sentence on the defendant. Although that stage will usually take only a very short time, there are a number of matters which must be borne in mind. Some steps require the consent of the defendant, others that he be given an explanation of what is entailed in the court order. Each of those requirements will be considered briefly, as will the question of the giving of reasons by the court. We shall also consider the need to avoid both improper reasons and the making of promises to the defendant, as well as some general matters. As a matter of convenience we have divided these matters up for discussion under the following heads:
(1) Consent of the defendant;
(2) The court shall explain;
(3) The giving of reasons;
(4) The adequacy of reasons; and
(5) Promises.

CONSENT OF THE DEFENDANT

7.02 We shall discuss the deferment of sentence in greater detail in the next chapter, but at this stage it is relevant to note that a court may not defer sentence without the consent of the defendant: Powers of Criminal Courts Act 1973, Section 1(3). The consent of the defendant must not be implied merely from a failure on his part to object to the proposal that the matter of sentence be deferred. "The accused should be asked personally whether he consents to that deferment."[1]

7.03 Consent is also obligatory when the court wishes to make a probation order. After explaining all the requirements of the proposed order to the defendant "in ordinary language" (which presumably does not mean ordinary lawyer's language) the court must make sure that the defendant "expresses his willingness to comply with its requirements"

---

1 *Fairhead* (1975) 61 Cr.App.R. 102 *per* James, L.J.

before making the order (Section 2(6)). The consent must be a genuine one, and not one extracted by means of a threat, whether express or implied, that the alternative is prison – if the court has no intention of imprisoning in any event.[2] It should be noted that there is no equivalent requirement for consent to be obtained from a juvenile before a supervision order is made, or from an adult made the subject of a suspended prison sentence coupled with a supervision order. Juveniles and adult suspended sentence defendants have the decision made for them by the court, without the option. There is one exception. The Children and Young Persons Act 1969, Section 12 (as amended) provides that night and certain other restrictions may only be added to a supervision order if "the supervised person or, if he is a child, his parent or guardian, consents to their inclusion".

7.04   A court may not make a community service order, even in respect of a 16-year-old, unless the defendant consents to the making of the order.[3]

7.05   Only the person to be bound can enter into a recognisance, that is, acknowledge or recognise his indebtedness or obligation to the Crown, and so his consent is an essential element, but that consent may be obtained with varying degrees of pressure. The Crown Court has the power formerly vested in assizes and quarter sessions to order:

> "the release, after respite of judgment, of a convicted person on recognisance to come up for judgment if called on, but meanwhile to be of good behaviour."[4]

7.06   If such a defendant declines to enter into a recognisance, the court must proceed to sentence him then, unless it decides to defer sentence, a matter which would also require his consent. Alternatively the court could adjourn for reports. Counsel would have to advise the defendant that a failure to enter into a recognisance might well lead to an immediate sentence of imprisonment.

7.07   The magistrates' court does not have the same power, but does have its ancient wide power (now shared by the Crown Court) to bind over, not only defendants who have been convicted, but also those acquitted in certain circumstances and, somewhat surprisingly, witnesses as well: Justices of the Peace Act 1968, Section 1(7). A person

2 *Marquis* (1984) 59 Cr.App.R. 228; *Barnett* [1986] Crim.L.R. 758.
3 Powers of Criminal Courts Act 1973, s. 14(2), as substituted by the Criminal Justice Act 1982.
4 Supreme Court Act 1981, s. 79(2); see further paras. 14.09ff *infra*.

required by the magistrates to enter into a recognisance to be of good behaviour or to keep the peace, can be imprisoned if he fails to enter into such a recognisance. In this case there is no pretence of consent being freely given. When one recalls the various decisions about consent in the criminal law, it is clear that the word may be said to have a very elastic meaning. Nowhere is this point better illustrated than in the sentencing stage.

7.08 There is one other occasion on which a person other than a defendant may be required to enter into a recognisance, and that is when a court dealing with a juvenile calls on his parent or guardian to enter into a recognisance to take proper care of and exercise proper control over him. Once again consent is required: Children and Young Persons Act 1969, Section 7(7).

THE COURT SHALL EXPLAIN

7.09 The Powers of Criminal Courts Act 1973 contains several sections that require the court to explain a particular order to the defendant in ordinary language. Explaining to the defendant that if he commits another offence during the period of a conditional discharge, he will be liable to be sentenced for the original offence, is simple enough.[5] The need to explain the requirements of a probation order and the consequences of a breach by the commission of a further offence, can be dealt with fairly simply also. Explaining a suspended sentence is straightforward, as is complying with the additional requirement that a supervision order attached to it must be explained separately.[6] It is only a little more complicated when one has to explain a partly suspended sentence.[7]

7.10 There is one order, however, which is not at all easy to explain, and that is the community service order, which Parliament expects to be preceded by a short lecture on the subject. Section 14(5) of the 1973 Act states:

> "Before making a community service order the court shall explain to the offender in ordinary language –
>   (a) the purpose and effect of the order (and in particular the requirements of the order as specified in section 15 of this Act);
>   (b) the consequences which may follow under section 16 if he fails to comply with any of those requirements; and

---

5   S. 7(3).
6   SS. 22(4), 26(11).
7   Criminal Law Act 1977, s. 47(2).

(c) that the court has under section 17 and power to review the order on the application either of the offender or of a probation officer."

Clearly the offender must be told at the very least that Section 15 requires him "to report to the relevant officer and subsequently from time to time notify him of any change of address" and to "perform for the number of hours specified in the order such work at such times as he may be instructed by the relevant officer". He ought to be told, since Section 15 insists on the point, that the work must be performed within a period of twelve months from the date of the order (subject to Section 17(1)). He must also be informed of the effect of Section 16 in case of any breach; that section has eight sub-sections and takes up more than a whole page of the statute book. Section 17 is equally long. In the circumstances sentencers may perhaps be forgiven by the Court of Appeal if they do not comply strictly with these statutory requirements.

The giving of reasons

7.11 A visitor from a country with an ideal system of justice (whose estimated time of arrival must necessarily be rather uncertain) might well make the comment that any important decision made in a court of law should be supported by a careful and accurate statement of the reasons for that decision. In England there are a number of critical occasions in the criminal trial which might surprise such a visitor, for no reasons are then given. Perhaps the most important one is the returning of the verdict of the jury in the Crown Court. The absence of any requirement for the giving of reasons is sometimes explained as being due to the untrained lay nature of the jury and its foreman: it would not be right to expect a layman to explain how he and his eleven colleagues had arrived at their decision. As the members of juries are routinely told that they are the judges of fact and not of the law, one might have thought that they could be expected to give their reasons for their conclusions on the facts. Many a defendant must have wanted to ask the jury to explain how they had arrived at their verdict, having regard to the evidence in the case and, one suspects, not a few lawyers would also have been interested to learn how some verdicts were reached. One suspects that many decisions of juries are arrived at by way of compromise, and that it would be impossible in many cases for the foreman to give an accurate account of how it was that each of the twelve members (or even eleven or ten) had arrived at the same conclusion. We shall, unfortunately, now never be able to discover how actual, as opposed to "shadow" or "simulated" juries work, as the Contempt of Court Act 1981, Section 8 has ruled out the possibility of any proper research on the subject.

7.12 In a magistrates' court the chairman will announce the decision of the court, which may be that of a simple majority (although that fact need not be made public) but he need not give any reasons for the decision of the court – subject to a few exceptions, some of which we have discussed earlier. Again, it is possible in such a case that the conclusion of the court was reached by way of a compromise, with two, or possibly all three members of the court using different routes to arrive at their particular conclusion. The same applies to the Crown Court when a judge is sitting with two magistrates as full members of the court. The accurate giving of reasons may be an almost impossible task at times when more than one decision-maker is sitting - whether the number be three or twelve.

7.13 Thomas has argued that reasons should at any rate always be given for sentencing decisions.[8] His four principal points were that natural justice demanded such a course; that it would lead to a rationalisation of sentencing generally; that it would lead to more consistency; and, finally, that an expression of reasons would make it easier to challenge the decision on appeal. As Devlin pointed out:[9]

> "It is of assistance to the defendant both in accepting what has happened, and, where he does not accept it, in preparing his appeal."

It must be borne in mind that a notice of appeal must give sufficient grounds for the appeal. It is not enough merely to state that the sentence was too severe.[10]

7.14 Another sound justification for the giving of reasons is that there are a number of people other than the defendant who need to understand the sentence. Writing for judges attending the American National Judicial College, Judge Mattina of New York gave his advice on the point succinctly:[11]

> "Explain your sentence fully – so that each of the interested parties understands :
> A. Defendant
> B. Victim
> C. Public
> D. Probation Department
> E. Prison Authorities
> F. Parole Board
> G. Appellate Courts
> H. Most importantly, YOU – the sentencing judge."

---

8   D.A. Thomas, "The Case for Reasoned Decisions" [1963] Crim.L.R. 243.
9   K. Devlin, *Sentencing Offenders in Magistrates' Courts* (1970) Sweet & Maxwell, p. 58.
10 Guide issued by the Registrar of Criminal Appeals (1983) 77 Cr.App.R. 138.
11 J.M. Burns and J.S. Mattina, *Sentencing* (1978) National Judicial College, p. 197.

To his first person on the list one should perhaps add the defendant's family, who will be immediately affected by the outcome.

7.15 We referred earlier to Parliament's reluctance to give legislative help to the courts on sentencing matters, and on the issue of the giving of reasons the legislature has remained almost completely silent. The explanation could be that it, and the relevant government departments, have appreciated the difficulties inherent in providing a realistic statutory framework for sentencing, such as would have to accompany any general direction to the courts that they must give reasons. It would be possible for a statute merely to state that reasons must always be given, or given by the Crown Court at any rate, but such a provision would not be of much help without some further statutory guidance providing, as a bare minimum, some clues as to the legislature's wishes (a) when fixing the maximum penalty, and (b) with regard to defendants not meriting such a maximum. Such legislation as exists relating to the giving of reasons is extremely limited, so the principal provisions can be described briefly.

7.16 (1) As we have seen already in Chapter 4, a magistrates' court is obliged to give reasons for proceeding without a social inquiry report in certain circumstances.

7.17 (2) A magistrates' court passing a sentence of imprisonment on a defendant over 21, who has not previously been subject to such a sentence, is required to "state the reason for its opinion that no other method of dealing with him is appropriate": Powers of Criminal Courts Act 1973, Section 20(2). Furthermore, that reason must be specified in the warrant of commitment and be entered in the court register. In practice the briefest of reasons is often given and recorded. As Walker has pointed out, the register sometimes records cryptic notes, such as "NODA", short for "No other disposal appropriate".[12] Merely stating the conclusion that no other disposal is appropriate is, of course, not giving the reason for the opinion. The Crown Court is also restricted in passing the sentence of imprisonment in similar circumstances, but is not obliged to give reasons for the opinion that no other method is suitable. It is helpful all round if the judges do in fact state their reason for imprisoning a defendant for the first time.

7.18 (3) The principal statutory insistence on reasons being given is to be found in the Criminal Justice Act 1982, Sections 2 and 6. In general

---

12   N. Walker, *Sentencing: Theory, Law and Practice* (1985) Butterworths, pp. 8, 310.

terms, Section 1(4) prohibits any court from passing a custodial sentence on a defendant under 21 (other than under the Children and Young Persons Act 1933, Section 53):

> "unless it is of the opinion that no other method of dealing with him is appropriate because it appears to the court that he is unable or unwilling to respond to non-custodial penalties or because a custodial sentence is necessary for the protection of the public or because the offence was so serious that a non-custodial sentence cannot be justified."

If a magistrates' court passes a custodial sentence on such a defendant, whether one of youth custody or to a detention centre, Section 2(4) requires the court to state its reason for the opinion that no other method is appropriate, stating why one of the three exceptions applies. It cannot be emphasised too strongly that the statutory obligation is not confined to stating the opinion or conclusion of the court: it is the *reason* for the opinion that must be stated and recorded. Apart from being entered in the register of the court, the reason must be specified in the warrant of commitment. The Crown Court is required to give its reasons in a similar way when passing a sentence of youth custody, though not when making a detention centre order.[13] There is no obligation on the higher court to record the reasons, but the shorthand writer will note any stated reasons in the normal way, save when an appeal from the magistrates' court is heard, when no shorthand note is taken. Once again, it is obviously helpful if the judge also states his reasons for finding that one or more of the statutory exceptions apply when making a detention centre order.

7.19 Any sentencer tempted to try a detention centre order as a first or second resort, rather than as a last resort as indicated by the Act, should ask himself why he is so tempted, and what the real reason for his choice of sentence is. It could be that he was persuaded on a visit to such an institution that young offenders could be most helped if they were to be sent to the detention centre at an early stage. The Home Office was clearly aware of this particular line of unhelpful advice when it warned the staff of young offender establishments on 20 May 1983:[14]

> "Visits to establishments by magistrates, judges and court officers are of course necesary to help them in their tasks . . . It would be quite wrong to use contacts such as visits to influence the courts' sentencing practice one way or the other . . . The evidence does not support the proposition that if establishments held young offenders earlier in their criminal careers this would reduce the level of their re-offending; indeed juveniles who do come into our custody have higher reconviction rates than young adults.

13 S. 6(1).
14 (1983) *Probation J. 30*, p. 95.

Furthermore, advice of that kind would be directly contrary to the provisions of the Criminal Justice Act which makes custody explicitly a last resort."

The suggestion is sometimes made that the Home Office seeks to exert influence, or too much influence, on the courts. This is a rare illustration of the executive trying in a positive manner to respect the independence of the judiciary and to keep it separate from the executive branch of government.

7.20 Parliament's intention was clearly to try and keep young offenders out of custody as much as possible, and the giving of reasons was obviously intended as one of the safeguards. Sentencers should be scrupulously on guard against deciding to pass a custodial sentence on a defendant under 21 without adequate reasons, and then seeking to justify the decision by stating reasons which are dredged up afterwards and which are not genuine. A juvenile court in the North-East of England was found to have entered no reasons at all in the register in four out of 99 cases of juveniles sentenced to youth custody or a detention centre, and to have given reasons in other cases which were less than adequate.[15] That court used the first exception (unable or unwilling to respond to non-custodial penalties) in the case of a boy whose only previous appearance in court had led to a conditional discharge. The "protection of the public" reason was given in a case in which a young defendant had stolen three handbags. The "seriousness" reason was given in the cases of several young property offenders of the type said by the Court of Appeal to be suitable, in the case of adults, for community service orders.

7.21 Magistrates have been criticised for giving a very flexible meaning to the words of the safeguards. In fairness to them one should point out that the word "serious" cannot have precisely the same meaning in a court where the maximum possible sentence is one of six months' incarceration, as it bears in a court with life imprisonment as the maximum. It might have been more helpful if Parliament had spelled out different criteria for the two courts.

7.22 In *Bradbourn*[16] the Court of Appeal considered the meaning of the word "serious". The court was there concerned with a 20-year-old woman shop assistant who was caught by security officers when she rang

---

15 P. Whitehead and J. MacMillan, "Checks or Blank Cheque?" (1985) *Probation J. 32*, p. 87. See also paras 10.22ff *infra*
16 (1985) 7 Cr.App.R.(S) 180.

up 15p in respect of a sale for which she was paid £2.15, pocketing the £2 difference. She was a first offender, but the security officers were involved because of similar losses in the past. She was sentenced in the Crown Court to three months' youth custody. The Court of Appeal substituted a conditional discharge (one month having been served) and stated that the seriousness exception, "so serious that a non-custodial sentence cannot be justified", referred to the sort of case in which right-thinking members of the public would feel that justice had not been done if the young offender received a non-custodial sentence. That is, seriousness refers to the facts of the case, and not merely to the charge. Similarly, in *Munday* [17] the Court of Appeal stated that none of the three exceptions could be said to apply in the case of a 17-year-old who had stolen property to the total value of £168 from six shops in the course of one afternoon, and whose only previous offence of theft had led to a fine of £40.

7.23 (4) Normally a sentence of four months' or less youth custody cannot be passed on a defendant: the correct sentence, if custody cannot be avoided, is a detention centre order for such a term. If a court concludes that a detention centre is ruled out only because of the defendant's mental condition, then it may pass a youth custody sentence even though the period is one of four months or less. In such a case Section 6(3) of the Criminal Justice Act 1982 obliges the court to "certify in the warrant of commitment that it passed the sentence of youth custody for that reason." In these circumstances not only the magistrates' court, but also the Crown Court is obliged to comply with the requirement. There is no requirement that the reason be stated in open court, but as a general rule it is probably desirable for the matter to be dealt with in open court, in carefully chosen terms, as well as in the warrant.

7.24 (5) If any court when dealing with a breach of a suspended sentence decides that it would be unjust to activate the whole of the original term unaltered, having regard to all the circumstances, then that court (whether Crown Court or magistrates' court) is required to state its reasons for such an opinion: Powers of Criminal Courts Act 1973, Section 23(1). Similar requirements apply to partly suspended sentences: Criminal Law Act 1977, Section 47(4).

7.25 (6) In motoring cases the court is required to give "special reasons" in special circumstances, but we need not discuss that esoteric branch of the law further at this stage. [18]

17 [1985] Crim.L.R. 752.
18 See paras. 15.48ff *infra*.

7.26 The foregoing are the principal statutory requirements relating to the giving of reasons, but there are other occasions when good practice requires such a course. In passing sentence a judge should, as a bare minimum, give reasons :

(1) If not following the recommendations of the social inquiry report;

(2) If passing an unusually severe sentence;

(3) If passing an unusually lenient sentence;

(4) If rejecting reasonable submissions put forward in the mitigation submissions, whether by the advocate or defendant in person. These four occasions need to be considered further.

7.27 (1) The defendant may well have been building up his hopes on the strength of the recommendations which he has been told are in the social inquiry report. For that reason, as well as the fact that the writer of the report should be given an explanation for the disagreement (both as a matter of courtesy and possible as a matter of training), it is helpful if the sentencer explains that the court has been unable to comply with the recommendation for sound reasons. Such reasons should then be stated. Often the principal reason will be that the court regards the offence as too serious to be dealt with in the recommended manner; on other occasions, the main reason will be the recent failure of probation of some other non-custodial disposal. The Court of Appeal has not, so far as the writers are aware, ever stated that the reasons for differing from a probation officer's recommendation relating to sentence should be given, but such a statement was made by the court in connection with a welfare officer's recommendation in a matrimonial dispute between parents over the custody of their child.[19] We mentioned earlier the undesirability of a court rebuking the writer of a report unjustly, but the point bears repetition at this stage.

7.28 (2) When a judge imposes an unusually severe sentence, and perhaps even if it is severe and not all that unusual, some explanation is due to the defendant and his family, as well as to the public and the Court of Appeal. As Shaw, L.J., remarked in *Newman:*[20]

> "Where sentences of that severity are imposed, it is not out of place for the learned judge to indicate the basis upon which he thinks that sentences of that magnitude are justified."

7.29 Godsland and Fielding have drawn attention both to the increased use made by the courts of the Children and Young Persons

---

19 *Stephenson v. Stephenson* [1985] F.L.R. 1140.
20 (1979) 1 Cr.App.R.(S) 252.

Act 1933, Section 53(2) and to the extent of the hardship, unintended as well as intended, that can follow on such an order.[21] Their suggestion that full reasons should be given whenever Section 53(2) is used is clearly a sensible one. A juvenile and his parents are entitled to hear in open court why the case is considered to be so serious that none of the usual provisions for defendants of that age can be used.

7.30 (3) If an unusually light sentence is imposed, the court should also give its reasons. The defendant and his family will on this occasion be too overjoyed to care very much about the reasons, but the victim, the public and the press should receive an explanation. The press is mentioned because nothing is worse for the courts, or indeed the public, than a headline to the effect, "Another ridiculously lenient sentence", particularly if, as so often is the case, the decision was in fact a proper one. A proper decision should always be capable of explanation, even though the formulation of reasons may not always be an easy task – particularly for the chairman of a bench of lay magistrates. If the reason for the exceptional leniency is a matter which cannot reasonably be made public, some circumlocution may be unavoidable. A judge clearly cannot announce in open court that the explanation for the apparent leniency is that the social inquiry or medical report shows that the defendant is dying (whether he knows it or not) unless counsel has mentioned the point in mitigation. Similarly, the fact that the defendant is still giving the police the names and addresses of serious criminals is not a matter for publication. Incidentally, information of the latter type affords one of the rare justifications for both counsel to see the judge in his room. However, such occasions for mystery are rare, and as a rule the court can easily state what the reasons are for the leniency extended on that occasion.

7.31 (4) If the defending advocate has put forward reasonable submissions in a professional manner, then, to use the expression of Shaw, L.J.,[22] "it is not out of place for the learned judge to indicate" the reason for the rejection of those submissions. Obviously there is no obligation on a sentencer to deal with every single point taken in a mitigation speech, but it can only help all round if the judge states why he has preferred another disposal in preference to the principal one urged on the court.

---

21 J.H. Godsland and N.G. Fielding, "Young Persons Convicted of Grave Crimes" (1985) *Howard J. 24*, p. 282.
22 In *Newman* (para. 7.28 *supra*).

The adequacy of reasons

7.32 To date there have been very few cases on the topic of the giving of reasons. In *R. v. Chesterfield Justices, ex parte Hewitt,*[23] Lord Widgery, C.J. referred to a "marked tendency in modern statutes to require Justices to give reasons for their sentences". He held that whilst statutory obligations to state reasons were mandatory,

"In my opinion a failure to perform that duty does not affect the validity of the sentence passed. If the defendant is aggrieved by the sentence, his remedy is to appeal."

7.33 The question of the adequacy of stated reasons has only received a limited amount of attention in the Court of Appeal, and the most helpful examination of what constitutes a proper giving of reasons is to be found in the High Court judgments of Nolan, J. and Mann, J. in two mental health cases, both concerned with convicted offenders: *Bone v. Mental Health Review Tribunal*[24] and *R. v. Mental Health Review Tribunal, ex parte Clatworthy,*[25] both in 1985. Both judgments emphasised that a distinction has to be made between a court or tribunal merely stating its conclusion, and stating the reasoning which brought it to that conclusion.

7.34 If any sentencer, and particularly a newly appointed one, has any difficulty in finding and stating his reasons for a given conclusion, that is, in stating the route by which he arrived at his sentence, then he might like to consider the advice given by Lord Lane, C.J. in connection with social inquiry reports.[26] The Lord Chief Justice suggested that the probation officer who was going to make an unusual recommendation might well first write out his reasons, and then examine them to see whether they made sense. So too with sentencing: it is better to take time and get things right, than to attempt to demonstrate one's efficiency by delivering judgments which are speedy and wrong. The sentencer should also bear in mind that not every statement preceding the imposition of a sentence is automatically a reason. Although it is perhaps a counsel of perfection, there is much to commend Ashworth's comment:[27]

"Statements that this is 'one of the worst cases of its kind', that there is 'no alternative' to passing a particular sentence and that 'full account has been

23 (1972) C.S.P. L9.2(b).
24 [1985] 3 All E.R. 330.
25 [1985] 3 All E.R. 699.
26 See para. 4.25 *supra.*
27 A. Ashworth, "Techniques of Guidance on Sentencing" [1984] Crim.L.R. 528.

taken of mitigating circumstances' should not be acceptable as *reasons*, for they do not disclose why the court chose three years rather than two, or a suspended sentence rather than a fine, and so on."

7.35 When passing sentence, and giving reasons for it, the sentencer should remember that the defendant is entitled to expect courtesy and restraint from the court. We have already mentioned the fact that the sentencer should not dwell unduly on the previous convitions, lest he give the impression that the defendant is being sentenced for his record.[28] Of course, it may be necessary to refer to one or more of those convictions to explain why the court has arrived at its instant decision. So too, there is merit in referring to previous convictions in general terms if the court is giving the defendant credit for having managed to avoid a court appearance for some years. Spent convictions, as we have seen, ought not to be referred to at all, unless such a course is unavoidable for some good reason.

7.36 It is entirely appropriate that the sentencer should mention any facts of the case which he has felt to be particularly significant. He is entitled to say that certain aspects of the case, which he should specify, make it more serious than the average. Conversely, he may explain that certain features – whether appearing from the facts of the case, or from reports, or from mitigation submissions – make the case less serious than it seemed at first sight. The odd word of encouragement is not out of place, whether addressed to a defendant who has managed to keep out of trouble until a recent isolated lapse, or to one who has appeared in court for the first time. As someone once put it: "Not every defendant needs to be knocked over the head with a judicial cudgel."

7.37 Homilies of an insulting or fatuous kind are best avoided altogether, and the sentencer should remember where he is, that is, in the Barchester magistrates' court or Crown Court, and not in the Lord Chief Justice's court. General pronouncements about crime in the country and statements about future policy are best left to the appropriate authorities. Apart from any other consideration, it is incredibly difficult to make wholly accurate statements about current, and *a fortiori*, future crime figures. Comments about the defendant's general fecklessness should be very sparingly used, if at all, and should never be regarded as justifying an increased sentence.[29]

7.38 When discussing counsel's duty during the mitigation stage, we pointed out that he must take great care not to blacken the character of

28 *Queen* (1981) 3 Cr.App.R.(S) 245.
29 *Loosemore* (1980) 2 Cr.App.R.(S) 72; *Reeves* (1983) 5 Cr.App.R.(S) 188.

absent third parties, merely because his client has made some wild allegations against them. The Bar *Code of Conduct* contains some suggestions about the restraint needed. It would be as well for the sentencer to apply similar principles to the sentencing stage and to refrain from criticising third parties, unless there are very exceptional circumstances making such a step unavoidable. Apart from anything else, critical comments may well, if reported in the press as they usually are, inhibit potential witnesses from giving evidence to a later inquiry set up to investigate the issues more fully. Such an inquiry may well be able to investigate the issues, and to allocate censure where necessary, more effectively than the criminal court, which had a totally different function to perform.[30]

7.39 We have already mentioned that certain explanations have to be given to the defendant in ordinary language. A statement of reasons should also be expressed clearly to the defendant. It will be of little use to him if couched in lawyer's language which is aimed only at the Court of Appeal or at the lawyers present in court. Plain language should always be used, particularly if the defendant has shown signs of having difficulty in understanding what is going on in court, and all essential points should be dealt with in open court in terms he can understand. As Devlin pointed out in the context of the magistrates' court:[31]

> "When it comes to sentence he should not only know what the court has decided but as far as possible why this course has been selected. Even where there is a legal obligation upon the court to explain the sentence as, for example, on the making of orders of conditional discharge or of probation, and the imposition of suspended sentences, this is often somewhat cursorily done, and it is less than adequate to follow the practice sometimes observed where the Chairman simply says that everything will be explained outside. It is the court's duty to do the explaining."

7.40 The sentencer should bear in mind not only the need to use the appropriate language, but should also refer realistically to the defendant's background, if such a course is thought desirable. For example, it is frankly nonsense to say to a very deprived young defendant that he has had every chance, when that plainly is not so according to the antecedents and the social inquiry report. The sentencer should remember that an earlier supervision order was not the same as a good home; that a community home with education was not the equivalent of a good private boarding school; that detention centre was not a glorious holiday

---

30 See *e.g. A Child in Trust*, Report of the Panel of Inquiry into the Circumstances surrounding the Death of Jasmine Beckford (1985) London Borough of Brent, p. 38.
31 *Op. cit.* (note 9 *supra*), p. 56.

camp; and that youth custody provided nothing like a university education. Fatuous comments discredit not only the sentencer making them, be he lawyer or layman, but can diminish respect for the courts as a whole. The sentencer should also be on guard against misinterpreting facts such as the defendant's smiling or manner of speaking in court. The fact that the defendant grins or gets his answers out with difficulty is much more likely to be caused by his feelings of apprehension and ill-ease with the surroundings than by surliness or arrogance.

PROMISES

7.41 It is imperative that sentencers should at all stages be on guard against making actual or implied promises about what may happen at a future date, either in court or later in a penal institution, unless the sentencer is personally able to keep that promise. If a judge indicates, in accordance with the guidelines laid down in *Turner*,[32] that he will make a probation order whether the defendant pleads guilty or is convicted by the jury, then he is in a position to keep the promise, provided the case remains in his list. He should ensure that the case does remain in his list, so that there is no danger of a later judge not implementing the promise.[33] Apart from that limited exception, express promises ought to be avoided at all times, and implied promises should also be guarded against by the court.

7.42 Apart from the plea discussion stage, the first occasion on which the promise is likely to rear its head is when sentence is, with the consent of the defendant, deferred to a later date not more than six months ahead. If the defendant is given the impression that he will receive a non-custodial sentence if he behaves well and receives a favourable report at the expiration of the deferment, it is wrong to pass a custodial sentence if he has indeed done well during that period.[34] Obviously similar considerations apply whenever a defendant is put back for a specific inquiry to be made, with the implied promise that a favourable response will lead to a probation order or other non-custodial disposal.[35] So too, if a defendant is put back solely for a report on his suitability for a community service order and that report is favourable, it is wrong thereafter to pass a custodial sentence.[36]

32   (1970) 54 Cr.App.R. 352.
33   *Moss and others* (1983) C.S.P. L7.2(c).
34   *Fletcher* (1982) 4 Cr.App.R.(S) 18.
35   *Ward* (1982) 4 Cr.App.R.(S) 103.
36   *Millwood* (1982) 4 Cr.App.R.(S) 281.

7.43 Some of the unfortunate incidents which have been revealed in the Court of Appeal in the above and similar cases have been largely caused by virtue of the fact that a different sentencer dealt with the case on the second occasion. A number of safeguards may prove helpful:

(1) The first sentencer should try to reserve the case to himself. This is a step which is not popular with administrators, but clearly justice comes before administrative convenience.

(2) If there is any reason to suppose that a second judge is likely to deal with the case, then all possible steps should be taken to ensure that he is given an accurate account of what occurred on the first occasion, preferably by means of a note from the first judge.

(3) To ensure that there is no misunderstanding about what occurred on the first occasion, the same advocates should appear on the second if possible, and certainly the defendant's representative should be the same. This applies even if the judge is the same. Croom-Johnson, J. gave useful advice in *Moss and others*:[37]

> "If the judge makes it clear that in asking for a report, or in exploring one possibility, he is not holding out any promise or expectation that a favourable report will necessarily lead to any recommended disposal being adopted, there can be no sense of injustice if he ultimately decides after mature consideration, on some other disposal, but if, as in *Gillam*,[38] there is something in the nature of a promise, express or implied, that if a particular disposal is recommended it will be adopted, then the sense of injustice will be created if it is not."

7.44 Whilst it is easy enough for a sentencer to avoid making an express promise, it is not so easy to avoid giving an impression to an anxious defendant that all may be well as long as a certain event occurs. In short, the implied promise is more of a menace than the express one, which can be more easily avoided. In *Ford*[39] the judge invited the defendant, during the mitigation stage, to name the supplier of his illegal drugs. He did so, but was sentenced to nine months' imprisonment nevertheless. The Court of Appeal reduced the sentence as the defendant had been given "false hopes" by the judge.

7.45 One promise that has in the past been found to cause considerable difficulties for the Prison Department is one to the effect that whilst the defendant must be sentenced to a term of imprisonment, he will receive treatment for his unfortunate mental or physical problem in prison. Sometimes a judge has given the defendant the clear impression

---

37 (1983) C.S.P. L7.2(c).
38 (1980) 2 Cr.App.R.(S) 267.
39 (1980) 2 Cr.App.R.(S) 33.

that he will be sent to Grendon Prison for psychiatric treatment. When the defendant discovers that he is not given the transfer or the treatment in question – because it is not appropriate – he feels a justifiable sense of having been misled by the court. The court should always avoid references to Grendon Prison and to treatment when passing a sentence of imprisonment.[40] It is otherwise, of course, when a hospital order or a probation order with a condition of treatment is being made: the above remarks relate to sentences to be served in an establishment run by the Prison Department.

---

40 *Thompson* (1983) 5 Cr.App.R.(S) 28.

CHAPTER 8

Deferment and Variation of Sentence

8.01 In most cases there will be no question of the sentence either being deferred or of it being varied after it has been passed. However, the provisions for such steps must be considered now, even though the question of deferment requires us to go back in time to before the last chapter.

DEFERMENT

8.02 Both the Crown Court and the magistrates' court are given the power by the Powers of Criminal Courts Act 1973, Section 1, as amended by the Criminal Law Act 1977, Schedule 12 and the Criminal Justice Act 1982, Section 63, to defer passing sentence on a defendant for up to six months. Such deferment shall be:

"for the purpose of enabling the court, or any other court to which it falls to deal with him to have regard in dealing with him, to his conduct after conviction (including, where appropriate, the making by him of reparation for his offence) or to any change in his circumstances."[1]

8.03 Like the suspended sentence, probation order and conditional discharge, the deferment of sentence is partly based on the principle of the sword of Damocles, but there is one important difference. The defendant subject to a deferment cannot be guilty of a breach of that order, but he will definitely have to return to court to be sentenced, whereas the defendant made the subject of any of the other orders mentioned will only be required to return in the event of a breach during the subsistence of the order in question. The deferred sentence period is in one sense a proving or probationary period, but as with the straightforward suspended sentence, there is no supervision attached: the defendant is on his own. This latter fact should be borne in mind by the sentencer deferring a decision and setting criteria for the defendant, and later when assessing his conduct and any change in his circum-

---

1 Powers of Criminal Courts Act 1973, s. 1 as amended.

stances.[2] The court may, of course, ask for a social inquiry report to be prepared for the return to court at the end of the deferred period.

8.04 The power to defer may only be exercised if the defendant consents, and he should be asked to consent personally, rather than by his representative.[3] If the defendant does not consent but the court nevertheless purports to defer sentence, then it would seem that there is no power to sentence him on his later return to court.[4] However, the failure of the sentencing court to deal with the defendant precisely within the time limit of the deferment is not necessarily a bar to the passing of sentence at a later stage. In *Ingle*[5] the defendant returned to court within the period of six months but was not then sentenced, as he was awaiting trial on other charges. The original court postponed dealing with him until after the expiry of the deferment period. The Court of Appeal said that such a course was legitimate and did not deprive the court of its power to sentence, but urged the courts not to take such a course unless there were strong reasons for doing so. In the case of a deferred sentence it is probably wiser for the sentencer to follow the advice of the Court of Appeal in *Ingle* and to deal with the defendant when he comes back, rather than the advice it gave in *Bennett*[6] to the effect that all matters against the same defendant should be dealt with by the same judge at the same time. There is no conflict between the two authorities, for in *Bennett* the court added the proviso that the practice of consolidating all matters before the same sentencer should be done "as far as possible." In *Anderson*[7] an administrative error led to the defendant only being called back for sentence after the expiry of the deferment peroid. The Court of Appeal held, as in *Ingle*, that there was still the power to sentence him then despite the error.

8.05 A sentencer must think hard before deciding to defer sentence. He must be sure not only "that it would be in the interests of justice to exercise the power", as required by Section 1(3) of the 1973 Act, but also precisely why he is in favour of such a step. He should first consider adjourning for a social inquiry report, or making a probation order (which can now be for as short a period as six months) or making a compensation order on its own or with some other order. The sentence should only be deferred if there is going to be some positive gain from

---

2 For the suggestion that some support during a period of deferment might be helpful, see M. Zander, *Diversion from Criminal Justice in an English Context*, Report of a NACRO Working Party (1975) Barry Rose, p. 28.
3 *Fairhead* (1975) 61 Cr.App.R. 102.
4 *McQuaide* (1974) 60 Cr.App.R. 239.
5 (1974) 59 Cr.App.R. 306.
6 (1980) 2 Cr.App.R.(S) 96.
7 (1983) 5 Cr.App.R.(S) 338.

such a step: it should not be deferred merely to give the sentencer more time to think. We have emphasised earlier the need for ample time to be taken over mitigation and sentencing decisions, but we were not seeking to suggest that as long as six months should be taken over the matter. As Lord Lane, C.J. put it in the guideline case of *George* in 1984:[8]

> "The power is not to be used as an easy way out for a court which is unable to make up its mind about the correct sentence. Experience has shown that great care should be exercised by the court when using this power."

8.06 Although the 1973 Act specifically refers to the possibility of reparation, Lord Lane thought that deferment would seldom be used for that purpose. What purpose is an appropriate one then? Lord Lane stated by way of example cases in which the court wished to see whether the defendant was going to make a real effort to find work, or whether there had been a real change in his attitude and circumstances. The reference to attitude doubtless included the possibility of some post-trial contrition. It is clearly important that the defendant should know exactly what is expected of him by the court which defers sentence. This is another occasion when the court must ensure that it uses language which is both intelligible to the defendant and precise. An injunction to the defendant that he should mend his ways and pull his socks up during the period of deferment is not good enough. It could lead to a dispute on his return to court as to how high the socks were to be pulled, and on how many occasions. A lack of clarity in stating what the court expected has been, according to the Lord Chief Justice in *George*, "a fruitful source of appeals". It is clearly also important that the case should come back before the original judge if possible, and that if such a course should not be possible, the second judge should be informed, preferably by a transcript or in writing by the first judge, as to the purpose of the deferment. There can be even less room for error if the first court's expectations are clearly stated in court and then reduced to writing, with a copy being given to the defendant at once, so that he can check during the period of deferment to see that he is doing his best to satisfy the court of his reform or whatever. As a further safeguard counsel for the defendant should attend court on the second occasion also, if possible.[9] Whatever the court's expectations of the defendant, when he returns for sentence in due course, the court should decide whether he has substantially done that which he was told would be expected of him. To demand complete, as opposed to substantial performance might well be unreasonable.[10]

---

8 (1984) 79 Cr.App.R. 26.
9 *Ryan* [1976] Crim.L.R. 508.
10 *Smith* (1979) 1 Cr.App.R.(S) 339; *Glossop* (1981) 3 Cr.App.R.(S) 347.

8.07 There can as a rule be one period of deferment only, but an exception is provided by the Powers of Criminal Courts Act 1973, Section 1(8A). Where a magistrates' court has deferred sentence on a defendant whom it later feels obliged to commit for sentence under the provisions of the Magistrates' Courts Act 1980, Sections 37 or 38, the Crown Court has the power to defer sentence for a second time in its own right. If during the period of deferment the defendant is convicted of another offence, even one committed before the deferment, then he can be dealt with for the original offence at once: there is no need for the deferment period to expire: Powers of Criminal Courts Act 1973, Sections 1(4) and 1(4A). The original court can sentence him for the original offence, or the second court may do so, subject to two provisos. As is usual with this type of legislation, the magistrates' court has no power to deal with a matter previously considered by the Crown Court; and the Crown Court, if dealing with a magistrates' court deferred matter, is limited to passing a sentence which the magistrates could have passed.

8.08 If a court is to deal with a defendant before the period of deferment has expired, it must ensure that there has been a conviction during that period : it is not enough that the defendant is suspected of a further offence,[11] or even that he has appeared in court and pleaded guilty to other offences, as in *Salmon*.[12] The defendant in *Salmon* had first received a six months' suspended sentence in the Crown Court, and had later pleaded guilty in a magistrates' court, which deferred sentence in respect of the fresh offence committed during the operative period of the suspended sentence. The Crown Court brought the defendant back for his breach of the suspended sentence during the lower court's period of deferment, that is, before the magistrates had finally disposed of the case by sentencing him for the fresh offence. The suspended sentence was activated by the Crown Court and the defendant appealed, arguing, successfully, that the magistrates might at the end of the period of deferment have made a probation order or some other order not amounting to a conviction. In short, courts must be careful not to jump the gun not only in suspended sentence cases, but also in cases of deferred sentences, and must be sure that there is a subsequent conviction before exercising their powers under the Powers of Criminal Courts Act 1973, Section 1(4) or 1(4A). Incidentally, if anyone should require an illustration of the fact that each new statutory provision further complicates an already complicated sentencing system, *Salmon* affords it.

11 *Benstead* (1979) 1 Cr.App.R.(S) 32.
12 (1973) 57 Cr.App.R. 953.

8.09 Morrish and McLean refer to the problem that can arise where two judges have disparate views on a given case – we are given to understand that this can occasionally happen:[13]

> "There is still the vexed question of the course to be taken by the judge who is ultimately to deal with the case, when he considers the course recommended by the original judge to be totally unrealistic; it is submitted that there is no reason why he should not insist that the original judge deal with the case finally, at whatever court at which he may then be sitting."

We would have thought, with respect, that such a course was undesirable for at least two reasons. It is not particularly helpful when a judge in open court displays his disagreement with a colleague of the same rank; and it is perhaps less than fair to force a defendant to attend at three different courts on four or more occasions spread over a period which may amount, if he was on bail before his trial, to 18 months or even two years in all. We can see no good reason why the second judge should not decide whether the defendant has done all that was expected of him by his colleague, and then make the appropriate final order.

8.10 In granting to the courts the power to defer sentence, Parliament expressly left untouched the existing power to bind over to come up for judgment when called upon, and to adjourn or postpone cases. Unfortunately, in Section 1(7) of the 1973 Act the legislature used the word "defer" in a misleading manner when referring to something other than deferment, for it provided:

> "Nothing in this section shall affect the power of the Crown Court to bind over an offender to come up for judgment when called upon or the power of any court to defer passing sentence for any purpose for which it might lawfully do so apart from this section."

VARIATION OF SENTENCE

8.11 As sentencing becomes increasingly complex, so inevitably errors creep into orders made by the courts, even though judge, counsel, solicitors and court clerks between them are supposed to know all the law and practice, so that, in theory, mistakes cannot occur. Very often errors or omissions are noticed before the defendant leaves the court and while all persons connected with the case are still present. At other times they are only discovered after a day or two. Sometimes more than

---

13   P. Morrish and I. McLean, *The Crown Court: An Index of Common Penalties* (11th edn. 1983) Barry Rose, p. 98.

a mere slip is involved. Fortunately, both the Crown Court and the magistrates' court have statutory powers to vary sentences within a limited time.

8.12 The Supreme Court Act 1981, Section 47 provides that the Crown Court may vary or rescind any sentence imposed, or other order made, within 28 days. If two or more defendants are jointly tried on indictment, the variation or rescission may take place not later than the end of the shorter of two periods specified, namely, 28 days after the conclusion of the joint trial, or 56 days after the sentence or other order in question was imposed. The joint trial is deemed to be concluded for these purposes on the latest of the following dates – the date on which any of the co-defendants is (a) sentenced, or (b) acquitted, or (c) on which a special verdict is brought in by the jury. The variation or rescission may only be made by the same judge who made the original order; he need not sit with any justices who may have sat with him originally, though there may well be occasions when he will consider such a course to be desirable.

8.13 A variation must be ordered in open court in the presence of the defendant and after counsel has been given an opportunity of being heard on his behalf.[14] The variation can lead to a more severe sentence, as was made clear in *Sodhi*.[15] The defendant had fired an air rifle at guests leaving a noisy neighbour's party and had injured one with a pellet. He was sentenced in the Crown Court to six months' imprisonment for malicious wounding. Some three weeks later, following the receipt of medical reports to the effect that the defendant was suffering from a paranoid psychosis which made him dangerous, the Crown Court varied the original sentence by making a hospital order pursuant to the Mental Health Act 1959, Section 60, with an unlimited restriction order under Section 65. The Court of Appeal was urged by his counsel to say that it was impermissible to increase a sentence in this way, but declined to do so. The original sentence, it was pointed out to the court, would soon have been served, whereas a hospital order could result in a very long period of detention indeed. This was clearly a correct submission, as was demonstrated in *R. v. Mental Health Review Tribunal, ex parte Clatworthy*,[16] in which an indecent assaulter, not suffering from any form of psychosis, was detained for 17 years, although the restriction order in his case had been limited to five years. In dismissing Sodhi's

14 *May* (1981) 3 Cr.App.R.(S) 165.
15 (1978) 66 Cr.App.R. 260.
16 [1985] 3 All E.R. 699.

appeal, Lawton. L.J. pointed out that not only was the defendant a danger to the public, but also to himself. Furthermore, he might well have been transferred to Broadmoor special hospital from prison and detained under the provisions of the Mental Health Act indefinitely in any event. The court held that there was jurisdiction to make the order increasing the sentence, and that in the unusual circumstances of the case it was proper to make it. In *Commissioners of Customs and Excise v. Menocal*,[17] the House of Lords confirmed that the courts had the widest powers to vary a sentence, provided the step was taken in time. However, even after the expiry of the statutory time limit, the Crown Court may exercise its inherent jurisdiction to correct minor mistakes in the record.[18] Where a variation under Section 47 may prove necessary because a hospital withdraws its undertaking to admit a defendant, the prison governor holding him must inform the court speedily so that the defendant can be brought back to court within the statutory period.[19]

8.14 The power to increase should clearly only be exercised in exceptional circumstances; the mere fact that the sentencer has had second thoughts about the matter, and has decided that the original sentence was too lenient, is not sufficient.[20] On the other hand, if a defendant has deceived the court during the mitigation stage and the court discovers that fact only after passing sentence, he can be brought back and re-sentenced within the statutory time limit.[21]

8.15 The Magistrates' Courts Act 1980, Section 142, gives very similar powers to the lower courts. The principal difference is that any variation or rescission there must take place within 28 days: there is no longer alternative as in the case of the Crown Court. Either all the original bench must sit for a variation, or a majority of the magistrates who sat on the first occasion.

---

17 (1979) 69 Cr.App.R. 157.
18 *Saville* (1980) 2 Cr.App.R.(S) 26.
19 *Archbold* (42nd edn.) para. 5–228; Prison Standing Orders 13, s. 185(1).
20 *Nodjoumi* (1985) 7 Cr.App.R.(S) 183.
21 *Hart* (1983) 56 Cr.App.R.(S) 25.

CHAPTER 9

Imprisonment

9.01 The question of whether a given offence is punishable by imprisonment or not obviously arises much more frequently in the magistrates' court than in the Crown Court. Rarely is there any problem: the Clerk to the Justices will advise the lower court if necessary; in the Crown Court nearly every offence is imprisonable. The question has to be resolved not only when a court is considering using imprisonment as the penalty, but also when it is looking at the possible use of other alternatives, for example a hospital order or a community service order, since those can only be imposed for an imprisonable offence.[1] The question also has to be answered when the court is seeing whether there has been a breach of a wholly or partly suspended sentence of imprisonment. In the Crown Court the issue of the power to imprison will arise whenever that court is limited to using the powers of the magistrates' court. There is one other occasion when the Crown Court judge must also be on guard, and that is where he is sentencing a defendant for a large number of assorted offences, including some fairly minor motoring matters. Occasionally judges have, in error, when passing a custodial sentence, imposed a concurrent sentence of one day's imprisonment for an offence which does not carry imprisonment at all. Although an appeal is unlikely in such cases, the error should obviously be avoided. Of far greater importance in practice are the statutory restrictions on the use of imprisonment. The first one need not be considered at any length despite its crucial nature: it is the requirement that the defendant be aged 21 or over. A court should remember that legislation is designed to protect young offenders from prison, and should not adjourn cases just to let their 21st birthday pass.[2] We shall deal with custodial sentences for defendants under 21 in Chapter 10. In the present chapter we shall consider some of the major points under the following headings:

    (1) Restrictions on first sentences of imprisonment;
    (2) Legal representation;

---

1 That fact in early days misled some magistrates into thinking that the community service order could only be used as an alternative to imprisonment, whereas Parliament had never explicitly said so.
2 *Arthur v. Stringer* (1986) The Times 11 October.

(3) The relevance of the maximum;
(4) Fixing the length of the term;
(5) Concurrent and consecutive sentences;
(6) The wholly suspended sentence;
(7) The partly suspended sentence;
(8) The extended sentence;
(9) Life imprisonment;
(10) Magistrates' powers of imprisonment; and
(11) Committal for sentence.

RESTRICTIONS ON FIRST SENTENCES OF IMPRISONMENT

9.02 Parliament has over the years made several attempts to inhibit the use of imprisonment, especially for those who are young and those who have not previously served a term in prison. It has to be conceded that the efforts have not been all that successful to date, but perhaps a combination of an increasing knowledge on the part of sentencers of the appalling conditions in overcrowded, insanitary prisons, coupled with an increasing scepticism about the ability of the prison system to affect the crime rate significantly, will lead to the statutory restrictions being more effective in future. Home Office research indicates that non-custodial disposals can be increased if sentencers consider and discuss them more often, as well as bearing in mind the shortcomings of custodial solutions.[3]

9.03 We have already discussed the need for a social inquiry report where the court is considering imposing a first sentence of imprisonment on a defendant over 21, but some elaboration is needed. Parliament has stated that such a sentence must not be passed unless "no other method of dealing with him is appropriate": Powers of Criminal Courts Act 1973, Section 20(1). It is clear from Section 20 that the restriction applies to anyone who has not been previously sentenced to imprisonment by any United Kingdom court, and that it also applies to a defendant who has been sentenced to imprisonment but has (a) had the sentence suspended and (b) not had any of it activated. Similarly the restriction also applies to defendants who have been in prison for contempt of court only. In order to strengthen these provisions, Parliament, by the Criminal Justice Act 1982, Section 62, added a new Section 20A to the 1973 Act. This provides that unless the court is of the opinion that a report is unnecessary,

---

3 D. Smith *et al.*, *Reducing the Prison Population* (1984) Home Office Research and Planning Unit Paper No. 23.

"the court shall in every case obtain a social inquiry report for the purpose of determining under Section 20(1) above whether there is any appropriate method of dealing with an offender other than imprisonment."

This obligation applies equally to the Crown Court and the magistrates' court, but only the lower court is obliged to state why it considers the obtaining of a report to be unnecessary, if such be the case, and to record the reason. We repeat our suggestion that it is perhaps equally desirable for the Crown Court judge to state why he considers it safe to proceed without first obtaining a report.

9.04   Whether the court considers the matter with a report or, exceptionally, without one, there is a further statutory obligation imposed by Section 20(1):

"for the purpose of determining whether any other method of dealing with any such person is appropriate the court shall obtain and consider information about the circumstances, and shall take into account any information before the court which is relevant to his character and his physical and mental condition."

It is difficult to see how the court could proceed to sentence at all without feeling the need to consider the circumstances. Much the same may be said of the obligation to take into account matters relevant to character and mental and physical condition; it would be a strange sentencer who considered himself able to sentence without taking all those matters into account. There is nevertheless probably some point in this legislative help for the courts. Taken as a whole Section 20, supplemented by the newer Section 20A, does make the point that imprisoning an adult for the first time should only be done as a deliberate, calculated matter of judgment, after all the alternatives have been ruled out, and after a proper amount of thought has gone into the making of the decision.

9.05   There will be some occasions when a court will feel driven to the conclusion that a custodial sentence cannot be avoided because of the seriousness both of the charge itself and of the facts of the case. An obvious example is a bad case of unprovoked violence involving the use of a dangerous weapon. The court may come to the conclusion that a social inquiry report could not possibly save the defendant from an immediate sentence of imprisonment, no matter what it might contain, and that such a report is therefore unnecessary. In such circumstances the court would clearly be prepared to read a social enquiry report which was already available, but it might well be reluctant to delay the passing of the sentence by ordering a report to be prepared. The general policy of the National Association of Probation Officers of declining to prepare reports on defendants pleading not guilty, means that many defendants have had no reports prepared in their case. If the court feels it must sentence without waiting for a report, then it may do so, stating reasons where required. On an appeal from a sentence passed in such circumstances, the higher court should obtain a social inquiry report, but Section 20A(5) permits the appellate court to proceed without one if it is itself of the opinion that in the circumstances a report is unnecessary. The following sub-section, incidentally, is a perfect example of unhelpful legislation:

> "(6) In determining whether it should deal with the appellant otherwise than by passing a sentence of imprisonment on him the court hearing the appeal should consider any social inquiry report obtained by it or by the court below."

The draftsman of this sub-section perhaps imagined a Lord Chief Justice in the Court of Appeal ordering a report and then declining to consider it when it arrived.

9.06 If a magistrates' court decides to imprison a defendant who has not served a sentence of imprisonment before, whether with or without the benefit of a social inquiry report, it must "state the reason for its opinion that no other method of dealing with him is appropriate." Stating the concluded opinion alone is not enough: the *reason* for that opinion must be stated, and recorded in the warrant of commitment and the register.[4] There is no similar obligation imposed on the Crown Court, but it would seem reasonable to expect a judge to tell a man why his case is one which justifies his confinement in a prison for the first time.[5]

LEGAL REPRESENTATION

9.07 The above statutory restrictions on first sentences of imprisonment are accompanied by further ones relating to representation. Section 21 of the 1973 Act provides that neither the Crown Court nor the magistrates' court may pass a sentence of the type discussed unless the defendant is either represented at the mitigation stage, or has turned down legal aid, or been refused it on the grounds that his means were adequate to pay for his own representation. In *McGinlay and Ballantyne*[6] Scarman. L.J. said:

---

4 S. 20(2).
5 See also A. Ashworth, "Justifying the First Prison Sentence" [1977] Crim.L.R. 553.
6 (1975) 62 Cr.App.R. 156.

"It does not need the authority of this court to say that it is extremely important that Section 21 should be followed by the courts of this country. It is in fact a declaration of the right of persons in jeopardy of their liberty to be legally represented before sentence curtailing liberty is passed."

To that observation one might perhaps add that the section does not apply every time a defendant is in jeopardy of such a sentence: it does not apply if he has previously served a sentence of imprisonment. Scarman, L.J. referred to all courts being obliged to observe the requirements of the section. In *R. v. Birmingham Justices, ex parte Wyatt*[7] the need for extreme care in the magistrates' court was made clear. The case is worth considering as it contained a number of useful points. The defendant Wyatt was neither represented nor offered legal aid at the sentencing stage before being sentenced to imprisonment by the magistrates. The omission may have been caused by the mistaken belief at an early stage of the proceedings that he had previously served such a sentence, for the recorded reason for the court's opinion that no other method of dealing with him was appropriate was (in all too common cryptic form): "Record: prison before". In fact the defendant had not been in prison before: he had merely had a suspended sentence which had not been activated and which, as we have seen, does not count for the present purposes.

9.08 Wyatt appealed to the Crown Court and there he was represented by counsel and solicitor. The court held that as the appeal was by way of rehearing, the defect in the lower court was adequately cured by the representation on appeal, and it left the sentence of imprisonment standing. The Divisional Court quashed it, pointing out that the Crown Court could impose a prison sentence only "if that is a punishment which that magistrates' court might have awarded".[8] Because of the requirements of Section 21, *that* magistrates' court had not had the power to imprison, and therefore the Crown Court on appeal had not got the power either.

THE RELEVANCE OF THE MAXIMUM

9.09 We have earlier sought to show that whilst the maximum sentence fixed by Parliament is sometimes a useful indication of the legislature's changing views of the relative gravity of different offences, at other times the maximum is so high that it is almost irrelevant in the

---

7 [1975] 3 All E.R. 897.
8 Courts Act 1971, s. 9(4), now Supreme Court Act 1981, s. 48(4).

majority of cases in which that particular offence is concerned. One of the features of English criminal law that surprises many visiting United States lawyers is the absence of any distinction between petty and other thefts. The maximum penalty of ten years for all offences of theft means that in practice the maximum has hardly ever been imposed. The Court of Appeal has over the years emphasised that the maximum should be reserved for the gravest instances of the offence in question, though it has added that it is not right for the sentencer to stretch his imagination so as to dream up the most serious circumstances possible.[9] Even if the facts are the most serious likely to come before a court, the requirement to give credit for a plea of guilty should be remembered – even though there have been instances of the Court of Appeal upholding a sentence of the statutory maximum despite such a plea. A defendant is certainly entitled to complain if given the maximum after pleading guilty, for he may well have relied on legal advice that he would be given credit for such a plea, having regard to the trend of the authorities discussed in Chapter 2.[10]

9.10 In very exceptional circumstances a court may even consider passing consecutive maximum sentences – but not many sentencers are likely to be confronted with facts as grave as those which had to be considered by Lord Parker, C.J., when he sentenced *Blake* in 1961[11] to three consecutive terms of 14 years for Official Secrets Act offences carrying such a maximum.

9.11 When Parliament indicates its changing views by increasing or reducing a maximum, then the court should take that into account – particularly if the change was a recent one. This is so particularly where a maximum has been reduced, as with cannabis-related offences. It would clearly be wrong for a sentencer to apply any guidance from the Court of Appeal which had been overtaken by statute. On the other hand, if the Court of Appeal's earlier decisions remain substantially relevant, then the sentencer must try to apply them in the light of the legislature's more recently expressed views. It need scarcely be added that the latter's views contained in a statute are undoubtedly binding on the courts, whatever the status of sentencing appeal decisions may be.

---

9 *Cade* (1984) 6 Cr.App.R.(S) 28; *Ambler* [1976] Crim.L.R. 266.
10 Paras. 2.15ff *supra*.
11 (1961) 45 Cr.App.R. 292. See para. 1.52 *supra*.

FIXING THE LENGTH OF THE TERM

9.12 Apart from the maximum, a number of other factors will have to be taken into account by the sentencer who has decided that a sentence of imprisonment cannot be avoided. One can summarise the matter by saying that practically everything must be given its appropriate weight, including all the matters discussed above, when the length of the term is being fixed. One or two of the relevant factors should be considered briefly here.

9.13 The judge will have the benefit of the guideline cases of the Court of Appeal, for example, in rape cases. He will also be able to check other decisions of the court in the *Encyclopedia of Current Sentencing Practice*, edited by Dr. David Thomas, and in his notes commenting on recent sentencing decisions in the *Criminal Law Review*. He will have the benefit of his own experience of similar cases which will help him to select the correct range for the particular offence, given the proved facts, and then to fix the most appropriate place in that range. In the latter task he will have regard to the circumstances of the defendant as disclosed by the various reports and the mitigation put forward. He may conceivably end up unsure as to which of two alternative sentence lengths is the more appropriate. In such a case he might care to follow the suggestion of Sheriff Nicholson, the author of the Scottish book on sentencing:[12]

> "In the circumstances it may be suggested that, if a judge is unable to explain with accuracy the reason for selecting the higher of two possible sentences of imprisonment, then there may be merit in choosing the shorter one."

9.14 Apart from relying on his own experience and on the decisions of the Court of Appeal, the sentencer will also have to try to have regard to the sort of sentences being passed by his judicial colleagues, for he will be conscious of the need to avoid disparity as much as possible. The recorder or assistant recorder having to pass sentence will have one advantage over the full-time judge, especially if he regularly appears as an advocate in the criminal courts in the course of his practice. He will have continuous and recent experience of the kind of sentences that other judges have been passing in similar cases elsewhere in other courts. The point is sometimes made that all full-time judges have the opportunity of discussing sentencing problems with colleagues. This is true, but such discussions are of limited value, as the colleagues who are

---

12   C.G.B. Nicholson, *The Law and Practice of Sentencing in Scotland* (1981) W. Green & Son, p. 240.

consulted are hardly ever placed in full possession of all the facts and rarely read all the documents. Furthermore, they never hear the mitigation put forward in their brother judge's court.

9.15 In fixing the length of the sentence the judge will not only have regard to what the Court of Appeal, his colleagues and he himself have been saying and doing about that particular class of offence, but he will also take a sideways glance at the sentences he has been passing for different types of offence. For example, when sentencing a burglar the judge will often bear in mind the sentence he passed on other burglars, on other dishonest offenders such as forgers or obtainers by deception AND on defendants committing offences of violence or of a sexual nature. He will try to ensure that his sentences on one class of offenders bear a reasonable relationship to those passed on other classes. We are not suggesting that crimes of violence, say, may not be singled out for higher sentences than offences involving fraud, but that one should always be able to relate one sentence to another even though the type of offence may be wholly different. This is particularly important in view of the research findings which show that some judges frown more on some types of offence than do most of their colleagues. The judge will also attempt to take public opinion into consideration, but if he is wise he will remember the difficulties involved in ascertaining what it is, and will keep in mind the dangers of relying only on the views of the newspapers he prefers, and those of his immediate circle of acquaintances.[13]

9.16 When two or more defendants are being sentenced for joint offences, particular care must be taken in fixing the sentence lengths to take account of the different parts played in the commission of the offence by each one, and their differing antecedents and mitigation. Unjust disparity must be avoided, and the various factors may lead to the need for what has sometimes been called "fine tuning."

9.17 The problems for magistrates are similar, whilst being both simplified and complicated by the low statutory maximum sentences permissible. The justices may consult their clerk, if necessary, on law and practice, but will usually be able to fix the length of imprisonment without any assistance from him. The need to keep an eye on their own sentences for different offences applies also to the magistrates, though perhaps more so when it comes to non-custodial decisions. This point is worth bearing in mind, for nothing infuriates the honest motorist more

13 See Ch. 1 *supra.*

than learning that he has been fined far more heavily than a "genuine" criminal appearing in the same court that day. Disparity is inevitable when one has so many different magistrates fixing sentence lengths. Some benches try to achieve some concordance with colleagues in the same county, but often have little idea of what is happening in another part of the country – even in the neighbouring county. The absence of reported cases and of guidance from the Court of Appeal means that efforts to avoid disparity essentially come from the Magistrates' Association, and then only to a limited extent. Further guidance can be given to the magistrates by their Crown Court liaison judge, but this will usually be limited both by the constraints of time and the inability of some judges to turn themselves into trainers of magistrates. This is so despite the fact that Crown Court judges are regularly having to "teach" the law to jurors.

CONCURRENT AND CONSECUTIVE SENTENCES

9.18 One matter which always requires careful attention is the decision as to whether a particular sentence should be ordered to run concurrently with another or consecutively. One of the basic rules of thumb over the years has been the so-called single transaction rule, but it is in practice not always easy to say at what point a given transaction was completed and when the next began. If a defendant is convicted of burglary and of going equipped with burglar's tools at the same time, it is clearly right to treat the two offences together and to make the second sentence a concurrent one. Incidentally, it is not correct to make the second sentence of equal length merely because it is being imposed concurrently. In our example the going equipped offence should result in a shorter sentence than the burglary. On the other hand if the same burglar were to assault a police officer trying to arrest him outside the house, a consecutive sentence would be called for and justified, as it would not have been an incidental part of the burglary transaction.[14]

9.19 The matter is slightly more complicated where two serious offences overlap, as where a robbery is committed with a firearm. In *Faulkner*[15] the Court of Appeal approved two consecutive three-year sentences passed on the defendant, who had been seen on a warehouse roof by an officer and who had then attacked him, striking him with the butt of his gun. The first sentence was for the assault on the officer; the

14 *Kastercum* (1972) 56 Cr.App.R. 298.
15 (1972) 56 Cr.App.R. 594.

second for possession of the firearm with intent. Lord Widgery, C.J. stressed the need for the courts to try and deter the carrying of firearms, and therefore held that the single transaction approach could not save the defendant from a consecutive sentence.

9.20 *Faulkner* was considered by Lord Lane, C.J. in *French*.[16] The defendant in that case had robbed a man in his own home, using a firearm to threaten him. The indictment contained both a count of robbery and one of possessing a firearm with intent. In view of the discussion in Chapter 3 above about the factual basis for sentencing, it is pertinent to note that Lord Lane gave three reasons for the addition of a firearm count to the robbery one:

> "First of all it is arguable, and indeed it is often argued, that a defendant ought not to be sentenced in respect of an offence with which he has not been charged or convicted. Secondly, the fact that an offence has not been charged might in some circumstances be taken as a concession by the prosecution that the offence was not committed. Thirdly, there may be occasions where possession of the offending weapon is disputed, or may be disputed, by the accused, and the sentencing judge would, if there were no firearm count in the indictment, be deprived of the jury's view on the matter."

On the issue of concurrent or consecutive sentences, the Lord Chief Justice gave the following helpful guidance about the totality principle:

> "We would emphasize that in the end, whether the sentences are made consecutive or concurrent, the sentencing judge should try to ensure that the totality of the sentences is correct in the light of all the circumstances of the case. In particular of course he must make sure – it goes without saying – that the defendant must not in effect be sentenced twice for carrying a gun."

If a judge finds himself having to sentence an armed robber who is charged only with the one count of robbery then, as long as the use of the firearm is conceded, his powers of sentence will be adequate to deal with the offence in any event.[17]

9.21 Over the years the Court of Appeal has pronounced quite often on the propriety of concurrent sentences where the victim is the same one, and of consecutive sentences where different victims are concerned. Many of the decisions have paled into relative unimportance in view of the guidance provided by Lord Lane in *French*: it is the total sentence which matters most.

---

16 (1982) 4 Cr.App.R.(S) 57.
17 *Turner* (1975) 61 Cr.App.R. 67.

9.22 Whatever conclusion the sentencer arrives at, he must state clearly which sentences are to be served concurrently and which consecutively. If there are two or more indictments against a defendant, then it is helpful if the judge states what the sentence is on each count and whether that sentence is concurrent or consecutive, and if he states as he finishes with each indictment: "Making a total of three years (or whatever) on the first indictment (or whichever)." He should deal with each indictment in the same way and make it clear whether the total sentences on each indictment are to run concurrently or consecutively to the other totals. Finally he should make a point of concluding with words such as, "Making a total of – years' imprisonment in all." If the defendant is already serving a sentence of imprisonment, it is important that the court should make it plain – if such should be the intention – that the fresh sentences are to be served after *all* previous sentences. If care is not taken at this stage, it is possible that the defendant's fresh sentences will commence when his current term has been completed, instead of at the end of all the consecutive terms he has earlier been ordered to serve. If it is the wish of the court to make the fresh sentence commence after all the existing sentences have been completed, then wording such as the following should be used: "This sentence passed on you today is to be consecutive to the total period of imprisonment to which you are already subject."[18]

THE WHOLLY SUSPENDED SENTENCE

9.23 When passing a sentence of imprisonment for two years or less, the court may suspend the operation of the sentence for a period of one to two years. The suspension is subject to the offender committing no further offence in Great Britain which is punishable by imprisonment during the operational period of the sentence: Powers of Criminal Courts Act 1973, Section 22(1). The total of the sentences passed, consecutive and concurrent, must not exceed two years, or there is no power to suspend: Section 57(2). Both the Court of Appeal in *O'Keefe*[19] and Parliament by Section 22(2) have made it clear that the suspended sentence must be treated by the courts as a sentence of imprisonment: it is not to be regarded as a conditional discharge with teeth[20], or as the equivalent of any other non-custodial sentence. It is a custodial sentence and must be regarded as such by sentencers. That means that a court must not consider imposing a suspended sentence unless it has

---

18 Practice Direction (1959) 42 Cr.App.R. 154.
19 [1969] 2 Q.B. 29.
20 *English* (1984) 6 Cr.App.R.(S) 60.

ruled out all the non-custodial alternatives and has come to the conclusion that a sentence of imprisonment cannot be avoided. It is only when the decision has been made, that a sentence of imprisonment must be passed, that the court should go on to consider the question of suspension. As we remarked earlier, this is not an easy exercise, and it requires a certain amount of mental gymnastics. (It is not without interest to note that even Thomas in his *Encyclopedia of Current Sentencing Practice* deals with the suspended sentence in his section on non-custodial measures, rather than in that dealing with imprisonment.) When imposing a suspended sentence the court must explain the consequences of a breach to the defendant in ordinary language. It is, of course, improper to lengthen a term of imprisonment *because* it is being suspended.[21]

9.24 Ever since the introduction of the suspended sentence there have been comments to the effect that many offenders having such sentences imposed on them will have great difficulty in surviving the operational period without committing any further imprisonable offence. From the start the possibility of adding a probation order for another offence has been ruled out (currently by Section 22(3)), but in certain circumstances a supervision order may be added. Section 26(1) provides that where a court passes a suspended sentence for a term of over six months for a single offence, it may add a suspended sentence supervision order for all or part of the operational period. Such an order requires the defendant to keep in touch with a probation officer and to notify him of any change of address. There are some material distinctions between such an order and a probation order. The first is one we have already mentioned: there is no need for the consent of the defendant to the making of the supervision order. The second is the important one that a breach of the supervision order only cannot be punished otherwise than by a fine of up to £400. The third is that the court may not attach any special conditions to a supervision order. The fourth is that supervision may in certain circumstances be added at breach proceedings.[22] Like the suspended sentence itself, the supervision order must be explained to the defendant by the court at the time of its imposition.

9.25 Where a defendant is convicted of another offence punishable by imprisonment and committed during the operational period of the suspended sentence, the court dealing with him must also deal with the suspended sentence. An exception is that a magistrates' court cannot deal with a suspended sentence of the Crown Court: it must either

21   *Mah-Wing* (1983) 5 Cr.App.R.(S) 347.
22   S. 26(10).

commit the defendant, in custody or on bail, to the Crown Court or notify that court in writing of the fresh conviction.[23]

9.26 Parliament has, by Section 23 given the courts four alternative options in cases of a breach, and one of them must be exercised:

(1) The court may order that the suspended sentence shall take effect with the original term unaltered;

(2) It may order that the sentence shall take effect with the substitution of a lesser term for the original term;

(3) It may by order vary the original order by substituting a new operational period expiring not later than two years from the date of the variation; or

(4) It may make no order with respect to the suspended sentence.

It should be noted that the last option must be exercised in a positive manner and not merely by default. The court must actually decide that no order is the correct outcome before choosing that option. It should then announce that decision. Section 23(1), as amended by the Criminal Justice Act 1982, Section 31, obliges the court to order the suspended sentence to take effect with the original term unaltered if a breach is established, *unless* it is of the opinion that it would be unjust to do so in view of all the circumstances, including the facts of the subsequent offence constituting the breach. Whenever the court concludes that full implementation would be unjust, it must state its reasons for that opinion. The court considering the breach must be acquainted with the facts of the original offence, otherwise it cannot properly consider the issue in the light of all the circumstances.[24] If the later offence, whilst being imprisonable, was of a trivial nature, then the second court will be slow to activate the suspended sentence, unless it was similar to the offence or offences which led to the suspended order. The mere fact that the later offence is of a different character will not necessarily be enough to save the defendant from the activation of the first sentence. If the original sentence of imprisonment was amply justified but was suspended on the basis of a "last chance" being afforded the defendant, the activation of the suspended sentence may well be the only proper result. It is only right to add that the Court of Appeal has not been entirely consistent in its decisions relating to the breach of suspended sentences.[25]

9.27 We have been discussing what should happen after a fresh conviction, but the court must be sure that there has indeed been, not

23   S. 24(2).
24   *Munday* (1971) 56 Cr.App.R. 220.
25   See A. Ashworth, "Techniques of Guidance on Sentencing" [1984] Crim.L.R. 525.

just a fresh offence, but also a conviction in the strict sense of the term.[26] It must be remembered that a discharge, whether absolute or con-ditional, and a probation order do not rank as convictions for present purposes.[27]

9.28 The court should consider the fresh offence first, provisionally fixing the penalty for that. If the sentencer comes to the conclusion that the suspended sentence should be activated with or without variation of the original term, he should as a general rule order that to take effect consecutively to the fresh sentence,[28] although the statute permits concurrent enforcements.[29] However, the sentencer should never lose sight of the totality principle, and may well decide that the fresh sentence he had in mind, followed by the whole of the original term, would make the total too long. He may decide that such a result would be unjust in all the circumstances. He would then be entitled to activate less than the whole of the original suspended term, stating his reasons for his opinion that activating the whole term would be unjust.[30] Alternatively, he might decide that the totality principle required him to scale down the sentence that he had in mind for the fresh offence, whilst adding the whole of the suspended term consecutively. In such a case he would be choosing the first of the four options set out above and would not be required to give reasons for that part of his decision. Once again, it would clearly be helpful if the sentencer were to explain both parts of such a sentencing exercise.

9.29 Normally, as we have seen, time spent in custody before sentence in connection with the instant offence counts as time served, in diminution of the total time to be spent in custody (subject to the parole minimum qualifying period). However, the Criminal Justice Act 1967, Section 67(1) does not bestow a similar benefit on a defendant who is subsequently given a suspended sentence which is later activated. This point should be borne in mind by sentencers, especially where a defendant has spent several months in custody awaiting trial. An example may emphasise the point. A defendant is in custody for six months awaiting trial and is then given a sentence of twelve months suspended for two years. If he is convicted of another offence punishable by imprisonment during the operational period of two years, he could well be sentenced to two years' imprisonment for that, with the

26 *Salmon* (1973) 57 Cr.App.R. 953 (discussed at para. 8.08 *supra* in connection with deferment).
27 Powers of Criminal Courts Act 1973, s. 13; *Barnes* [1986] Crim.L.R. 573.
28 *Ithell* (1969) 53 Cr.App.R. 310.
29 Powers of Criminal Courts Act 1973, s. 23(2).
30 *Bocskei* (1970) 54 Cr.App.R. 519.

twelve months being ordered to be served consecutively, making three years in all. He will get no credit for the six months served on remand before the first sentence was passed. It might be said that it serves him right and that he should have stayed out of trouble, but the Court of Appeal has indicated that the time served should be borne in mind and allowed for when the suspended sentence length is initially being fixed.[31]

THE PARTLY SUSPENDED SENTENCE

9.30   The government and the legislature hesitated over the introduction of the partly suspended sentence, and one sometimes wishes they had continued to hesitate. It has the dubious distinction of being the most complicated sentence in practice, and its utility is open to question, even though some judges appreciate it. Lord Lane, C.J., in the guideline case of *Clarke*,[32] suggested that it might be considered in the following circumstances:

> "In general the type of case that we have in mind is where the gravity of the offence is such that at least six months' imprisonment is merited, but when there are mitigating circumstances which point towards a measure of leniency not sufficient to warrant total suspension. Examples are always dangerous, but we venture very tentatively to suggest a few: first of all, some serious "one off" acts of violence which are usually met with immediate terms of imprisonment; some cases of burglary which at present warrant 18 months' or two years' imprisonment, where the offender is suitably qualified in terms of his record; some cases of fraud on public departments or some credit card frauds where a short immediate sentence would be insufficient; some cases of handling involving medium-range sums of money; some thefts involving breach of trust; some cases of stealing from employers."

Lord Lane went on to quote with approval the Advisory Council's view that partial suspension would be suitable where serious first offenders or first-time prisoners would be adequately deterred by serving a part of he sentence only. This perhaps begs the question whether a shorter sentence, without the suspended tail, could not more often provide adequate deterrence on the "clang of the prison gates" principle.

9.31   Lord Lane stated that the court felt that the sentence might also be used for those whose last term of imprisonment had been some considerable time earlier, and where more than a short sentence of

---

31   *Deering* (1976) C.S.P. D5.5(c); Practice Direction (1970) 54 Cr.App.R. 208.
32   (1982) 4 Cr.App.R.(S) 197. See also *Sentences of Imprisonment: A Review of Maximum Penalties* (1978) H.M.S.O. para. 282.

immediate custody was called for, both to mark public disapproval and as general deterrence.

9.32 The provision for the sentence was originally put onto the statute book by the Criminal Law Act 1977, Section 47, but was brought into force only after amendment by the Criminal Justice Act 1982, Section 30. The power to suspend part of a sentence exists only in the case of an adult who has been sentenced to a term of imprisonment of not less than three months and not more than two years. The comment of Lord Lane about the minimum of six months being merited has to be seen in the light of the fact that Parliament changed the statutory minimum period to three months shortly after *Clarke*. The upper limit is the same as that for the wholly suspended sentence; the lower limit is unique. Two other minima are incorporated in the legislation. The part ordered to be suspended must not be less than a quarter of the whole term, and the minimum part to be served must be 28 days. The Home Secretary may alter these periods by statutory instrument.

9.33 The approach to be used by the court when considering the possible use of the partly suspended sentence was also laid down in *Clarke* in the excerpt we quoted earlier,[33] which should be consulted. Parliament stressed that the partly suspended sentence should not be used unless a wholly suspended sentence is inappropriate: Criminal Law Act 1977, Section 47(1A). Just as the Court of Appeal pointed out in *Mah-Wing*[34] that it is improper to lengthen a sentence merely because it is suspended, so in *Clarke* Lord Lane warned of the partly suspended sentence:

> "Great care must be taken to ensure that the power is not used in a way which may serve to increase the length of the sentence."

9.34 The part held in suspense will not be served unless the defendant is convicted of an offence punishable by imprisonment committed during the whole period of the original sentence. Even then, as with the fully suspended sentence, the court has several options open to it, in this case three:

(1) The court may restore the part of the sentence held in suspense, thus requiring him to serve it;

(2) It may restore some of the suspended part only;

(3) It may decide to make no order: Criminal Law Act 1977, Section 47(3) and (4).

If the court is of the opinion that in all the circumstances it would be

---

33 At para. 6.08.
34 (1983) 5 Cr.App.R.(S) 347 (see para. 9.23 *supra*).

unjust to exercise the first option and to make the defendant serve the remainder of the term of imprisonment passed, then it must resort to one of the other two options. It is only if it exercises the third option and makes no order that the court is obliged to state its reasons – unlike with the wholly suspended sentence, where the obligation to activate the whole and to give reasons is wider.

9.35   As in the case of the wholly suspended sentence, it is not good practice to impose a partly suspended sentence at the same time as an immediate term of imprisonment.[35] Whenever a court is dealing with a breach of a wholly or partly suspended sentence, the sentencer should remember that he is not passing the original sentence, but merely dealing with it because of the breach. The second court's powers are strictly limited to those given by the legislation. If the second court activates a suspended sentence which was earlier passed and followed by a breach, there is no power to suspend a part of the activation.[36]

9.36   We have referred earlier to the appeal of the sword of Damocles to some sentencers, and we have now seen various sanctions based on the threat of future punishment in the event of further offending. Although the duration of the threat is fixed and clear from the outset where there is a conditional discharge or probation order for two years, it varies on other occasions. The defendant who, say, has a term of imprisonment for twelve months imposed on him, which is then suspended for two years, also knows that he is at risk for two years. If he should commit any imprisonable offence on the last day of the period at risk, he may – subject to parole and/or remission – have to serve the whole year consecutively to any fresh sentence – unless he is lucky enough to come before a judge who regards the date of the fresh offence as a mitigating factor. The defendant who has half of his twelve months' sentence of imprisonment suspended will serve six months, less remission, and then be at risk only until the end of the year following on the date of his sentence. He will be at risk to the extent of six months, which once again is likely to be ordered to be served consecutively to any additional sentence for a fresh offence which constitutes a breach. The defendant who is sentenced to twelve months' imprisonment to be served immediately will come out of prison after eight months if he has the benefit of remission only, but possibly after seven months if he obtains parole. If he is released after eight months he is in no danger at all from the previous sentence (save that it will figure in his antecedents if he is convicted again later) and he will be at risk only for one month if

---

35   *Sapiano* (1968) 52 Cr.App.R. 674; *McCarthy* (1982) 4 Cr.App.R.(S) 364.
36   *Gow* (1983) 5 Cr.App.R.(S) 250.

released after seven. His maximum liability on recall will be to serve to his two-thirds date, or 30 days, whichever is the longer.

9.37 It may seem strange that the most serious offender, the one who receives the longest sentence effectively, should be free of risk the earliest, and that the mildest offender of the three should be the most at risk. However, that result can be justified by the concept that the more one has paid for one's offence in terms of time served in prison, the less one should be subject to the risk of further incarceration. Parliament realised that there was perhaps something to be said for having certain persistent offenders subject to some control after the expiry of two-thirds of a sentence of immediate custody, and accordingly created the extended sentence, which we must now consider briefly.

THE EXTENDED SENTENCE

9.38 The introduction of the extended sentence was Parliament's third attempt to provide satisfactory legislation to deal with the persistent offender, but it is being used by the courts for only about twenty of the 80,000 Crown Court defendants annually.[37] The current provisions permit the court in certain limited circumstances to exceed a statutory maximum sentence, and also to make an order which has practical consequences for the persistent offender after release from prison. The power to exceed the maximum has only been used in three extended sentence cases out of about 650 in the period 1967-84, mainly because most maximum sentences for serious offences are ten years' imprisonment at least, but partly no doubt because of a distaste on the part of sentencers for any remedy which smacks of punishing a defendant twice for the same offence. The power to increase the normal supervision for habitual offenders has proved more attractive to the courts, and is no doubt responsible for the survival of the extended sentence provision. Without the licence provisions the extended sentence would by now probably have followed preventive detention into the penal histories.

9.39 There are the following six pre-requisites before a court may impose an extended term of imprisonment on a persistent offender, according to the Powers of Criminal Courts Act 1973, Section 28:
(1) The defendant must be convicted on indictment of an offence punishable with imprisonment for a term of two years or more;
(2) That offence must have been committed less than three years from

37 *Home Office Research and Planning Unit Bulletin* (1986) No. 21.

(i) the date of a previous conviction of an offence punishable on indictment with such a term (though not necessarily dealt with on indictment) or

(ii) his final release from prison after serving a sentence passed on such a conviction;

(3) The defendant must have been convicted on indictment on at least three previous occasions since attaining the age of 21 of offences punishable as aforesaid;

(4) The total length of the sentences must have been five years or more. Furthermore

(i) at least one of those previous sentences must have been one of preventive detention (and there are still a number of graduates of that defunct institution) or

(ii) on at least two of those occasions a sentence of imprisonment or corrective training was passed, one of which was for imprisonment for three years for a single offence, or two of which were for two years each for single offences. A suspended sentence is not a qualifying one unless activated and served.

(5) The statutory notice provisions of Section 29 must have been scrupulously obeyed; and

(6) The court must be satisfied "by reason of his previous conduct and of the likelihood of his committing further offences, that it is expedient to protect the public from him for a substantial time." It is clear from the authorities that the word "substantial" has been interpreted so as to come right down to four years.

9.40 When such a sentence is imposed the court must issue an extended sentence certificate, stating the term imposed. The extension of the normal maximum authorised by Section 28 is up to five years for any maximum below that total, and up to ten years for any maximum between five and ten years. The House of Lords decided in *Director of Public Prosecutions v Ottewell*[38] that there was power to pass an extended sentence and to issue the certificate even though the normal maximum was not in fact exceeded by the court. The defendant had been sentenced to two consecutive sentences of two years' imprisonment for two assaults occasioning actual bodily harm. As the existing maximum of five years could theoretically have been passed for each offence consecutively, the maximum possible sentence had been ten years in all.[39] In fact the sentence passed totalled four years only, one year below the maximum possible for a single offence. The House held that the Court of Appeal had been wrong to hold that the section

---

38 (1968) 52 Cr.App.R. 679.
39 *Blake* (1961) 45 Cr.App.R. 292.

applied only to an extension above and past the statutory maximum for an offence. (The House of Lords decision falls into the category sometimes politely described as "difficult".)[40]

9.41 Since *Ottewell* the Court of Appeal has on several occasions commended the extended sentence for its licence provisions, even where the normal maximum is not exceeded.[41] As we pointed out earlier, a prisoner who is subject to an extended sentence will remain in custody or on licence for the whole of his sentence, instead of being free of all restraint, as most prisoners are, after serving two-thirds of the sentence. Incidentally, the desirability of a defendant coming out of prison subject to both the supervision and the help of the probation service, is at the heart of the parole scheme. It is often considered to be in the public interest that even a serious offender should come out with some supervision during a licence period, and subject to recall, rather than staying in prison until the two-thirds stage, when he is entitled to come out "cold", without any after-care provision – unless he should ask for voluntary after-care.

9.42 From what has been said above it should be clear that great care must be taken by the court and counsel to ensure that all the requirements of the statute have been followed. The absence of even one only of the six prerequisites rules out the making of an extended sentence order. The court should ask the defendant whether he has received the notice served under Section 29 and whether he admits the convictions set out in it. If he does not, there must be adequate proof before the matter proceeds further. Clearly, the sentence should not be imposed merely because the defendant satisfies the formal criteria relating to convictions. The facts of the offence and all the circumstances, including the defendant's history and the contents of any reports on him, must be considered before the conclusion is reached that an extended sentence is needed "to protect the public from him for a substantial time." The professional criminal rather than the fairly petty persistent offender should be the kind of defendant considered for this exceptional kind of sentence, and the defendant who has kept out of trouble for some time should have that fact taken into account in his favour, despite a bad earlier record.[42]

---

40 For a full discussion see J.E. Hall Williams, *The English Penal System in Transition* (1970) Butterworths, p. 209.
41 See *e.g. Cain* (1983) 5 Cr.App.R.(S) 272.
42 *Kenway and Cunningham* (1985) 7 Cr.App.R.(S) 457.

LIFE IMPRISONMENT

9.43 Some 25 years ago the life sentence was a rarity, but now we have over 2000 lifers in custody at any given time. The increase is due partly to the abolition of capital punishment, coupled with the mandatory sentence of imprisonment for life as the only penalty for murder by the Murder (Abolition of Death Penalty) Act 1965. In part it is due to the increase in serious crimes, most of which have in law been punishable by life imprisonment for many years. In part the increase may be due to some concern, probably unjustified, about the possibility of the premature release of dangerous offenders who are made the subject of hospital orders.[43]

9.44 As many of the Court of Appeal decisions show, the sentencer faced with a discretionary life maximum is in a dilemma. Whilst his principal concern in very grave cases must be for the protection of the public, he has to bear in mind his duty to be just towards the defendant. Every man who has committed two rapes is a potential third-time rapist, and the temptation must often exist to consider a life sentence in order to protect women in general, in other words, to play safe. A long determinate sentence could in such a case also protect the public for a considerable time, especially as rape is one of the offences subject to the Home Secretary's restrictions on parole announced in November 1983. How long must a determinate sentence be to afford adequate protection? How long is justified by the offences committed, and how much extra because of the danger of further offences? These are the sort of questions that the sentencer must agonise over – not only the High Court, but increasingly also the Circuit judge authorised to try cases of that gravity. The Court of Appeal has in the past referred to a life sentence, which is subject to release on licence at any time in theory, being more merciful to the defendant than a long determinate sentence. However Lawton L.J., speaking with great authority, countered that proposition most forcefully in *Pither*:[44]

> "This court is of the firm opinion that sentences of life imprisonment, passed in the circumstances described, are not merciful. It may well be that a man who is sentenced to life imprisonment may be released fractionally earlier than one who is sentenced to a fairly long determinate sentence. He may be; but he may not. What this court has to bear in mind is the anguish which must be felt, even by the most hardened young thugs, if they are in prison, sentenced to life imprisonment, and have no idea, as the years go by, when (if at all) they will be released."

43 N. Walker, *Sentencing: Theory, Law and Practice* (1985) Butterworths, p. 359.
44 (1979) 1 Cr.App.R.(S) 209; *cf.* Lawton, L.J.'s remarks in *Rose* (1973) C.S.P. A7.3(a), F3.2(h) discussed at para. 11.28 *infra*.

Even when released, the life prisoner will remain on licence for the rest of his days and subject to recall, even without his committing another offence. He may even be recalled to prison by the Home Secretary in appropriate emergency situations without the Parole Board being consulted in advance.[45] We are not seeking to suggest that these powers are unnecessary, but merely wish to underline the point made by Lawton, L.J. that a life sentence is a very drastic one compared with nearly all determinate sentences.

9.45 In recent years a number of safeguards for defendants seem to have emerged from the Court of Appeal, although the decisions are not all consistent – understandably in such a difficult area. In *Pither* Lawton, L.J. added:

> "Secondly, this court has laid it down as a matter of principle that life sentences for offences other than homicide should not be imposed unless there are exceptional circumstances in the case. One of the most usual type of exceptional circumstances is that there is a marked degree of mental instability, which may or may not amount to a mental disorder within the Mental Health Act 1959."

9.46 In *Wilkinson* [46] Lord Lane, C.J. approved this approach. He there said of a defendant who was in such a mental state that he was dangerous to the life and limb of members of the public:

> "It is sometimes impossible to say when that danger will subside, and therefore an indeterminate sentence is required, so that the prisoner's progress may be monitored by those who have him under their supervision in prison, and so that he will be kept in custody only so long as public safety may be jeopardised by his being let loose at large."

Wilkinson had pleaded guilty to a large number of robbery and burglary charges, and had a bad record. His violence had been confined to tying up the owners of some of the houses he had burgled. In a sense he was a danger, but not essentially to life and limb. He was described by the Lord Chief Justice as being no different from any other bad burglar or robber. A sentence of eleven years' imprisonment was substituted for the life sentence which had been passed. A life sentence should not even be contemplated unless the case is serious enough to warrant a very long sentence.[47]

9.47 As we mentioned earlier, a medical report should normally be before the court whenever a life sentence is contemplated.[48] If the

---

45 Criminal Justice Act 1967, s. 62(2). See also *Weeks v. United Kingdom* (1987) The Times 5 Mar.
46 (1983) 5 Cr.App.R.(S) 105.
47 *Hodgson* (1967) 52 Cr.App.R. 13.
48 *De Havilland* (1983) 5 Cr.App.R.(S) 107; para. 4.33 *supra*.

sentencer has a particular type of sentence in mind that has not been referred to in court at all during the mitigation stage, then, as we have suggested above, it is desirable for the judge to invite counsel to address him on the point. *A fortiori*, a judge should not pass a life sentence without any previous mention by anyone of the possibility of such a drastic sentence.[49]

9.48 When passing a sentence of life imprisonment for murder – but for no other offence, not even manslaughter by reason of diminished responsibility – the trial judge may make a recommendation to the Home Secretary as to the minimum number of years he considers the defendant should serve. As this is a recommendation only, it is not binding on the Home Secretary or the Parole Board, and it is not appealable.[50] Many judges decline to make any such recommendation, and one can understand why: it is pretty pointless. There is very little risk of any Home Secretary releasing a dangerous murderer prematurely. The Parole Board panel considering life cases always includes a High Court judge and a psychiatrist among its members, and both the trial judge and the Lord Chief Justice must be consulted. It also seems fair to say that no Home Secretary would see any political mileage in the premature release of a notorious murderer.

MAGISTRATES' POWERS OF IMPRISONMENT

9.49 The powers of the magistrates' courts in relation to imprisonment are scattered about the Magistrates' Courts Act 1980, so we must briefly consider the effect of Sections 22, 31-33 and 132-3 – although some other sections are also relevant. A magistrates' court may not impose a sentence of imprisonment for less than five days.[51] The general upper limit is one of six months in respect of any one offence, even though that offence had earlier had a higher maximum penalty attached to it. If Parliament expressly excludes this general limit from applying to a specific offence and permits a higher maximum, then the court may of course pass an authorised sentence of more than six months.[52] The general limit does not apply either to any power of the magistrates'

---

49 *MacDougall* (1983) 5 Cr.App.R.(S) 78.
50 The Parliamentary All-Party Penal Affairs Group has advocated the repeal of the minimum recommendation, with the alternative suggestion that if it is retained it should (a) be appealable, and (b) be made subject to the requirement that the judge should give reasons for his recommendation: *Life Sentence Prisoners* (1985) Barry Rose.
51 s. 132.
52 S. 31(1) and (2).

court to impose a term of imprisonment for non-payment of a fine, or for want of sufficient distress to satisfy a fine.[53]

9.50 When passing a sentence of imprisonment the magistrates' court may, like the Crown Court, order the fresh sentence to commence on the expiration of any other term of imprisonment passed by any court. Subject to a major exception in the case of the summary trial of offences triable either way, there is a general limit imposed on the lower court with regard to consecutive sentences. Such sentences may not on aggregate exceed six months (Section 133(1)). However, if at least two of the terms of imprisonment imposed were in respect of offences triable either way that were in fact tried summarily, then (subject to what follows) the maximum total may be twelve months. The maximum is *not* raised if the offences triable either way were tried summarily pursuant to Section 22(2) because of the low value involved in a criminal damage charge. To complicate matters slightly further, the lower maximum of three months' imprisonment applies to such offences when so tried (Section 33). On summary conviction of any offence triable either way that is listed in Schedule 1 of the Act, the magistrates' court may pass a maximum sentence of six months, unless the Crown Court has no power to imprison for such an offence on indictment (Section 32(1)).

Committal for sentence

9.51 Where the magistrates have tried a defendant for an offence triable either way, other than a low value criminal damage offence, then under the provisions of Section 38 Magistrates' Courts Act 1980:

> "if on obtaining information about his character and antecedents the court is of opinion that they are such that greater punishment should be inflicted for the offence than the court has power to inflict, the court may . . . commit him in custody or on bail to the Crown Court for sentence in accordance with the provisions of section 42 of the Powers of Criminal Courts Act 1973."

We are in this chapter considering imprisonment for the adult offender only, but Section 38 applies to any defendant who is not less than 17 years of age. Section 42 of the 1973 Act enables the Crown Court to deal with the defendant who has been committed for sentence as if he had just been convicted of the offence in question on indictment. In theory a committal for sentence can lead to a much heavier sentence. For example, the defendant convicted by the magistrates of a single theft might be alarmed to learn that the maximum in his case had been

---

53 S. 31(3); see also s. 133(4) and (5).

increased 20-fold by the committal for sentence: the maximum had leapt from six months to ten years. In practice he need not worry unduly, for experience over the years has shown that the higher courts (whether quarter sessions or later the Crown Court) often pass a sentence, after such a committal by the lower court, which is one that the magistrates could have passed themselves. Devlin suggested that there were two possible explanations:[54]

> "First, that in a very substantial percentage of cases, the higher tribunal has taken a different view of the gravity of sentence merited by the offender; and secondly, that magistrates have perhaps taken the opportunity to commit for sentence under section [38] when simply in a dilemma as to how to deal with an offender rather than because they have thought that greater punishment was required."

A third explanation is to be found in the point we made earlier, namely, that in the period between the two court appearances circumstances often change significantly. The Crown Court will have before it more information than the committing magistrates had. The probation service will invest more time in the case; solicitors will take it more seriously; employers will agree to come to court as character witnesses; and other members of the community may rally round when the defendant is clearly in serious trouble. Although "greater punishment" loomed large in the minds of the committing magistrates, that is, retribution and/or deterrence and/or incapacitation, more constructive alternatives will often have appeared by the time the case comes on in the Crown Court. Particularly if he is on bail during this "mini-probation" period, the defendant may also take steps which may impress the Crown Court favourably, such as finding work and making good his victim's losses. The moral to be drawn, perhaps, is that sometimes not enough effort is put into the problems of sentencing in the magistrates' court, whilst the spur of a Crown Court appearance shakes up more people than just the defendant. Defence lawyers would do well to bear this point in mind when representing a defendant in the lower court.

9.52 When committing for sentence the magistrates' court may also send up certain summary offences committed by the defendant for sentence at the same time: Criminal Justice Act 1967, Section 56. The Crown Court will then be able to sentence the defendant for all his offences at the same time, and thus avoid some of the undesirable effects of two courts having to deal with the same man. In respect of the summary offences the Crown Court's powers of sentence will be the same as those of the lower court.[55] In certain limited circumstances a

---

54 K. Devlin, *Sentencing Offenders in the Magistrates' Courts* (1970) Sweet & Maxwell, p. 122.
55 *Cattell* [1986] Crim.L.R. 823.

magistrates' court may commit court may commit a defendant for sentence to another magistrates' court, if that court agrees: Magistrates' Courts Act 1980, Section 39.

9.53 When a defendant has been sentenced in the Crown Court following a committal for sentence, his rights of appeal to the Court of Appeal are considerably curtailed, when compared with those of the defendant who has been convicted in the Crown Court. The principal restriction, imposed by the Criminal Appeal Act 1968, Section 10, is that there is no appeal against a sentence of imprisonment or youth custody imposed after a committal for sentence, unless the term exceeds six months.

CHAPTER 10

Attendance Centre Orders and Custodial Sentences For Young Offenders

10.01 In this chapter we bring together discussion of the custodial sentences for young offenders:

(1) Detention centre orders;

(2) Youth custody orders;

(3) Detention under Section 53(2), Children and Young Persons Act 1933;

(4) Detention in default or for contempt;

(5) Custody for life; and

(6) Detention during Her Majesty's Pleasure;

and also attendance centre orders. The latter, which are discussed first, can be conveniently included in this chapter because they are limited in their application to offenders under the age of 21, and because they are seen by some as occupying an intermediate position between custodial and non-custodial measures which enables at least a "whiff of custodial grapeshot" to be experienced when such an order is made.

Supervision and care orders, which are also limited to children and young persons, are dealt with more appropriately in Chapter 13 under the heading of probation, as they are to some extent analogous measures.

Other methods of dealing with young offenders are also available for dealing with adults and are covered in the appropriate chapters concerned.

ATTENDANCE CENTRE ORDERS

10.02 An attendance centre order requires the attendance of the person concerned at a specified centre, usually for periods of three hours at a time at fortnightly intervals on a Saturday morning or afternoon. Originally available only for young males aged ten to 16, it has now been extended to offenders of both sexes aged ten to 20 who have pleaded or been found guilty of an offence punishable with imprisonment in the case of an adult (Criminal Justice Act 1982, Section 17). In practice, however, because by Section 17 an order cannot be made unless a centre is available in the area for the appropriate sex and age group of offender concerned, this measure is not likely to be available for girls and the older male age group except in the largest centres of population.

10.03 According to the fourth edition of *The Sentence of the Court* (at p. 48) the aims of an order are:

> ". . . to impose, in loss of leisure over a considerable period, a punishment that is generally understood by young people and to encourage them, in a disciplined environment, to make more constructive use of their leisure time."

It goes on to make the point that an order will not usually be appropriate in the case of offenders with long records of offences or who need removal from bad surroundings or prolonged supervision but that in the right case an order may be made "as an alternative to custody for an offence of some gravity". The attendance centre order can therefore be seen as both deterrent and, insofar as it is used as an alternative to a custodial sentence, reformative in aim. However, those in favour of such centres probably concentrate upon the deterrent aspects of the loss of leisure, the inconvenience involved and the semi-institutional nature of the routine. Viewed in this way, attendance centre orders are perceived as giving offenders a foretaste of institutional life, something which is likely to act as a deterrent for those otherwise likely to commit further offences.

10.04 The programme of typical attendance centres, which will in many cases be run from schools, youth clubs and church halls by off-duty police officers, will involve firm discipline, physical training and instruction in handicrafts, motor vehicle maintenance, etc.

Restrictions on the use of attendance centre orders

10.05 As indicated above, by Section 17 an offender must be between ten and 20 and convicted of an offence punishable with imprisonment in the case of an adult. An order is also available where the court has the power to impose a custodial sentence in default of the payment of a fine etc. or for failing to do (or abstain from doing) anything required to be done or left undone, or where it has the power to deal with an offender for failure to comply with the requirements of a probation order or a supervision order.

10.06 The court must also have been notified that an attendance centre is available for the sex and age group concerned and is reasonably accessible, i.e. not further away than 15 miles or a journey of not more than 1½ hours, except in the case of children under 14 when the limits are ten miles and 45 minutes' journey time. By Section 17(3), unless there are special reasons, the offender must not have previously served a custodial sentence.

An attendance centre order should not for obvious reasons be combined with any custodial order or with probation or supervision imposed on the same occasion.

Requirements of the order

10.07 By Section 17(4) the *minimum* period which may be ordered is 12 hours except where the offender is under 14 and the court believes that 12 hours would be excessive. The *maximum* period is 24 hours (where 12 hours is considered in all the circumstances to be inadequate by the court), unless the offender has reached the age of 17, when 36 hours may be ordered (Section 17(5)). Where several offences are dealt with at the same time, the total hours ordered to be served must still not exceed the maximum (or be less than the minimum), but where an offender already subject to an attendance centre order is sentenced again with another order, the total of the hours outstanding on the old order and those specified in the new order *may* exceed the maximum (Section 17(6)).

10.08 The order must under Section 17 specify the centre and the date and time of first attendance, but thereafter attendance is at the direction of the person in charge, who as far as practicable is required to avoid interference with school or working hours. By Section 17(11) not more than three hours' attendance at any one time and no more than one attendance per day may be required.

Breach of an order

10.09 Where there is a failure to attend as ordered or a breach of the rules of the centre, the offender may be brought back to an appropriate magistrates' court, the order revoked and the offender dealt with afresh or, in the case of an order made by the Crown Court, he may be committed by the justices either in custody or on bail to the Crown Court for appropriate action there.

10.10 However, the Act is silent as to what step the court can take if the offender is in breach of an attendance order imposed for non-payment of a fine. Clearly the offender cannot be sentenced again for the original offence. Presumably the outstanding fine will have to be resurrected and alternative methods of enforcement considered. Perhaps this is why attendance centres seem so rarely used to enforce the payment of fines.

Discharge and variation

10.11 An order may be discharged by the offender or the officer in charge of the centre applying to a magistrates' court or to the Crown Court when the latter has reserved to itself the power to discharge.

It is also possible on application for the court to vary the day or hour specified for first attendance or, where it is satisfied that the offender has changed or proposes to change his address, to substitute another named centre to which as a result of his move the offender has reasonable access.

Where the order has been made in default, for example, of the payment of a fine and the fine is then paid in full, the order ceases to have effect: where part payment is made the total number of hours which the offender is required to attend is reduced proportionately (Section 17(13)).

CUSTODIAL SENTENCES

10.12 The powers available to deal with offenders under the age of 21 depend upon their age classification and the court before which they appear. Those aged 10 to 16, except in the circumstances set out below, are tried and sentenced by the juvenile court. Those aged 17 and over are tried by the magistrates' court or by the Crown Court as adults. Apart from prolonged detention (see below), in respect of children aged 10 to 13, the courts are not empowered to make any form of custodial sentence save for that involved in a "residential" care order (see paras. 12.49ff *infra*). Young male offenders aged 14 to 20 may be made the subject of detention centre orders and those aged 15 to 20 of youth custody orders, whereas young female offenders aged 15 to 20 may only be sentenced to youth custody. On the other hand, young offenders of both sexes under 17 may be sentenced to prolonged detention by the Crown Court if tried on indictment. In addition, where appropriate, offenders aged 15 and 16 may be committed by the juvenile court, and those aged 17 to 20 by the adult magistrates' court to the Crown Court under the Magistrates' Courts Act 1980, Sections 37 and 38 respectively.

10.13 It is therefore obvious that the exact age of a young offender may be critical in deciding what may be done with him. The recent case of *Arthur v. Stringer*,[1] together with the case of *Daley*,[2] makes it plain that the power to adjourn for sentence must be exercised judicially and must not be done simply for the purpose of enabling the defendant to attain a higher age group, thereby making him liable for a more serious sentence.

10.14 Unless charged with homicide, a person under 17 must be tried summarily except when charged jointly with an adult who is committed for trial on indictment or where the juvenile court refuses jurisdiction and commits the offender to the Crown Court for trial under the Magistrates' Courts Act 1980, Section 24(1). So far as the latter is concerned, this can occur in the case of a juvenile aged 14 to 16 charged with an offence such as is mentioned in the Children and Young Persons Act 1933, Section 53(2) (under which young persons convicted of certain grave crimes may be sentenced to be detained for long periods – see below) and the court considers that if found guilty, it ought to be possible to sentence the accused in accordance with that power.[3]

10.15 A juvenile who is charged jointly with an adult and pleads or is found guilty by a magistrates' court must be remitted for sentence to the juvenile court unless it proposes to discharge him, fine him, order him to pay compensation or order his parent to enter a recognisance to exercise proper control: Children and Young Persons Act 1969, Section 7(8). However, so far as the Crown Court is concerned, Lord Lane, C. J. in *Michael Lewis*[4] made the point that since the passing of the Criminal Justice Act 1982, there had been "an alignment of the sentencing powers of the higher courts and the lower courts and the concept of the juvenile court being the sole proper forum in which to deal with juveniles now seems to this court to be out of place." Accordingly when applying Section 56(1) of the 1933 Act a court must consider whether it is satisfied "that it would be undesirable to . . . remit the case to a juvenile court . . ." The Lord Chief Justice then set out a list of what might constitute possible reasons for making it undesirable to do so: that the judge who presided over the trial might be better informed as to the facts and circumstances; that there was an unacceptable risk of disparity if co-defendants were sentenced in different courts on different occasions; that remitting the case might lead to delay, duplication of proceedings and fruitless expense; and the provisions for appeal, which were that appeal against conviction would be to the Court of Appeal and against

1 (1986) The Times 11 October.
2 (1982) 146 J.P. 263.
3 See *R. v. South Hackney Juvenile Court ex p. RB (a minor) and CB (a minor)* (1983) 77 Cr.App.R. 294 for guidance by the Divisional Court on this procedure.
4 (1984) 79 Cr.App.R. 94.

sentence to the Crown Court. It was also observed that it might be desirable to remit a juvenile where a report has to be obtained and the judge would be unable to sit when the report would be available.

10.16 By virtue of the Criminal Justice Act 1982, Section 1(4), before a detention centre or youth custody order can be made, the court must be of the opinion that no other method of dealing with the offender is appropriate, because it appears to the court that he is unable or unwilling to respond to non-custodial penalties, or because a custodial sentence is necessary for the protection of the public, or because the offence was so serious that a non-custodial sentence cannot be justified. Thus the court must first exclude all non-custodial orders as being inappropriate. To do this it must obtain and consider information about the circumstances of the offence, and must take into account any information before the court as to the character and physical and mental condition of the defendant (Section 2(1)), and accordingly a social inquiry report should be obtained unless the court considers it unnecessary to do so (Section 2(2) and (3)). In the case of a magistrates' court making a detention centre or youth custody order, it must state its reasons in open court for making the order by reference to Section 1 together with its reasons for not seeking a report, record the reasons in the committal warrant and enter them in the court register (Section 2(4), (6) and (7)). Furthermore, before making such an order both the magistrates' courts and the Crown Court must ensure that an unrepresented defendant is informed of his right to apply for legal aid and give him an opportunity to do so: it may only proceed if the application is refused because the defendant does not appear to be eligible or if he fails to apply or refuses representation after having been informed of his rights (Section 3). Before making a youth custody order, the court must be of the opinion that the appropriate term of the custodial sentence is in excess of four months (Section 6).

Detention centre orders

10.17 Detention centre orders are available for males aged 14 to 20 convicted of offences punishable with imprisonment in the case of an adult. There are no detention centres for females. The minimum term is 21 days and the maximum is four months, except (1) as regards the minimum, when detention is imposed for failure to comply with the compulsory supervision requirements of the sentence which is itself an offence and punishable with up to 30 days,[5] and (2) as regards the

5 Criminal Justice Act 1982, s. 15(11).

maximum, when the maximum sentence of imprisonment available for the offence as an adult is less than four months (Section 4(2)). A detention centre order may not be made where the court considers it to be unsuitable because of the offender's mental or physical condition (Section 4(5)(a)). Furthermore by Section 4(5)(b) an offender who has served or is serving a sentence of (1) imprisonment; (2) detention under the Children and Young Persons Act 1933, Section 53; (3) Borstal training; (4) youth custody; or (5) custody for life, cannot be made the subject of a detention centre order unless there are special circumstances that warrant such a course (Section 4(6)). Consecutive orders may be made provided the total term does not exceed four months (Section 5(1) and (2)).

10.18   According to the Detention Centre Rules 1983, Rule 4, the aims of the new detention centres are:

> ". . . to provide disciplined daily routine; to provide work, education and other activities of a kind that will assist offenders to acquire or develop personal resources and aptitudes; to encourage offenders to accept responsibility, and to help them with their return to the community in co-operation with the services responsible for their supervision."

However their aims are described, detention centres are probably associated in the minds of most people with the need of the individual offender for a "short, sharp shock" in order to "bring him to his senses". A stay in a detention centre is meant to be short and strenuous and the virtue of the brevity of the experience in contrast to the disadvantages of longer forms of custody is recognised by the shortness of the sentence that may be imposed.

Youth custody orders

10.19   Youth custody was introduced by the Criminal Justice Act 1982, Section 6 as a replacement for Borstal training and imprisonment for young offenders. Originally it was intended as the only custodial sentence for young offenders. As presently organised youth custody is designed to provide training and generally it is less regimented than the detention centre regime. Youth custody orders are available for males and females aged 15 to 20 but can only be imposed where the court considers that a custodial sentence in excess of four months is necessary. However, where the offender is male, and is considered unsuitable for a detention centre, or who has served a previous custodial sentence as specified in Section 4(5) and (6), or is a female aged 17 to 20, youth custody may be reduced to a minimum of 21 days at the discretion of the court (Section 7(6)). As with detention centre orders, so too, following release from youth custody, a breach of the conditions of supervision may be punished by a youth custody sentence of less that 21 days: (Section 15(11)).

10.20 The maximum term of youth custody for an offender under the age of 17 is 12 months (Section 7(8)). However, the decision in *Oliver*[6] makes it clear that in imposing sentences of youth custody a court is not bound to take account of a youth custody order already being served and accordingly may impose a term of up to 12 months notwithstanding that the aggregate of the two terms exceeds 12 months.

Again the maximum term for the offence to which an adult would be subject must not be exceeded (Section 7(1)).

10.21 Within the limit of 12 months, consecutive sentences may be imposed in the normal way. Thus where appropriate a juvenile court may impose up to 12 months' youth custody in respect of two offences when six months is imposed consecutively on each. It follows that there is no point in committing an offender under 17 to the Crown Court for a youth custody sentence under the Magistrates' Courts Act, 1980, Section 37 where there are two such offences on which he can be sentenced by the magistrates themselves.

10.22 In practice the courts have not found the restrictions on the use of detention centre and youth custody orders in Section 1(4) of the Criminal Justice Act 1982 easy to interpret. Indeed in research published in 1985 under the title of "All Things to All Men: Justifying Custody under the 1982 Act,"[7] Elizabeth Burney described finding "a quite astonishing degree of neglect of the 1982 sentencing formulae"[8] with the result that "in the majority of cases courts break the law by failing to follow the statutory formula or failing to record it".[9] Frances Reynolds, in her own research "Magistrates' Justification for making Custodial Orders on Juvenile Offenders"[10] pointed out that the courts had had difficulty in applying the "protection of the public" and "serious offence" formulae in particular, claiming that the former had often been "frequently linked with recidivism rather than dangerousness".[11] According to Frances Reynolds, the results of the introduction of these powers so far as juvenile courts were concerned, were that (1) custodial orders were being made "considerably earlier in a delinquent career and much lower down the tariff" and (2) sentencing aims were "shifting quite

6 (1983) 5 Cr.App.R.(S) 477.
7 [1985] Crim.L.R. 284.
8 At p. 287. See also para. 7.20 *supra*.
9 At p. 288.
10 [1985] Crim.L.R. 294.
11 At p. 295.

explicitly towards deterrence and retribution even in cases where, previously, the need for social work intervention would have been self-evident".[12]

10.23 In *Bradbourne*[13] Section 1(4) was described as being "pregnant with ambiguities". In this case Lawton, L.J. dealt with the requirement that the offence must be "so serious that a non-custodial sentence cannot be justified," observing that whereas it might help "academics lecturing in criminology" to have definitions of other parts of the sub-section, to attempt to do so in this case would be *obiter*. But so far as the "so serious" category was concerned, he said it came to this:

> ". . . the kind of offence that when committed by a young person would make right thinking members of the public, knowing all the facts, feel that justice had not been done by the passing of any sentence other than a custodial one."

The court concluded that in this case, involving a 20-year old woman of previous good character, stealing £2 from the till was not so serious that a non-custodial sentence could not be justified, and substituted a conditional discharge for three months' youth custody. In general it would seem that only burglaries and thefts at the top of the scale of seriousness will be "so serious" that a non-custodial sentence could not be justified and even when burglaries involve dwelling houses, usually thought to be grave enough to warrant immediate imprisonment in the case of adults, they will not necessarily attract custodial sentences in those under 21.[14] However, where burglaries of dwelling houses indicate greater planning and sophistication or are repeated then custodial sentences will be upheld.[15] Robbery, in particular the "mugging" of elderly people, will normally result in sentences of custody,[16] but again it is an offence which involves a wide range of conduct and seriousness and will not necessarily be "so serious" that a non-custodial sentence cannot be justified. Similarly offences of unprovoked violence and sustained assaults, violence at football matches or with intent to resist arrest, "glassings", assaults involving other dangerous weapons like knives, and affrays are all likely to involve immediate loss of liberty. Again, as the decision in *Dewberry and Stone*[17] makes plain, whereas arson is an offence which is normally regarded as serious, there are cases, and this was held to be one, where the conduct falls into "the lower range of criminality for arson". In this case Dewberry, aged 17

12 At p. 297.
13 (1985) 7 Cr.App.R.(S) 180.
14 *Bates* (1985) 7 Cr.App.R.(S) 105.
15 *Pilford* (1985) 7 Cr.App.R.(S) 23.
16 *Fleming and Dodge* (1984) 6 Cr.App.R.(S) 222.
17 (1985) 7 Cr.App.R.(S) 202.

with no previous findings of guilt, together with a number of young men including Stone, set fire to a parka which had been placed against the door of a temporary classroom. About £200 worth of damage was done and Dewberry was sentenced to 12 months' youth custody. On appeal 50 hours of community service was substituted.

10.24 As regards the protection of the public, the Court of Appeal has stressed the point in relation to youth custody that the sentence should not be longer than is warranted by the offences for which it is passed, in the hope that the offender will benefit from the sentence. In the case of *Hart and Hart*,[18] the appellants, who were twin brothers aged 20, pleaded guilty to burglary having removed three bars from the window of a hut in a car park with the intention of stealing a radio set. They ran away when an alarm sounded. Both had previous convictions for relatively minor offences and there was medical evidence that they had psychological difficulties which were thought to require their treatment for a significant period in a controlled environment. They were not eligible for hospital orders and the local authority declined to accept them on the basis of a guardianship order. They were each sentenced to two years' youth custody. In giving the judgment of the Court, Mustill, J. made the following observations:

> "The state makes no provision for persons such as these men, the more so since they are their own worst enemies. But the Courts cannot, in our judgment, properly be allowed to draw themselves either into casting men loose without regard to the fact that they are criminals who have been and may in the future be a serious problem to the community, or at the other extreme impose sentences not merited by the offences themselves, with the aim of trying to patch up gaps in the Social Services. There are gaps in the Social Services through which these men have fallen or have thrust themselves. But is is not the task of the Courts to remedy these deficiencies. The Courts must take the offenders and the sentences as they find them."

The sentences were reduced to 12 months.

10.25 Finally, on the inability or unwillingness of the defendant to respond to non-custodial penalties, as yet the Court of Appeal does not seem to have directly concerned itself with this restriction, although experience suggests that the lower courts will frequently have imposed custodial sentences on this ground alone or in association with one or other of those already discussed.

10.26 In general terms, once can say that the principles used in determining the length of sentence of youth custody are similar to those

18 (1983) 5 Cr.App.R.(S) 385.

which apply to calculation of the length of imprisonment in an adult, with the youth of the offender being taken into account as a mitigating factor. Thus a defendant under the age of 17 should normally be given credit for a plea of guilty by imposing a term less than the maximum of 12 months.[19]

10.27 The Court of Appeal also made it clear in *Tyre*[20] that the fact that one co-defendant is under 17 and therefore subject to the maximum of 12 months' youth custody should not restrict the sentence imposed on a co-defendant over the age of 21.

10.28 In *Dobbs and Hitchings*[21] it was held that where a court had in mind to impose a youth custody sentence in circumstances in which in the case of an adult a partly suspended sentence of imprisonment would be appropriate, the youth custody sentence should be for a term equal to the part of the sentence which an adult would be ordered to serve in the first instance. This somewhat convoluted formulation is the result of the inability of the courts, which the Lord Chief Justice lamented in this case, to impose fully or partially suspended sentences of detention or youth custody.

10.29 Remands in care involving time spent in custody or in secure accommodation should be taken into account when fixing the length of a sentence of youth custody, as otherwise they will not count towards sentence.[22]

Detention under Section 53(2) Children and Young Persons Act 1933

10.30 Where a child or young person (i.e. under 17) is convicted on indictment of an offence punishable in the case of an adult with 14 years' imprisonment or more[23] and the court considers that none of the alternative methods is appropriate, it may sentence the offender to detention in accordance with the direction of the Secretary of State, for such period as it determines, not exceeding the maximum sentence of

19 See *Stewart* (1983) 5 Cr.App.R.(S) 320, *Fleming and Dodge* (note 16 *supra*), and *Pilford* (note 15 *supra*); an exception is where the court could have imposed a sentence under s. 53(2) Children and Young Persons Act 1933 and accordingly 12 months' youth custody represents a considerable discount: *Reynolds* [1986] Crim.L.R. 125.
20 (1984) 6 Cr.App.R.(S) 247.
21 (1983) 5 Cr.App.R.(S) 378.
22 *Murphy and Duke* [1986] Crim.L.R. 571.
23 And not being a sentence fixed by law. The power to order detention may also be exercised where the offender is convicted of a common law offence: *Bosomworth* (1973) 57 Cr.App.R. 708.

imprisonment for the offence available in the case of an adult: Children and Young Persons Act 1933, Section 53(2).

10.31 It is clear from the words of the section that before invoking this power the court must be satisfied that no other method of dealing with the offender is appropriate – not only excluding non-custodial methods but also, as was indicated in *Butler*,[24] ruling out 12 months' youth custody. In so doing the court will necessarily take into account the restrictions on custodial sentences set out in Section 1(4) of the Criminal Justice Act 1982 and should only proceed to sentence under Section 53(2) where it finds that the criteria contained in these restrictions have been met and decides that 12 months' youth custody is insufficient. If a sentence under Section 53(2) is being considered, it is obvious that a social inquiry report will be required.[25] It is hardly necessary to add that good practice suggests that reasons for the decision should also be given.[26]

10.32 It is also hardly necessary to draw attention to the fact that the power to impose long-term detention under Section 53(2) arises only as a result of conviction on indictment and not on committal for sentence.[27]

10.33 Of course long-term detention is particularly appropriate when a child or young person has committed an offence of great gravity and appears likely to represent a danger to the public for a considerable period in the future. In *Fuat, Storey and Duignan*[28] the appellants were convicted of robbery and attempted murder, having attacked a man in the street and robbed him of cigarettes and matches. In the course of the attack the man was knocked to the ground and then struck on the head with a brick by one of the appellants. Storey was ordered to be detained for 20 years, the other two for ten years each. In the course of his judgment, Lord Widgery, C.J. made the following observations:

> "In this case the concern of the public and the possibility of future danger is underlined, in our opinion, by the fact that no trace of mental illness is discoverable in any of these three young men, and absolutely no kind of motivation or reason at all in their background, history or any other source is to be found. If they can do acts of this kind in those circumstances once, obviously there is a danger they will do them with equal lack of excuse again, and the safety of the public and the protection

---

24 (1984) 6 Cr.App.R.(S) 236.
25 *Barton* [1977] Crim.L.R. 435.
26 *Massheder* (1983) 5 Cr.App.R.(S) 442.
27 *McKenna* (1985) 7 Cr.App.R.(S) 348; *Corcoran* (1986) 8 Cr.App.R.(S) 118.
28 (1973) 57 Cr.App.R. 840.

of the public from similar incidents is a factor which has to be in forefront of the sentencing exercise."

He then went on to say that detention under Section 53(2) was an appropriate means of dealing with this kind of sentencing difficulty, describing it as an entirely flexible procedure in which, as the subject develops and his character matures, the Home Secretary can direct him to appropriate training and eventually secure his release when that release is possible and consistent with the safety of the public.

10.34 Detention for life may be ordered where the offender appears likely to be a public danger for the foreseeable future;[29] but it was held in *Tunney*[30] that detention for life should not be imposed unless it was clearly necessary for the protection of the public to do so, Shaw, L. J. making the point as follows:

"The Court has to strike a balance between correction of an offender coming before the Court to answer for wrong-doing and the protection of the public. It seems to this Court that it is wrong in a case where the offender is not inherently a dangerous criminal to say that in order to safeguard the interests of the public we must exclude all possible risk that there might be a relapse into further wrongdoing. It is wrong for the Court to abdicate its function of deciding what the justice of the case requires, and to transmit the responsibility of deciding when she can be released to authorities and institutions or doctors under whose care and observation she comes.

This Court must face up to the matter and decide itself what the measure of risk is and fix an appropriate term; that is to say the term which is the maximum period for which she will be in custody."

In this case the appellant had set fire to her bed at a secure unit where she was detained. She pleaded guilty to arson and was ordered to be detained for life. On appeal the sentence was varied to detention for three years.

10.35 At the other end of the scale it is now clear that detention under Section 53(2) may properly be used as a sentence of general deterrence, even when the cases do not fall into the category of being very grave or exceptionally serious cases as was required in *Oakes*.[31]

10.36 In *Butler*[32] the appellant, a boy of 16, pleaded guilty to six counts of burglary and asked for 23 other offences, many of them burglaries, to be taken into consideration. Three of the burglaries charged related to residential premises when the occupiers were away;

---

29 *Flemming* (1973) 57 Cr.App.R. 524; *Bryson* (1973) 58 Cr.App.R. 464.
30 (1975) C.S.P. E4.3(c). See also paras. 1.79, 1.80 and 9.43ff *supra*.
31 (1983) 5 Cr.App.R.(S) 389.
32 (1984) 6 Cr.App.R.(S) 236.

damage was done in two of the houses, one to the extent of £2,000. The three other counts related to burglaries of shop premises. The total value of the property stolen was in excess of £5,000. The appellant had previous findings of guilt for burglary and assault occasioning actual bodily harm, and had previously been sentenced to three months at a detention centre. He was sentenced to two years, detention under Section 53(2) and it was argued on his behalf that as the offences were not so serious or exceptional as to warrant detention under Section 53(2) the proper sentence would have been a term of youth custody which would not, because of his age, have been more than 12 months. The Court of Appeal disagreed. Boreham, J., who gave the judgment of the court which was presided over by the Lord Chief Justice, said:

> "It seems to us . . . that the crucial question in circumstances such as those is this: were there other methods which were suitable and adequate for disposing of this matter? Narrowing that question to the particular circumstances of this case, was twelve months' youth custody adequate to reflect the gravity of the offences? No doubt in considering that question the Court will hesitate before making use of Section 53(2) and will confine itself, if it properly can, to twelve months' youth custody. But where such a sentence is clearly inadequate, then in our judgment the court should take advantage of Section 53(2) and pass the appropriate term of custodial sentence."

10.37 It was made plain in *Dewberry and Stone*[33] that an order for detention under Section 53(2) should not normally be less than two years on the basis that the difference between anything much less and 12 months was not so great that it could be argued that 12 months' youth custody was inadequate. In *Storey and others*[34] it was also held that in determining the length of a punitive or deterrent sentence, the youth of the offender would be a mitigating factor as compared with a similar offence committed by an adult. This case involved the setting fire to a school causing £37,000 worth of damage. The three appellants, who were just under or just over 16 at the time, pleaded guilty to arson. None had previous findings of guilt and there were reports to the effect that none was considered likely to repeat the offence. There was no evidence of psychological disturbance. They were sentenced to five years' detention under Section 53(2) and this was reduced on appeal to three years, the court indicating that with offenders of this age the gravity of the offence should be assessed more with regard to the appellants' intentions rather than to the cost of putting right the damage done and that a period of detention should not be set so long that they could not see the end of it.

---

33 (1985) 7 Cr.App.R.(S) 202.
34 (1984) 6 Cr.App.R.(S) 104.

10.38 Guidance on the inter-relationship between long-term detention and youth custody was given by Lord Lane, C.J. in *Fairhurst and others*.[35] In this case the point was made that the poles of judicial opinion were represented by *Oakes*[36] and *Butler*,[37] both of which with hindsight seemed to have gone too far in opposite directions. A balance had to be struck on the one hand between the desirability of keeping youthful offenders under the age of 17 out of long terms of custody and on the other the necessity of ensuring that serious offences committed by youths of that age should be met with sentences adequate to provide both the appropriate punishment and also the necessary deterrent effect – and in certain cases to provide a measure of protection for the public.

10.39 The Lord Chief Justice accordingly made it clear that it was not necessary in order to impose a sentence under Section 53(2) that the crime committed should be one of exceptional gravity, but said that equally it was not good sentencing practice to pass such a sentence simply because 12 months' youth custody seemed to be on the low side. He also emphasised that if an offence merited a sentence of less than two years but more than 12 months for an offender over 17, then in respect of an offender under 17, the sentence should presumably be one of youth custody, the point being that it could not be said that the differences between a sentence of, for example, 21 months' and one of 12 months' youth custody was so great that 12 months could be regarded as an inappropriate term. However a sentence of less the two years' detention could be imposed concurrently or consecutively on one offence when the offender was charged with another offence of sufficient gravity for a sentence under Section 53(2) of two years or more to be ordered.[38]

10.40 Turning to the problem of a defendent under the age of 17 charged with two offences, one carrying a sentence of 14 years of more, the other with a lower maximum, the court pointed out that generally speaking it was not proper to pass a sentence under Section 53(2) on the first matter which it would not otherwise merit, in order to compensate for the fact that 12 months' youth custody was inadequate on the second. But where it could truly be said that the offender's behaviour in respect of the second matter was part and parcel of the events giving rise to the first, then such a sentence might properly be passed.

35 (1986) 8 Cr.App.R.(S) 346.
36 (1983) 5 Cr.App.R.(S) 389.
37 (1984) 6 Cr.App.R.(S) 236; see para. 10.36 *supra*.
38 *Gaskin* (1985) 7 Cr.App.R.(S) 28.

10.41 As regards the difficulty of consecutive or concurrent sentences where the first offence carried a maximum of 14 years or more for an adult but where the second carried a maximum penalty of less than 14 years, or where it came before the Crown Court as a result of a committal for sentence under the Magistrates' Courts Act 1980, Section 37, it was pointed out that it was undesirable for sentences of Section 53(2) detention and youth custody to be passed consecutively or concurrently with each other.[39] The only way out might be to impose no separate penalty on the second matter.[40]

10.42 Finally the court drew attention to the fact that detention centre and youth custody orders were reduced by the time spent in custody awaiting trial or sentence but pointed out that this rule did not apply to sentences of detention under Section 53(2).

Detention in default or for contempt

10.43 By the Criminal Justice Act 1982, Section 9, where a young offender aged 17 to 20 is in default of payment of a fine or other sum, or is in contempt of court or guilty of any kindred offence, the court may commit him to be detained for a term not exceeding the term of imprisonment that it would have had the power to impose had not imprisonment for young offenders been abolished. Before making such an order the court must be of the opinion that no other method of dealing with him is appropriate (Section 1(5)). By Section 2(1) the court is required for the purpose of determining whether there is any other appropriate method of dealing with such an offender to obtain and consider information about the circumstances and shall take into account any information before the court which is relevant to his character and physical and mental condition. It is not necessary to obtain a social inquiry report nor is it necessary for the defendant to be legally represented. By Section 2(5) and (7) a magistrates' court dealing with such an offender must state in open court the reason for its opinion that no other method of dealing with him is appropriate and cause that reason to be specified in the committal warrant and entered in the court register.

Custody for life

10.44 Offenders aged 18 to 20 convicted of murder must be sentenced to custody for life under the Criminal Justice Act 1982, Section 8(1). By

---

39 *Gaskin* (note 38 *supra*); *McKenna* (1985) 7 Cr.App.R.(S) 348.
40 If there were a successful appeal on the first matter, the Court of Appeal would be entitled under the Criminal Appeals Act 1968 s. 4(2) to pass whatever sentence seemed appropriate on the second count: *Dolan* (1976) 62 Cr.App.R. 36.

Section 8(2) there is a discretionary power to sentence an offender aged 17 to 20 who commits an offence punishable with life imprisonment in the case of an adult to custody for life, but this is a power that would only be appropriate in the most serious cases. *Turton*[41] is recent authority for the proposition that it should not normally be imposed unless the offender is subject to a marked degree of mental instability.

Detention during Her Majesty's pleasure

10.45 In the case of young persons aged 14 to 17 convicted of murder, the court must impose detention during Her Majesty's pleasure under the Children and Young Persons Act 1933, Section 53(1).

---

41 [1986] Crim.L.R. 642.

CHAPTER 11

Mentally Abnormal Offenders

11.01 So for as the Crown Court is concerned, the question of mental impairment arises primarily at two stages in the criminal process. First, at the trial stage when a defendant is either found unfit to plead under the Criminal Procedure (Insanity) Act 1984, Section 4, or on raising the defence of insanity, when he is found not guilty by reason of insanity under Section 2. In both of these situations the defendant will be ordered to be detained under the Mental Health Act 1983, Section 41. Neither constitutes a sentencing problem and accordingly both fall outside the scope of this book.

11.02 It is with the question of impairment at the second (sentencing) stage that the sentencer in all trial courts becomes concerned and complex problems of disposal arise, when the offender has pleaded guilty or been convicted, and is then found to be suffering from certain forms of mental disorder. At this stage the sentencer is concerned with the offender's mental state at the time of sentence and although that condition may also be a continuation of his condition at the time of committing the offence, it may on the other hand be an intervening condition, with the result that there is no causal connection between the offender's mental disorder and the offence in respect of which sentence is to be imposed.[1]

11.03 In this chapter we shall accordingly discuss the following matters:
(1) Hospital orders;
(2) Definitions of abnormality;
(3) Alternatives to hospital orders (including psychiatric probation orders and guardianship orders);
(4) Restriction orders; and
(5) Use of imprisonment.

---

1 See *McBride* (1972) C.S.P. F2.2(a).

HOSPITAL ORDERS

11.04 A court may make a hospital order under the Mental Health Act 1983, Section 37, subject to the following requirements.

(1) The offence in respect of which the person is convicted must be punishable by the court concerned with imprisonment.

(2) The court must be satisfied by the evidence of two registered medical practitioners that:

(a) the offender is suffering from mental illness, psychopathic disorder, severe mental impairment or mental impairment; and

(b) the mental disorder warrants the offender's detention in a hospital for medical treatment and in the case of psychopathic disorder or mental impairment that such treatment is likely to alleviate the condition or prevent deterioration.

(3) The court must be of the opinion, having regard to all the circumstances (including the nature of the offence, the character and antecedents of the offender, and the other available methods of dealing with him), that a hospital order is the most suitable method of dealing with him.

(4) The court must be satisfied that arrangements have been made for the offender's admission to the hospital specified by the medical evidence within 28 days of the making of the order (pending which the court may order conveyance to and detention in a place of safety).

It is also to be noted that new powers were introduced under the Mental Health Act 1983 to provide alternatives to remand to prison for medical reports. Thus by Section 35 a person may be remanded to hospital for periods up to a total of 12 weeks for a report on his mental condition. A Crown Court may also remand an accused person to hospital for treatment provided there is evidence from two registered practitioners that he is suffering from a mental disorder that requires treatment by means of detention in hospital and that a bed is available (Section 36). By Section 38 a court may also make an interim hospital order for an initial maximum period of 12 weeks, renewable for further periods of up to 28 days to a maximum of 6 months. Before making such an order, the court must be satisfied that in substantial terms the conditions exist for making a full order, with the addition that one of the registered medical practitioners must be employed at the hospital where the person is to be detained. Such an order enables the doctors to assess from more prolonged examination how the person is likely to react to the regime in a psychiatric hospital.

11.05 As there is no procedure by which a person may be found unfit to plead in the magistrates' courts, by Section 37(3) of the 1983 Act, where a person is charged before the justices with an offence in respect of which a hospital order based on *mental illness* or *severe mental impairment* could be made, the magistrates may make a hospital order without convicting him if satisfied that the accused "did the act or made the omission charged".

11.06 The effect of a hospital order is detention for one year in the first instance, renewable where the responsible medical officer considers further detention necessary for the protection of the public or in the interests of the offender's health.

Definitions of abnormality

11.07 In Section 1 of the Act, the general term "mental disorder" is defined as "mental illness, arrested or incomplete development of mind, psychopathic disorder, and any other disorder or disability of mind". Of the special categories of disorder listed in Section 37, mental illness is not defined, but the remaining three categories are defined in Section 1 as follows:

> "'Severe mental impairment' [formerly severe subnormality] means a state of arrested or incomplete development of mind which includes severe impairment of intelligence and social functioning, and is associated with abnormally aggressive or seriously irresponsible conduct on the part of the person concerned . . .
> . . . 'mental impairment' [formerly subnormality] means a state of arrested or incomplete development of mind (not amounting to severe mental impairment) which includes significant impairment of intelligence and social functioning and is associated with abnormally aggressive or seriously irresponsible conduct . . .
> 'psychopathic disorder' means a persistent disorder or disability of mind (whether or not including subnormality of intelligence) which results in abnormally aggressive or seriously irresponsible conduct on the part of the person concerned; . . ."

Alternatives to hospital orders

11.08 Ordinary principles suggest that even where the conditions for making a hospital order are satisfied, the alternatives of making a psychiatric probation order or a guardianship order should be considered first.

11.09 The conditions for making a *psychiatric probation order* are set out in the Powers of Criminal Courts Act 1973, Section 3. This section enables the court to make such an order including a requirement that the offender shall submit to treatment by or under the direction of a duly qualified medical practitioner "with a view to the improvement of the offender's mental condition". Before making an order with such a requirement, the court must be satisfied on the evidence of a duly qualified medical practitioner (approved for the purposes of the 1983 Act, Section 12) that the mental condition of the offender is such as "requires and may be susceptible to treatment" but *not* such as to warrant detention under a hospital order. The period of probation may be not less than six months and not more than three years, and the treatment required may be for the whole of the period or during such part of it as may be specified in the order.

11.10   The treatment required must be one of the following:
  (1) Treatment as a resident patient in a hospital or mental nursing home (not a "special" hospital);
  (2) Such treatment as a non-resident patient as may be specified; or
  (3) Such treatment by or under the direction of such duly qualified medical practitioner as may be specified.
Again before making such an order the court must be satisfied that arrangements have been made for the offender's treatment.[2]

11.11   The Court of Appeal has indicated that a psychiatric probation order may be employed in cases where the offender has committed offences of substantial gravity such as arson with intent to endanger life[2a] and indecent assault,[3] but has stressed that it should not be employed in serious cases unless there is a reasonable chance that it will succeed in its object.[4]

11.12   The *guardianship order* is provided as a direct alternative to a hospital order and is subject to the same statutory restrictions. Its effect is to place the offender in the care of the local authority social services department and could perhaps be particularly useful where an offender is reluctant to accept treatment under a probation order but where detention in hospital is not warranted and there is no immediate risk to the public.

11.13   Equally, although an offender may be suffering from some mental disorder for which treatment and facilities are available, the circumstances of the offence may only indicate that some lesser non-custodial disposal is appropriate, such as a discharge, a fine or ordinary

2 For the power to include a requirement of treatment for a mental condition in a
   supervision order in respect of children, see the Children and Young Persons Act 1969,
   s. 12(4) and (5). See also Chapter 12, note 52 *infra*.
2a *Hoof* (1980) 2 Cr.App.R.(S) 299.
3 *McDonald* (1983) 5 Cr.App.R.(S) 419.
4 *West* (1975) C.S.P. F1.2(c).

probation. The converse is also true, *i.e.* that although an offender may, for example, have a condition treatable under a psychiatric probation order (and indeed may very much wish to be given the opportunity of such an order), the offence may be too grave for it to be dealt with in this way, or the offender too dangerous for the risk to be taken. These are matters which go to the root of the sentencing process, but the problems sometimes arise in a different or more pronounced form where the court feels obliged to consider other forms of custodial sentence as alternatives to hospital orders.

11.14   The point to be made is that even where all the conditions set out in Section 37 are satisfied, there is no obligation on the court to make a hospital order. Indeed as already indicated, before making a hospital order, the court must consider that it is "the most suitable method" of dealing with the offender, which presupposes consideration of all the other methods available first, including other forms of custody. Anxious though the court may be to consider treatment for abnormal offenders, it would be unrealistic for it to discount or give lower priority to the risk of danger to the public in situations where the only security available under a hospital order is that of a local hospital without secure accommodation: in other words where the court making the order knows that there is no access to a regional secure unit or to a special hospital. This is not the place to discuss social policy in relation to medical and social service provision for the mentally ill. It is sufficient to note, as others have done, that while the relevant recommendations of the Butler Committee[5] remain unimplemented, financial stringency in recent years has brought about the reduction of places or beds in psychiatric hospitals and that during this period, the prison population has continued to rise. It is also well known that a significant proportion of the prison population at any one time is mentally ill.[5a] It is against this background that the sentencer may reflect upon the realistic nature of the methods of disposal available. Once a hospital order is made, responsibility rests with the hospital or the Home Secretary.

RESTRICTION ORDERS

11.15   As already indicated, the Mental Health Act 1983, Section 41, enables a restriction order to be made, where, having regard to

---

5 *Report of the Committee on Mentally Abnormal Offenders* (1975) H.M.S.O. (Cmnd 6244).
5a See *e.g.* Butler Committee Report (note 5 *supra*) para. 3.19.

(1) The nature of the offence;

(2) The offender's antecedents; and

(3) The risk of further offences if released,

the court thinks that it is necessary for the protection of the public from "serious harm". Restriction may be for a specified period or without limit of time. Before a restriction order is made at least one medical practitioner must give oral evidence as to the offender's condition.

11.16 It is emphasised that only a Crown Court may make a restriction order, and in *Gardiner*[6] Lord Parker, C. J. went to considerable lengths to spell out the effects of a hospital order in relation to the additional safeguards provided by restriction orders (then made under the Mental Health Act 1959, Sections 60 and 65 respectively) as follows:

"It must be borne in mind that when only a hospital order is made:

(1) It is only authority for the patient's detention for one year in the first instance. This authority can be renewed if the medical practitioner in charge of the treatment of the patient (whom I will call the "responsible medical officer") reports to the hospital managers that it appears to him that further detention is necessary in the interests of the patient's health or safety or for the protection of others. The hospital managers, however, are not bound to act on such a report and may refuse to extend the period and accordingly discharge the patient. Further, if the patient is 16 or over, he or his nearest relative can apply, at certain intervals, to a Mental Health Review Tribunal, who may in any case direct the patient's discharge and must do so, if satisfied that he is no longer suffering from a mental disorder or that his further detention is not necessary.

(2) The patient can be discharged at any time by the hospital managers, whose power is unlimited, or by the responsible medical officer, whose power is again unlimited, or by a Mental Health Tribunal as already stated.

(3) Once discharged, the patient is no longer liable to recall.

(4) A patient who is absent without leave cannot be retaken into custody and indeed ceases to be liable to be detained: (a) if he is over 21 and is classified as psychopathic or sub-normal, after six months' absence, (b) in any other case, after 28 days' absence.

If, however, a restriction order is made in addition to a hospital order; (i) there is authority to detain the patient for at any rate the duration of that order, though the Secretary of State may terminate it at any time if satisfied that it is no longer required for the protection of the public; (ii) the patient can be discharged only with the consent of the Secretary of State or by the Secretary of State himself; (iii) the Secretary of State has power in discharging the patient himself to make the discharge conditional, in which case the patient remains liable to recall during the period up to the expiration of the restriction order. This power is particularly useful as a means of keeping a discharged patient under the supervision of a probation officer or mental welfare officer for a longer period than

---

6 (1967) 51 Cr.App.R. 187.

S–H

would be possible if there were no restriction order; (iv) lastly, a patient who is absent without leave may be taken into custody again at any time."

He went on to emphasise the role of the restriction order in protecting the public from the discharge of "dangerous" patients, making the point that without a restriction order

". . . it is inevitable that the hospital's first concern is the welfare of the patient and this does result in some cases in a patient who is subject to a hospital order alone securing his discharge earlier than he would do if he were also subject to a restriction order."

He then added that a Home Secretary might refuse to order the release of a patient no longer in need of treatment, in order to guard against "the possibility of relapse leading to further crime". The Lord Chief Justice made it clear that he was not suggesting the making of restriction orders in every case but added that it was "very advisable" that such orders should be made in "all cases" where it was considered necessary to protect the public. He said:

"Thus in, for example, the case of crimes of violence, and of the more serious sexual offences, particularly if the prisoner has a record of such offences, or if there is a history of mental disorder involving violent behaviour, it is suggested that there must be compelling reasons to explain why a restriction order should not be made."

11.17   The requirement that a restriction order should be imposed to protect the public from "serious harm" was the result of an amendment to the Mental Health Act 1959, Section 65 by the Mental Health (Amendment) Act 1982, following a recommendation by the Butler Committee that a restriction order should not be employed in respect of the "petty recidivist because of the virtual certainty that he will persist in similar offences in the future".[7]

11.18   To date "serious harm" has not been interpreted by the Court of Appeal but decisions prior to the 1982 Act made it clear that a restriction order may be made even where the offender has no previous history of violence.[8] It has also been held that a restriction order may be made where there is no evidence of a propensity to future violence provided there is a risk of the offender absconding and gaining his freedom by remaining at large for the statutory period.[9] In *Smith*[10] the appellant pleaded guilty to twenty counts of obtaining by deception involving relatively modest sums of money by means of fraudulent

---

7   *Op. cit.* (note 5 *supra*), para. 14.24.
8   *e.g. Smith* (1974) C.S.P. F2.4(b).
9   *Toland* (1973) C.S.P. F2.4(c).
10   Note 8 *supra*.

betting tip schemes and asked for 738 similar offences to be taken into consideration. But as Lawton, L.J., who gave the judgment in the Court of Appeal said, this was an unusual case in that although at first sight the offence of fraud was not one which would attract a restriction order, according to the medical evidence, the motive for the offences was the appellant's attempt to get his own back on those of his family about whom he had paranoid delusions. He went on to say that "antecedents" were not confined to previous convictions and included the whole history of the appellant which in this case included a history of incipient schizophrenia which had developed into the full mental illness. Lawton, L.J. then went on to say:

> "Was there a risk of his committing futher offences if at large? Having regard to his paranoid delusions and his desire to protect himself by carrying around a loaded air pistol and a sword stick, it seems to us that the doctors were justified in the conclusions which some of them reached, that he would be likely to commit offences of a violent nature."

11.19 In *Toland*,[11] the Court of Appeal upheld the imposition of a restriction order in the case of an appellant, aged 19, who was convicted of burglary and was described an "an anti-social person" and "a pest", mainly it seems because of a propensity to abscond and commit offences while unlawfully at large. As Roskill, L.J. concluded:

> ". . . he is somebody from whom the public is entitled to be protected because when he is put in open hospitals he absconds and, of course, unless a restriction order is made he may through absconding obtain ultimate freedom."

11.20 The point is that the assessment of the need for protection from "serious harm" must arise from a consideration of a totality of the three matters set out in Section 41 of the Mental Health Act 1983. In *Eaton*[12] a hospital order combined with an unlimited restriction order was substituted for a term of 18 months' imprisonment in respect of a woman convicted of damaging two panes of glass in a telephone kiosk to the value of £4, where it is difficult to believe that apart from her history of behavioural problems, a sentence of imprisonment would have been justified. The Court of Appeal concluded that her condition merited her treatment in Rampton and that "all the evidence" was in favour of a hospital order. In the limited report of this case in Thomas's *Encyclopedia of Current Sentencing Practice* the court went on to decide from the medical reports that the appellant was a danger to the public and that on "ordinary principles" a restriction should be made. In *Allison*,[13]

---

11 Note 9 *supra*.
12 (1975) C.S.P. F2.4(d).
13 (1977) C.S.P. F2.4(d).

where hospital and restriction orders were imposed in respect of the appellant, who had pleaded guilty to the theft of a purse containing £4.80 from his sister, Michael Davies, J., giving the judgment of the court which was presided over by Lord Widgery, C.J., dismissed the appeal saying, "The fact that the offence itself was of a minor character is neither here nor there." He then went on to say that the period of time for which the appellant was treated depended entirely on his progress.

11.21 It is clear from the above decisions and from the decision in *Haynes*[14] that restriction orders should not be imposed on a tariff basis. Although the Court has the discretion to impose restrictions for fixed periods, whether a fixed period or an unlimited order is imposed depends not on the seriousness of the offence, but on the medical evidence as to the period at the end of which it would be safe to allow the release of the offender.

11.22 It is of interest that although by Section 41 the court is obliged to consider the evidence of two doctors, of whom one must give oral evidence, it is clear from the decision of the Court of Appeal in *Royse*[15] that it is not obliged to follow the medical recommendations as to the need to impose a restriction order. As Dunn, L.J. observed in giving the judgment of the court:

> "The section puts the responsibility squarely on the shoulders of the judge . . . if, in his opinion, it is necessary for the protection of the public to do so, whether or not the doctors advise such an order should be made . . ."

11.23 As a magistrates' court cannot make a restriction order, if it considers such an order is desirable it should commit the offender to the Crown Court under Section 43 for both a hospital order and a restriction order to be made there. The disadvantage of this procedure is that if the Crown Court decides that such orders are not appropriate, it is limited to the other sentencing powers available to the magistrates. Accordingly Section 43(4) provides that, if a magistrates' court is of the opinion that greater punishment than it could impose itself is merited, *unless* a restriction order combined with a hospital order is made, it should commit the offender for sentence under the Magistrates' Courts Act 1980, Section 38 which gives the Crown Court unfettered powers of sentence. The Mental Health Act 1983, Section 44, enables a magistrates' court, in the case of an offender in respect of whom the requirements for the making of a hospital order are satisfied, to commit to hospital pending disposal by the Crown Court.

---

14 (1981) 3 Cr.App.R.(S) 330.
15 (1981) 3 Cr.App.R.(S) 58.

11.24   If a court is considering making a restriction order, the defendant should be legally represented.[16]

USE OF IMPRISONMENT FOR ABNORMAL OFFENDERS

11.25   The sentencing problems really begin when either a hospital order cannot be made or for various reasons such an order is not considered appropriate. It may simply be that the conditions for making an order are not satisfied, perhaps because the doctors cannot agree on the diagnosis, or because the conditon (*e.g.* personality disorder) does not fall within one of the statutory categories, or because in the case of psychopathic disorder or mental impairment the condition is not susceptible to treatment. In such cases the whole range of sentencing options arise but against the background of the medical considerations.

11.26   Once again the main sentencing problems are likely to be in regard to whether and if so, for how long, a custodial sentence should be imposed. If there is no realistic opportunity for treatment within the penal system and if they are faced with what is patently bizarre, seriously anti-social or potentially dangerous behaviour, courts may be tempted to order longer sentences than would otherwise have been imposed in order to protect the offender from himself or more likely to protect the public. As many have pointed out, there is a tendency both to over-predict and to over-estimate "dangerousness" and indeed to exaggerate the degree of protection provided by a custodial sentence. However where a custodial sentence is decided upon, the guiding principle that the Court of Appeal has indicated should be applied (while sometimes falling short of its own standard) is that of proportionality. That is to say, where an offender suffering from mental abnormality cannot be accommodated, or for some other reason cannot be made the subject of a hospital order, for example, because he is a danger to the community, it is wrong in principle to impose a sentence of imprisonment which is out of proportion to the gravity of the offence simply to ensure that he is contained. As has already been indicated, the general principle is supported by ample authority and is illustrated by the decision in *Clarke*,[17] where a young woman with a record of convictions for relatively minor offences was originally sentenced to 18 months' imprisonment for criminal damage a flower pot valued at £1. It seems that she had been made the subject of a hospital order on a previous occasion but had been released. On this occasion she had

---

16   *Blackwood* (1974) 59 Cr.App.R. 170.
17   (1975) 61 Cr.App.R. 320.

deliberately committed the offence on returning to hospital and refusing to leave. On appeal Lawton, L.J. said it was wrong to impose such a sentence in order to protect both the public and the appellant from herself and went on to say:

> "Her Majesty's Courts are not dustbins into which the social services can sweep difficult members of the public. Still less should Her Majesty's judges use their sentencing powers to dispose of those who are socially inconvenient. If the courts become disposers of those who are socially inconvenient, the road ahead would lead to the destruction of liberty. It should be clearly understood that Her Majesty's judges stand on that road barring the way."

He went on to say that sentences should fit crimes and that the crime in this case was breaking a flower pot worth £1 in a fit of temper. The sentence was varied to a fine of £2.

11.27 However, in the case of *Scanlon*,[18] although Waller, L.J. made it clear that it was "absolutely wrong for the criminal courts to be put in a position of having to apply the provisions of the criminal law and sentences of imprisonment simply because there (were) no proper facilities in hospitals for this appellant", sentences of three years' imprisonment for criminal damage to the door of her flat and possessing an offensive weapon (a carving knife) which he said he found "very difficult to justify", were upheld in order to protect the public. In this case, it seems that the decision in *Clarke* was not cited, but since then the general principle set out above and applied in *Clarke* has been followed in a number of cases such as *Hook*[19] and *Foster*.[20]

11.28 The question of danger to the community was considered in the interesting case of *Rose*[21], where the appellant, who was 16 at the time of the offence, was sentenced to 18 years for manslaughter, robbery and indecent assault. The medical evidence was that he was suffering from a personality disorder which did not fall within the provisions of the Mental Health Act 1959 but which would make him a danger to the public in the future. The judgement of Lawton, L.J. is worth setting out at some length as illustrating the principles to be applied in what one might regard as one of the more extreme situations. He said:

> "The basis of the plea of manslaughter was clearly that the appellant had not got the requisite intention which would have been necessary to prove a case of murder. The learned judge, however, being conscious that this appellant was likely to be a danger to the public for a considerable time,

---

18 (1979) 1 Cr.App.R.(S) 60.
19 (1980) 2 Cr.App.R.(S) 353.
20 (1981) 3 Cr.App.R.(S) 112.
21 (1973) C.S.P. A7.3(a), F3.2(h).

passed a sentence which would have in his view have given protection from him.

In our view the appropriate course in a case like this would have been to have passed a sentence of life imprisonment, the reason being that the appellant had a personality disorder and marked emotional immaturity, and it would have been both in the public interest and in mercy to this young man for the date of his release to be left to the prison authorities. They would have been able to watch him grow up and no doubt when the appropriate time came that they could be certain that he was no longer a danger to the public they could have taken the appropriate steps to procure his release. But since the Judge had decided to pass a determinate sentence then this Court has to consider whether in all the circumstances the sentence was of the appropriate length and it has come to the conclusion it was not."

The sentence was reduced to ten years.

11.29   On the other hand in *Gouws*[22] the appellant's sentence of six years' imprisonment, described by Skinner, J. as "severe for simple arson," was upheld on the basis of the danger to the public. Gouws had a long history of disturbed behaviour and was thought to be suffering from severe psychopathic disorder, but was not considered to be acceptable to a special hospital. It is plain that it is not easy to reconcile this case with the principle set out above.

---

22   (1981) 3 Cr.App.R.(S) 325.

CHAPTER 12

Community Service and Probation

12.01 In this chapter we discuss the two main measures in which the probation service is involved: community service and probation. In the former we deal with such matters as:

(1) Use of the order;
(2) Social inquiry reports;
(3) Length of the order;
(4) Breach;
(5) Revocation; and
(6) Extension of the period of work.

Under probation we discuss:

(1) Criteria for making an order;
(2) Requirements of the order;
(3) Breach;
(4) Commission of a further offence; and
(5) Discharge.

We also consider supervision orders and intermediate treatment as well as care orders to deal with young offenders.

COMMUNITY SERVICE

12.02 The community service order was introduced in 1972 for offenders aged 17 and over and was extended to offenders aged 16 in 1982. It is now governed by the Powers of Criminal Courts Act 1973, Section 14 (as amended) which enables courts to make a community service order, *i.e.* to order the carrying out of unpaid work under the direction of "the relevant officer", in respect of offenders aged 16 and over convicted of an offence punishable with imprisonment. The number of hours that may be ordered to be completed is not less than 40 and not more than 240 (120 in the case of an offender aged 16).

12.03 Before an order is made the offender must have consented and the court must have considered a report about him and his circumstances and be satisfied that he is a suitable person to perform such work. The court must be further satisfied that arrangements can be made for the offender to perform the work which is to be ordered in the petty sessions area in which he resides or will reside (Section 14(2) and (2A)).

12.04 In order that an informed consent may be given Section 14(5) requires that the court should explain in ordinary language the purpose and effect of the order and its requirements and consequences together with the possibilities for review by both parties. The requirements of the order are set out in Section 15 and are as follows:

(1) The offender must report when required to the relevant officer and notify him of any change in his address.

(2) The offender must perform the work at the times instructed until the hours specified in the order have been completed.

(3) The work must be completed within 12 months unless the time period is subsequently extended by the court in accordance with Section 17(1).

Section 15(3) requires that so far as possible work should not be ordered which would conflict with the offender's religious beliefs or interfere with his work or attendance at school, etc.

12.05 According to Walker[1] the history of community service illustrates what he calls the "ambiguity" of penal measures: the appeal both to punishment and reform (set out in the passage to which he refers from the Wootton Report,[2] which in 1970 recommended the measure). Since its introduction there has been much discussion about whether the community service order was only to be used as an alternative to imprisonment or not. Certainly the Home Office Circular No. 230/1972 on the Criminal Justice Act 1972 said that the courts and the public would see it as such, and the third edition of *The Sentence of the Court* described that as its primary purpose. However in *Lawrence*[3] Lord Lane, C. J. indicated that its use was not restricted in this way, observing that a short period of community service would usually be reserved for cases where the court did not intend to impose a custodial sentence. Accordingly the fourth edition of *The Sentence of the Court*[4] recognises that although it was originally regarded as "a realistic alternative for a custodial sentence", as a result of "subsequent custom and practice" the order had come to be regarded as a sentence in its own right.

1 N. Walker, *Sentencing: Theory, Law and Practice* (1985) Butterworths, p. 279.
2 *Non-Custodial and Semi-Custodial Penalties*, Report of the Advisory Council on the Penal System (1970) H.M.S.O.
3 (1982) 4 Cr.App.R.(S) 69.
4 At p. 41.

12.06 Having said that, it is obviously important for court clerks to make a note of what is said when the order is made so that if the Chairman or judge states that a community service order is to be a direct alternative to a custodial sentence, this can be taken into account in the event of proceedings for breach (see below). It is equally important to note when community service is expressed *not* to be as an alternative to imprisonment, lest on breach the offender is given a custodial sentence that he would not have received in the first place.

12.07 A good deal of research activity has been directed towards this new measure[5] and much has been claimed for it at various times. However, sober reflection on the reconviction rates (imprecise a yardstick though they may be) suggests that community service is no more "successful" at reducing crime than any other measure. It is, however, cheaper than imprisonment and perhaps more importantly, probably does less harm to offenders in terms of contamination and social damage. More than that, as the Wootton Committee pointed out, in some circumstances it gives effect to the old adage that "the punishment should fit the crime", emphasises reparation to society and provides the offender with the possibilities of developing a positive outlook to his own circumstances and offending.

12.08 However, as Judge Peter Goldstone pointed out in an article "A Fresh Look at Community Service Orders",[6] in which he addresses many of the practical problems to be found in making and enforcing community service orders, community service should not be used where the defendant needs:

> "the help and support and disciplinary guidance of the probation service . . . Orders should not be made to encourage the work-shy, or to show the idle the errors of their ways. They are a penal alternative – not a social reform."

Use of community service

12.09 In *Clarke*[7] Lord Lane, C.J., giving guidance on the use of partially suspended sentences of imprisonment, said that before imposing such a sentence the court should ask itself the following question:

---

5 See *e.g.* J. Sussex, *Community Service by Offenders – Year One in Kent* (1974) Barry Rose; K. Pease *et al.*, *Community Service Orders* (1975) H.O.R.S. Report no. 29; K. Pease *et al.*, *Community Service Assessed in 1976* (1977) H.O.R.S. Report no. 39; K. Pease and W. McWilliams (eds.), *Community Service by Order* (1980) Scottish Academic Press; Stephen Shaw, *Community Service – A Guide for Sentencers* (1983) Prison Reform Trust.
6 *The Magistrate* (May 1982), p. 71.
7 (1982) 4 Cr.App.R.(S) 197.

"First of all, is this a case where a custodial sentence is really necessary? If it is not, it should pass a non-custodial sentence. But if it is necessary, then the court should ask itself secondly this: can we make a community service order as an equivalent to imprisonment, or can we suspend the whole sentence? That problem requires very careful consideration. It is easy to slip into a partly suspended sentence because the court does not have the courage of its own convictions. That temptation must be resisted. If it is possible to make a community service order or to suspend the whole of the sentence, then of course that should be done."

12.10 The result of some kind of satisfaction with the positive aspects of the measure, together with its "penal ambiguity", has been a willingness on the part of the Court of Appeal to extend the use of community service to deal with a wide range of offences, including offences of a seriousness that would have ruled out community service in the past. Thus it seems clear that even with relatively serious violence, community service may be properly imposed, particularly where a defendant is of previous good character, has committed an isolated act of violence and perhaps has only done so as a result of provocation.[8] However, it has been emphasised that community service should not be imposed for a case of serious violence resulting in grave injuries.[9] Where to draw the line is obviously a matter of some difficulty, but perhaps the appellant in *West*[10] was rather fortunate in having his sentence of six months varied to one of 150 hours community service. In this case the appellant pleaded guilty to two counts of assault occasioning actual bodily harm and one of criminal damage. While driving his car he became annoyed at the driving of another vehicle. He cut in front of it, forcing it to stop, and then attacked it with a pick axe handle which he took from the boot of his car. He smashed all the windows of the car and the driver and passenger suffered cuts from flying glass. His record was described as indifferent but its "outstanding feature" was that his last conviction for violence had been nine years previously when he was in his early twenties. It was said that it was abundantly clear that his conduct merited punishment and that "he should not be allowed to get away with such outrageous behaviour," but community service was thought to be adequate.

12.11 It also seems clear that community service is not necessarily wrong in principle for burglary of commercial premises and theft of goods of substantial value or even on occasion, burglary of dwelling houses.

---

8 *McDiarmid* (1980) 2 Cr.App.R.(S) 130.
9 *Heyfron* (1980) 2 Cr.App.R.(S) 230.
10 (1983) 5 Cr.App.R.(S) 206.

12.12   In *Brown (M.A.)*[11] the appellant, aged 19, with no previous convictions, pleaded guilty to burglary at the premises of his employer, allowing his keys to be used by his co-accused to unlock the stock room. Goods worth £2,850 were stolen. The appellant was sentenced to Borstal training: his co-defendant, an older man with a substantial criminal record, was sentenced to 12 months' imprisonment. McCullough, J., giving judgment, observed:

> "We have come to the conclusion that, but for the availability nowadays of orders for community service, a custodial sentence is entirely appropriate, having regard for the breach of trust. But this case is tailor-made for a community service order. We have here a first offender – indeed the position could have been the same if he had what I might call a 'light' criminal record; he came from a stable home background with a wife and a young child; he had a good work record; and it now appears that a job is available to him. There is apparently genuine remorse and the risk of re-offending appears slight."

12.13   As regards burglaries of dwelling-houses, even a person with good character, must as a general rule expect a custodial sentence, especially for offences committed at night. However, in a number of cases the Court of Appeal has decided that community service may be imposed in cases of burglary of dwelling-houses even if the defendant has previous convictions for similar offences, provided the circumstances are sufficiently "exceptional". Thus in *Afzal*[12] the defendant had "undergone a change", and in *Stanbury*[13] there was a long interval between the offences with substantial reform in the meantime. In *Seymour*[14] the Court of Appeal found evidence of a change of heart in an 18-year-old who pleaded guilty to burglary of a dwelling-house, was arrested after a chase through several back gardens and who had been sentenced on a number of previous occasions for burglaries. In the course of his judgment, May, L.J. said:

> "Where one has an offence of burglary committed by a young man of this age, who has already had so substantial a past record of burglary offences, the Court naturally thinks long and hard before taking the view that a sentence other than a custodial sentence, so as to remove the convicted burglar from circulation for a time for the protection of the public, should be imposed. A sentence other than a custodial one is perhaps justified, however, particularly in the case of a young offender, if there is any indication that he is beginning to realise the extent of his past criminality and the situation to which offences of a similar nature will take him if they are persisted in . . ."

11   (1981) 3 Cr.App.R.(S) 294.
12   (1981) 3 Cr.App.R.(S) 93.
13   (1981) 3 Cr.App.R.(S) 243.
14   (1983) 5 Cr.App.R.(S) 85.

Social inquiry reports

12.14 It is undeniable that when community service is ordered in this way for this degree of gravity of offence it makes for a certain inconsistency not only in actual sentencing but also in approach. Probation officers have received criticism on occasions for a lack of realism in their recommendations but if the Court of Appeal is prepared to put community service so high up on the tariff, the service is bound to explore the possibilities of community service even in the case of relatively grave offences and even where the offender's criminal record is bad. Similarly counsel will be bound to follow it up in mitigation with the risk that this brings of creating unrealistic expectations on the part of the offender. A further difficulty that arises out of the requirement that a report should be obtained before an order may be made is that it has been held that when a court adjourns for this purpose and the report shows the offender to be suitable for such an order, the court ought to make it because otherwise feelings of injustice would be aroused in the accused.[15]

12.15 The point that emerges from these and other decisions is that where a court adjourns for the purposes of obtaining a social inquiry report and the defendant's assessment for community service, it should make it clear where is is appropriate to do so that these reports are simply required to complete the picture and that "all the options are open" when the case comes back for the offender to be sentenced.[16]

Length of order

12.16 Calculating the length of an order has in some cases created problems for the courts. Dr. Pease, one of the leading researchers in the field, has drawn attention to what he has described as "the random and seemingly inexplicable way" in which courts have determined the appropriate length of an order.[17] A number of courts have devised their own tariffs based on a related scale of imprisonment, but it seems clear that given the complicated nature of the factors to be taken into consideration, such as the nature and extent of the offender's family and working commitments and other personal circumstances, these will have a limited value. The nearest that the courts have got to providing this

---

15   *Gillam* (1980) 2 Cr.App.R.(S) 267; *Ward* (1982) 4 Cr.App.R.(S) 103; *Rennes* (1985) 7 Cr.App.R.(S) 343.
16   *Stokes* (1983) 5 Cr.App.R.(S) 449.
17   See also research of Dr. Warren Young published in *Community Service Orders* (1979) Heinemann.

kind of guidance was in the case of *Lawrence*,[18] where it was indicated that 190 hours was appropriate for a burglary meriting 9-12 months' imprisonment.[19]

12.17 As far as consecutive orders are concerned, Section 14(3) of the Powers of Criminal Courts Act 1973 makes it clear that when two or more offences are dealt with at the same time the court should not exceed the maximum of 240 hours or 120 hours in the case of a 16 year old. Similarly in *Evans*[20] Geoffrey Lane, L. J. expressed the view that in respect of orders made at different times by different courts it was undesirable that at any one time there should be orders in existence that exceeded the maximum prescribed by statute. As the community service order is to be regarded as a sentence in its own right, a person should not be fined for the same offence.[21] But there would appear to be nothing wrong with imposing community service on one offence and a fine on another if the circumstances, including the means of the offender, so indicate. It is also bad practice to impose a sentence of imprisonment suspended or unsuspended on the same occasion.[22]

Breach of community service order

12.18 By Section 16(3) of the Powers of Criminal Courts Act 1973, if a magistrates' court is satisfied that an offender is in breach of any of the requirements set out in Section 15 without reasonable excuse, it may:

(1) Impose a fine of up to £400 (which does not prejudice the continuance of the order); or

(2) If the order was made by a magistrates' court, revoke the order and deal with the offender in any way in which he could have been dealt with on conviction if the order had not been made (except that it may not commit the offender to the Crown Court for sentence);[23] or

(3) If the order was made by the Crown Court, commit the offender to the Crown Court to be dealt with there.

At the Crown Court, a fine of up to £400 may be imposed or again, the order may be revoked and the offender dealt with afresh – Section 16(5).

---

18 (1982) 4 Cr.App.R.(S) 69.
19 For a fuller discussion see *e.g.* K. Pease, "Community Service and the Tariff" [1978] Crim.L.R. 269; A. Willis *et al.*, "Community Service and the Tariff" [1978] Crim.L.R. 540; Edgar Jardine *et al.*, "Community Service Orders, Employment and the Tariff" [1983] Crim.L.R. 17.
20 (1977) 64 Cr.App.R. 127.
21 *Carnwell* (1978) 68 Cr.App.R. 58.
22 *Starie* (1979) 1 Cr.App.R.(S) 172; *McElhorne* (1983) 5 Cr.App.R.(S) 53; *Ray* (1984) 6 Cr.App.R.(S) 26.
23 *R. v. Worcester Crown Court and Birmingham Magistrates' Court ex p. Lamb* (1985) 7 Cr.App.R.(S) 44; *Daniels* [1986] Crim.L.R. 824.

12.19 In dealing with him for the original offence, the court must have regard to the gravity of that offence and any mitigation, *i.e.* not punish him for the failure to perform the community service order.[24] It follows that an offence which would not have justified a sentence of imprisonment originally will not justify such a sentence on breach. It also follows that an offence for which community service was imposed as an alternative to imprisonment will, in the event of non-compliance with the conditions without reasonable cause, often in practice result in imprisonment.[25] However, it is not like breach of a suspended sentence, and a custodial sentence would usually be inappropriate where the offender has completed a substantial proportion of the work required under the order.[26]

12.20 Where a court deals with an offender subject to a suspended sentence by imposing a community service order for the latest offence, but making no order on the suspended sentence, it may not later activate the suspended sentence if the offender is subsequently in breach of the community service order.[27]

12.21 The Court of Appeal has so far not adequately resolved the difficulty of dealing with the application of the criteria for a custodial sentence where a defendant under 21 is brought back for breach of a community service order.[28]

Revocation of an order

12.22 By section 17(2), if it seems in the interests of justice to do so, a magistrates' court may revoke an order made by a magistrates' court or revoke it and deal with the offender for the original offence, or if the order was made by the Crown Court, commit him to that court, which has similar powers under Section 17(3). These powers may only be exercised on application by the offender or the relevant officer. Revocation of the order and dealing with the original offence could be the result of the offender having been sentenced to custody for another offence since the making of the community service order. In determining the appropriate sentence to be imposed, credit should again be given to the offender who has already performed a substantial part of the

24 *Simpson* [1983] Crim.L.R. 820.
25 *Garland* (1979) 1 Cr.App.R.(S) 62.
26 *Paisley* (1979) 1 Cr.App.R.(S) 196; *Williams* [1986] Crim.L.R. 754.
27 *Temperley* (1980) 2 Cr.App.R.(S) 127.
28 *Gittings* [1985] Crim.L.R. 246.

order.[29] Further powers to revoke orders exist under Section 17(4A) and (4B) where custodial sentences are subsequently imposed by courts other than the original courts, but under these subsections there are no powers to deal with the original offence.

Extension of the period of work

12.23 Either the offender or the relevant officer may at any time apply to the court for the 12-month period of the work to be extended. If it appears that it is in the interests of justice having regard to the circumstances which have arisen since it was made, the court may so order (Section 17(1)).

PROBATION

12.24 The statutory roots of probation can be said to lie in the system of binding offenders over to come up for judgment when called upon to do so under the Summary Jurisdiction Act 1879 and in the provisions of the First Offenders Act 1887. The latter statute allowed for voluntary guidance and supervision by police court missionaries, many of whom became official probation officers when the service was established by the Probation of Offenders Act 1907. In due course this was followed by the Criminal Justice Act 1925 (as amended), which set up what was to develop into a comprehensive organisation for probation in England and Wales. The present powers of the court to impose probation orders are governed by the Powers of Criminal Courts Act 1973, Sections 2-4.

12.25 By Section 2(1) a probation order may be made in the case of an offender aged 17 or more "instead of sentencing him" where the court is of the opinion that having regard to the circumstances and the character of the offender, it is expedient to do so. The order requires the offender to be under the supervision of a probation officer for a specified period of not less than six months and not more than three years.

12.26 Probation is primarily reformative in the sense that its aim is the re-establishment of the offender in the community. It seeks to provide support for the individual which will help him to avoid committing further crime and thus as probation helps the offender to become more responsible for his own actions, it in turn helps to protect society as a whole. In addition there is inevitably an element of discipline in the

---

29 *Anderson* (1982) 4 Cr.App.R.(S) 252; *Baines* [1983] Crim.L.R. 756; *Whittingham* [1986] Crim.L.R. 572.

submission of the offender while at liberty to the supervision of the probation officer. In considering these aspects of probation, the Morison Committee[30] observed that in seeking to protect itself against crime and show disapproval of the wrongdoer, it was axiomatic that society should seek the minimum interference with the life and liberty of offenders, and continued:

> "We see probation as epitomising [this] principle because while it seeks to protect society through the supervision to which the offender is required to submit, it both minimises the restrictions placed upon him and offers him the help of society in adjusting his conduct to its demands. It seeks to strengthen the offender's resources so that he may become a more responsible member of the community, which must also play a part in rehabilitating him. The offender is conditionally entrusted with freedom so that he may learn the social duties it involves . . ."[31]

Emphasis upon the reformative aspects of probation is to be found in the fact that Section 2 empowers the court to make a probation order *instead of sentencing* the offender. It is specifically provided that costs and compensation may be ordered to be paid at the same time (Section 12(4)). However by Section 2(4) payment of sums by way of damages for injury or compensation for loss shall not be included in the *requirements* of an order. Similarly a court may order a driver's licence to be endorsed or disqualify a person put on probation from driving.

12.27 It has also been held that while it is clearly improper to impose a fine in respect of the same offence for which an offender is placed on probation, there is nothing wrong in principle in making a probation order on one charge and imposing a fine on another.[32] On the other hand, a probation order should not be made concurrently with a custodial sentence.[33] This may not be done even by "extending" an existing order at the time of the imposition of a sentence of imprisonment so as to provide support and supervision on release.[34] Similarly, a probation order cannot be made at the same time as a person is sentenced to immediate imprisonment for contempt.[35] Nor can a probation order be made at the same time as the court passes a suspended sentence for another offence: Powers of Criminal Courts Act 1973, Section 22(3).

30 *Report of the Departmental Committee on the Probation Service* (1962) H.M.S.O. (Cmnd 1650).
31 Para. 13.
32 *Bainbridge* (1979) 1 Cr.App.R.(S) 36.
33 *Evans* (1959) 43 Cr.App.R. 66.
34 *Emmett* (1969) 53 Cr.App.R. 203.
35 *Socratous* (1984) 6 Cr.App.R.(S) 33.

Criteria for making a probation order

12.28 The formal conditions prescribed by statute are:

(1) That the offender has attained the age of 17 (Section 2(1));

(2) That a probation order is, in the opinion of the court, expedient (Section 2(1)); and

(3) That the offender consents (Section 2(6)).

In considering whether it is expedient to make a probation order the court will have to look at all the circumstances of the case, including the nature of the offence and the character of the offender. Some guidance on the criteria to be applied in reaching this decision was given 25 years ago by the Morison Committee which concluded that there was an *a priori* case for use of probation where four conditions existed:

(1) The circumstances of the offence and the offender's record must not be such as to demand, in the interests of society, that some more severe method be adopted in dealing with him.

(2) The risk, if any, to society through setting the offender at liberty must be outweighed by the moral, social and economic arguments for not depriving him of it.

(3) The offender must need continuing attention, since otherwise, if condition (2) is satisfied, a fine or discharge will suffice.

(4) The offender must be capable of responding to this attention while at liberty.[36]

As far as (1) is concerned, the Court of Appeal in dealing with a succession of offenders with long records of previous convictions has frequently over the years observed that probation should be used at the "psychological moment for leniency".[37] It has also emphasised that a probation order may be appropriate in the case of a persistent offender who would otherwise receive a long sentence of imprisonment, in an attempt to give him a "last chance" or to save him from perpetual recidivism or institutionalisation.[38]

12.29 In *Bradley*[39] the appellant, a man of 33 with a long criminal record, pleaded guilty to seven counts of burglary and asked for eight other burglaries and one other offence to be taken into consideration. Twelve of the burglaries involved dwelling-houses. The court varied the four-year sentence of imprisonment to probation in an attempt to break the appellant's pattern of crime and prevent him becoming institutionalised, Stocker, J. observing that the court was "prepared to take what must be of course a calculated risk in the hope that the public will in the

---

36 Report (note 30 *supra*), para. 15.
37 *Weston* [1967] Crim.L.R. 377.
38 *McNamee* (1979) 1 Cr.App.R.(S) 126; *Green* (1979) 1 Cr.App.R.(S) 110.
39 (1983) 5 Cr.App.R.(S) 363.

long term be better protected by such a period of probation as that to which the applicant may be subject". He added that there was "the risk that that very lenient course will not succeed, but if the attempt is even to be made, it would appear that this is the moment to make it."

12.30 It was held in *Heather*[40] that where there is a danger that an offender will become hopelessly addicted to drugs, a probation order might be appropriate in order to counter that risk, even though a substantial sentence of imprisonment might otherwise be justified. In that case the appellant pleaded guilty to robbery at a chemist's shop where an assistant was threatened with a knife and drugs were demanded of the pharmacist. He was sentenced to five years' imprisonment which on appeal was varied to three years' probation.

12.31 In coming to a decision about the suitability of probation in the particular case, the court will normally have had the benefit of a social inquiry report which will have canvassed the desirability of such a course in terms of the Morison criteria set out above. While it is possible for the court to make a probation order without the advice of the probation service, prudence suggests that this is a practice that should not be encouraged. In the first place unaided assessments by the court are, from the very nature of the circumstances in which they are made, likely to be unreliable. Secondly, it seems unfair to impose an offender on the probation service without it having had the opportunity of assessing the chances of success and of making representations to the court: it is one thing to take a calculated risk and put the offender on probation against the advice of a probation officer, it is another to do so without consulting the service at all. Thirdly, where probation is a realistic possibility, it is often useful to allow a pause to occur before the order is made – the point is that it is a procedure that requires the consent of the offender and it may be important that he should be given an opportunity for proper reflection.

12.32 In order for it to be an informed consent, the court must first have explained in ordinary language the effect of an order, including any additional requirements, and the effects of non-compliance as well as of the commission of a further offence during the course of the order (Section 2(6)). It is unrealistic to think that the consent will be a free choice and it is likely that in most situations an offender will see probation as the least of the evils that could be visited upon him, but the

---

40 (1979) 1 Cr.App.R.(S) 189.

courts should try to avoid the situation where the possibilities are so reduced that the defendant makes a decision on the stark alternatives of probation or else imprisonment.[41]

Requirements of the order

12.33 The basic order simply requires that the offender be under the supervision of a probation officer of the petty sessions area in which he resides for the period specified. By Section 2(3) the court may also include such requirements as it "considers necessary for securing the good conduct of the offender or for preventing the repetition by him of the same offence or the commission of other offences" and, in furtherance of this object, what are sometimes called the standard conditions are frequently inserted:

(1) The accused shall be of good behaviour and lead an industrious life.

(2) The accused shall inform the probation officer immediately of any change of address or employment.

(3) The accused shall comply with the instructions of the probation officer as to reporting to the officer and as to receiving visits from the probation officer at home.

The first has been criticised[42] as being imprecise and inappropriate, particularly insofar as leading an industrious life in terms of getting and keeping a job may be beyond the offender's powers in times of high unemployment, and there is some force in this point. However, in reinforcing the requirement to be of good behaviour or more explicitly, not to commit further offences, the court is simply underlining the consequences if he does re-offend.

12.34 Apart from the special statutory requirements described below, the court is in addition free to insert any condition that might be expected to assist in ensuring the offender's good conduct and avoiding repetition of his offence. On the face of it this is a wide discretion and in the past it has been used in such a way as to require the probationer not to associate with a named person or not to go to a particular public house or night club. But it will be obvious that this kind of negative requirement should be employed with great care. In 1936 the *Report of The Committee on Social Services in Courts of Summary Jurisdiction*[43] drew attention to some "extravagant conditions" which it said were "hardly likely to win the respect and co-operation of the probationer," viz:

41 *Marquis* (1974) 59 Cr.App.R. 228.
42 See Stephen Savage, "Conditions in Probation Oders" (1985) 149 J.P. 105.
43 H.M.S.O. (Cmd 5122).

"A young man of 18, charged with attempting to steal one shilling's worth of cigarettes, was bound over on the condition that he should not smoke cigarettes for twelve months, that he should be in the house winter and summer at nine o'clock, and that he should go to church at least once every Sunday.

Two boys placed on probation for theft were ordered not to attend a cinema for two years.

Our attention was drawn to one case where a man and a woman who were charged jointly were forbidden to speak to one another. This condition was apparently more honoured in the breach than the observance as they were married within a month."[44]

The effect of the House of Lords' decision in *Cullen v. Rogers*[45] is that except as is now provided by Section 4A and 4B (below), the requirements under Section 2(3) of the 1973 Act must not import into the probation order anything that can be construed as a sentence or punishment. Accordingly courts should avoid inserting requirements that are oppressive. They should also not include requirements that are too wide or uncertain or with which it would be impossible to ensure compliance. There is no power to include a condition that the defendant leaves the country and does not return.[46]

12.35 Under the Act (as amended) the courts are empowered to include four special additional requirements:

(1) A condition of residence under Section 2(5), *i.e.* a requirement that the probationer shall live in a particular place for a period, usually suitable lodgings or a hostel recommended by the probation service where it is believed that the probationer is more likely to keep out of trouble than in his home surroundings;

(2) A condition of medical treatment under Section 3 (see Chapter 11);

(3) Day centre requirements under Section 4B; and

(4) Requirements under Section 4A.

12.36 Section 4B(6) defines a day centre as "premises at which non-residential facilities are provided for use in connection with the rehabilitation of offenders". Such centres must be under the broad supervision of the probation service and with the approval of the probation committee. Before making a day centre requirement, the court must consult a probation officer and be satisfied both that arrangements can be made for the probationer to get to the centre and that the person in charge is willing to have him (Section 4B(2)). The

---

44 At para. 54.
45 [1982] 1 W.L.R. 729.
46 *McCartan* [1958] 1 W.L.R. 933.

requirement does not specify the number of days on which he must attend, but by Section 4B(3) the maximum number of days on which he can be instructed by the probation officer to attend is 60. While at the centre he must obey instructions given by those in charge. By Section 4B(4) instructions as to attendance should avoid interference with the probationer's work or school attendance. See *Cardwell*[47] for general considerations applicable to day centre requirements.

12.37   Under Section 4A the court is enabled to include requirements that the probationer (a) attends at a specified place other than a day centre; (b) participates in specified activities; or (c) refrains from participating in specified activities. Before making a requirement under Section 4A the court must have a report from a probation officer and be satisfied that it is feasible to secure compliance with the requirement.

Breach of probation

12.38   Breach of probation relates only to breach of the requirements of the order, and inevitably falls within the discretion of the probation officer to enforce. However it is the view of some observers that except for the most trivial breaches, the offender should be brought back before the court, if only to be warned of the serious consequences of a further lapse. Whether there is a breach is initially for the probation officer to decide and in many courts officers are encouraged to consult members of the bench (through probation liaison committees in magistrates' courts) before taking action.

12.39   The court's powers, where it is the court that made the order or the supervising court, are to impose a fine up to £400, or in the case of offences punishable with imprisonment, make an attendance centre order (if available) while allowing the probation order to continue. Alternatively, it can make no order on the breach. Where the probation order was originally made by a magistrates' court, the court dealing with the breach may instead sentence the offender for the original offence and thus, of course, even make a new probation order. This is so even where this would have the effect of extending the period covered by probation to more than three years from the date of the original order.[48]

12.40   Where the original order was made by the Crown Court, the supervising magistrates' court can impose a fine for breach but cannot deal with the original offence. Where it thinks that the latter course is

47 (1973) 53 Cr.App.R. 823.
48 *R. v. Havant JJ. ex p. Jacobs* [1957] 1 W.L.R. 365.

desirable it should commit the probationer on bail or in custody to the original court for him to be sentenced there. The Crown Court's powers are similar to those of the magistrates' courts (Section 6(6)). The decision to sentence or commit for sentence on the original offence will normally only be employed in cases where the probation order has demonstrably failed.

Commission of a further offence

12.41 Although also sometimes called "breach", where the probationer is subsequently convicted of a further offence *committed* during the currency of the probation order, the court empowered to deal with the matter may dispose of the original offence as if the offender had just been convicted of it.[49] Once more this includes the power to make a fresh order. However it was pointed out in *Thompson*[50] that if a person who has broken the terms of probation by the commission of a further offence is put on probation again without proper reflection,

> "it greatly weakens the force of probation orders, it brings the machinery of the probation service into contempt and public harm would result therefrom."

There may well be cases where there are temporary lapses in the pattern of rehabilitation which it would be in the public interest to disregard – save for a warning to the defendant—but it is clear that there cannot be a licence to commit offences. It is not the aim of probation to provide supervision and support while the probationer continues to commit further crime. Much will depend upon the nature and circumstances of the offence subsequently committed, and in some cases the commission of some technical offence, or one of strict liability where the intention of the offender was negligible, or where the offence was of a totally different character, may be relevant in deciding what course to take.

Discharge

12.42 A probation order may be discharged by the supervising court (except where the order was made by the Crown Court reserving to itself the power of discharge) on the application of the probation officer or the probationer himself before the expiry of the order (Section 5(1) and Schedule 1). Similarly a conditional discharge may be substituted for the balance of the probation period (Section 11(1)).

---

49 S. 8. There is no power to extend an existing probation order analogous to the power to extend the operational period of a suspended sentence: *Mullervy* (1986) 8 Cr.App.R.(S) 42.
50 [1969] 1 All E.R. 60.

SUPERVISION ORDERS

12.43 Broadly speaking a supervision order is equivalent for the age group 10 to 16 of probation in the case of an adult offender. It is available on the finding of guilt for any offence or upon discharging a care order made in criminal proceedings (Children and Young Persons Act 1969, Section 7). A supervision order may be made for any period of time not exceeding three years. Like probation, supervision is intended to introduce an element of control over the young offender's lifestyle by providing for the supervision of a local authority social worker (normally in the case of the age group 10 to 13) or probation officer (normally for 14 to 16-year-olds). It may require the juvenile to live with a specified person (Children and Young Persons Act 1969, Section 12(1)). It is the duty of the supervisor to advise, assist and befriend the supervised person.

12.44 Supervision orders may also include requirements to take part in Intermediate Treatment programmes, which allow for the involvement of the juvenile in schemes of constructive and supervised activities.

12.45 Intermediate Treatment requirements fall into two kinds. First there is Intermediate Treatment for a maximum of 90 days where the implementation and direction of the requirements are left to *the discretion of the supervisor* – what is sometimes called "discretionary". Intermediate Treatment under Section 12(2) as substituted by the Criminal Justice Act 1982, Section 20[51]. By this the conditions with which the supervisor may require the juvenile to comply are:

(1) To live at a place or places specified for a specified period or periods;

(2) To present himself to a person or persons specified at a place or places specified on a day or days specified;

(3) To participate in activities specified in the directions on a day or days specified.

Before the court may require compliance with such conditions it must be satisfied there is a scheme under Section 19 in existence for the area in which the juvenile resides or will reside (Section 19(12)). A copy of the scheme must be sent to the Clerk to the Justices for the court in the area to which the scheme relates.

---

51 The account in this chapter of these provisions and those that follow is necessarily limited to an outline only, and for a detailed analysis the reader is referred to specialist works, in particular Richard A. H. White (ed.), *Clarke Hall and Morrison on Children* (10th ed.) Butterworths.

12.46 In the second form of Intermediate Treatment, detailed requirements are included in the order. This is sometimes called "stipulated" Intermediate Treatment, by which the offender may be *required by the court* to do anything the supervisor could have required him to do under "discretionary" Intermediate Treatment (Section 12(3C)(a). Similarly under Section 12(3C)(b) the court may prescribe a *night restriction* order by which for not more than 30 nights in the first three months the supervised person may be required to remain at a place or places specified (one of which must be where he lives) for a period not exceeding ten hours per night from 6 p.m. to 6 a.m. The court may also require the supervised person to *refrain from participation* in specified activities under Sections 12(3C)(c).

12.47 In all cases of "stipulated" Intermediate Treatment, before such requirements are included in a supervision order the court must:

(1) Have consulted the supervisor as to the offender's circumstances and be satisfied as to the feasibility of securing his compliance with the requirements;

(2) Be satisfied that the requirements are necessary to secure the offender's good behaviour or to prevent a repetition of the offence or the commission of other offences; and

(3) Have obtained the consent of the offender (or, where the offender is under 14, of his parent or guardian) (Section 12(3F)).

The court must not include in "stipulated" Intermediate Treatment orders requirements involving the co-operation of other persons without their consent, conditions of medical treatment or the requirement to reside with a specified individual (Section 12(3G)).[52]

12.48 Orders without conditions may not be made the subject of breach proceedings. The only remedy is an application to discharge the order. If any condition is attached and a breach of it is established, the juvenile court may order a person who has not reached the age of 18 to pay a fine of up to £100 or make an attendance centre order (Section 15(2A)). Where the supervised person is over 17 but under 18, the juvenile court may also discharge the order and deal with the supervised person for the original offence under section 15(2) and (4). If the supervised person has reached the age of 18 or more, a magistrates' court may, as well as punishing the breach in the usual ways, if it discharges the supervision order impose any punishment which it would have the power to impose if it then had the power to try him for the

---

52 Provisions for the inclusion of a requirement for medical treatment are set out in Section 12(4).

offence – subject to a limit of six months and a fine of £2,000 for either way or indictable offences (Section 15(4)(b)).

CARE ORDERS

12.49 Where a juvenile is found guilty of an offence punishable in the case of an adult with imprisonment, the court may make a care order under the Children and Young Persons Act 1973, Section 7(7) placing him in the care of the local authority. The effect of such an order is to transfer all the rights of the parents to the local authority, who from then on have the responsibility for deciding how the care order is to be implemented (Child Care Act 1980, Section 10). Normally, however, the juvenile will be dealt with by being allowed to remain at home under the charge and control of his parents (but subject to the right of the local authority to place him elsewhere); being boarded with foster parents; or being required to reside in a community home or some voluntary home specified by the local authority.

12.50 Before a court makes a care order it must be satisifed that a care order is appropriate because of the seriousness of the offence and that the juvenile is in need of care and control which he is unlikely to receive unless the court makes an order (Section 7(7A)). Where a care order is made in respect of an offender aged 16, it lasts until he is 19; otherwise it lasts until he attains the age of 18 (Section 20). It is also necessary that the juvenile be legally represented unless he has failed to apply for legal aid when given the opportunity to do so or has been refused legal aid on the basis of his parents' means (Section 7A).

12.51 The so-called "residential" care order was introduced by the Criminal Justice Act 1982, which inserted a new Section 20A into the 1973 Act. By this new section a juvenile court or Crown Court dealing with a juvenile found guilty of an offence punishable with imprisonment who is already in care as a result of a criminal matter, may add a residential condition to the existing care order. The effect of the residential condition is that for a period not exceeding six months as specified by the court, the local authority may not discharge its duties under the care order by allowing the juvenile to remain in the control of a parent or guardian *etc.*, but has to send him away from home, usually to a community home. When the residential condition expires the local authority regains its discretion to place the child. A second residential condition may be made for another offence which could extend the period to more than six months.

12.52 Before making such an order the court must consider it is appropriate because of the seriousness of the offence and after obtaining and considering information about the circumstances, be of the opinion that no other method of dealing with the juvenile is appropriate: (Section 20A(3)). Once again the juvenile must be legally represented or have not applied for or been refused legal aid (Section 20A(4)).

CHAPTER 13

Fines, Compensation and Costs

13.01 Fines, compensation and costs have been included in the same chapter because they are the three financial orders most commonly employed by the courts. Furthermore, when the means of the individual offender are limited and these three measures are used in combination the courts have to consider both the "totality principle" in relation to the total sum ordered to be paid on the same occasion and also the priority and the allocation of the offender's resources between the different orders, compensation taking precedence over the other two.

The new powers to make confiscation orders under the Drug Trafficking Offences Act 1986, which are also financial measures, have been included in Chapter 15 with other ancillary measures.

FINES

13.02 The deterrent and retributive effect of fines was emphasised by the Report of the Advisory Council on the Treatment of Offenders (*Alternatives to Short Terms of Imprisonment*) in 1957, which recorded its agreement with those representatives of the police who were

> "firmly of the opinion that the deterrent value of the fine is underrated by the courts and that fines are more appropriate for many acquisitive and personal offences than the courts apparently think."[1]

However, the report also drew attention to a point which is sometimes sharply brought home to the courts, that unless care is employed in the fixing of the fine, it acts positively as an encouragement to crime in that the offender feels obliged to commit further offences in order to obtain the resources from which the fine may be paid. This is a clear illustration of the deterrent nature of the fine breaking down, not because the penalty is not severe enough, but because on a subjective assessment by the offender of the amount he can pay measured against the risks of being caught, it is too severe.

---

1 At para. 24.

13.03 Another problem is that of fine enforcement. Where someone is determined not to pay and is equally determined not to go to prison, the cost of the long-drawn-out business of attempting to enforce the fine can be very great indeed.

13.04 In the case of persons convicted in the Crown Court or committed to that court for sentence under the Magistrates' Courts Act 1980, Section 38, there is no limit on the fine that may be imposed (Criminal Law Act 1977, Section 32(1), and the Powers of Criminal Courts Act 1973, Section 42(1)). However where an offender is committed to be dealt with under the provisions of the Criminal Justice Act, 1967, Section 56, the fine is limited to what the magistrates' courts could have inflicted after summary trial.

13.05 So far as magistrates' courts' powers are concerned, briefly summarised the position is as follows:

(1) The maximum fine for an offence triable either way included in the Magistrates' Courts Act 1980, Schedule 1, is currently £2,000, and with some exceptions (certain drugs offences) that for such offences not listed in Schedule 1 is £1,000 or such larger sum as may be prescribed by the statute creating the offence.[2]

(2) The maximum for summary offences depends upon the level on the standard scale of fines appropriate for the offence under the Criminal Justice Act 1982, Section 37(2).

(3) The maximum fine for a young person is £400,[3] and for a child it is £100.[4]

Use of the fine

13.06 Use of the fine is governed by a number of factors. It is most appropriate when a deterrent or retributive sentence is thought to be required but when the offence itself is not considered to be sufficiently grave to justify a custodial sentence and when the offender's circumstances, record and degree of involvement, *etc.*, are such as to suggest that a fine will meet the interests of society and the needs of the individual.

13.07 In deciding how much the offender should be fined, the court should first relate the amount of the fine to the gravity of the offence (as

---

2 Magistrates' Courts Act 1980, s. 32.
3 Magistrates' Court Act 1980, s. 24(3).
4 1980 Act, ss. 24(4) and 36(2).

reduced by mitigation).[5] It should then consider that amount in relation to the offender's means in the sense of ascertaining the means before the fine is finally determined.[6] Indeed in the magistrates' court there is a statutory duty to consider, among other things, the means of the offender when fixing the amount of the fine "so far as they appear or are known to the court" (Magistrates' Court Act 1980, Section 35).

13.08　Having determined the amount of the fine to be imposed, the court should then decide whether the offender should be allowed time to pay (Powers of Criminal Courts Act 1973, Section 31(1)).

13.09　Reference is sometimes made to the tariff so far as fines are concerned. This is somewhat misleading because although the Magistrates' Association does produce guidance for magistrates on suggested penalties for motoring offences, this does not amount to anything like a comprehensive national tariff of fines in the way that a tariff of imprisonment has been developed for use in the Crown Courts. Indeed the Magistrates' Association specifically makes the point that its "suggestions" on motoring offences are not to be regarded as a tariff but as a starting-point if that is thought locally useful. It is not inappropriate, however, to talk of local tariffs of fines generally applied by local benches of magistrates on the basis of agreed ranges of fines to be employed in their areas for certain kinds of offences.

13.10　Such research as has been carried out suggests wide variations between fines used for similar offences by different benches across the country.[7] Those who produce the kind of local tariffs referred to above will no doubt wish to look at the guidance produced by adjoining petty sessional divisions so as to reduce major discrepancies and perhaps in this way, gradually produce a tariff that *will* allow for greater national consistency while taking into account, where appropriate, local considerations.

13.11　What the Court of Appeal has repeatedly stressed is that on the basis of looking at the offence first and the offender second, a fine

---

5　*Jamieson* (1975) 60 Cr.App.R. 318; *Fairbairn* (1980) 2 Cr.App.R.(S) 315; *Messana* (1981) 3 Cr.App.R.(S) 88.
6　*Rizvi* (1979) 1 Cr.App.R.(S) 307.
7　See *e.g.* (anon.), "Disparity in Sentencing" (1986) 150 J.P. 196; R. Tarling, *Sentencing Practice in Magistrates' Courts* (1979) H.M.S.O., H.O.R.S. no. 56.

should not be used when the gravity of the offence requires the use of a custodial sentence.[8] The matter was succinctly summarised in *Lewis*[9] where it was observed:

> ". . . the first consideration in a matter of this sort is whether the accused person should go to prison or whether he can be properly dealt with by way of a fine . . . Once the court has decided that a fine is appropriate then there are obviously in each case many factors which may follow, but amongst the factors which the court must consider one can mention first the amount involved in the fraud, which in this instance was enormous, secondly, the amount obtained out of it by the accused if known...; thirdly, his capacity to pay."

It is right to say that this case must now be read subject to the decision in *Clarke*,[10] the guideline case on partly suspended sentences which we discussed in Chapters 6 and 12,[11] but in broad terms it still indicates the proper approach in terms of deciding when the fine ought to be employed.

13.12 What has obviously to be guarded against is creating the impression that the wealthy offender can buy himself out of prison by paying a heavy fine.

13.13 In summary, once the court has decided that it is not necessary to impose a custodial sentence, but that a deterrent or retributive sentence, rather than anything more constructive, is required, then the answer is that a fine may be imposed. Once the appropriate fine has been decided upon, on the basis of the gravity of the offence taking into account the mitigation put forward, this notional figure has to be adjusted by reference to the offender's means. It may be reduced by his lack of means but it may not be increased by his wealth.

13.14 Having said that, it was held in *Messana*[12] that although the fine appropriate to the gravity should not be increased by the offender's wealth, the court should "ensure that the fine did have the effect of punishing him". The report does not make it clear how this should be done and indeed the commentary in the 1981 *Criminal Law Review*[13] concludes that there is "some ambiguity" in the suggestion, but one way could be to reduce the number of instalments or the period of payment in order to ensure that the fine had some "teeth". However, this would

8 *Thompson* (1974) C.S.P. J1.2(a); *Sisodia* (1979) 1 Cr.App.R.(S) 291.
9 [1965] Crim.L.R. 121.
10 (1982) 4 Cr.App.R.(S) 197.
11 Paras. 6.08ff and 12.09 *supra*.
12 (1981) 3 Cr.App.R.(S) 88.
13 At p. 506.

have little effect in the case of an offender whose means did not require time to pay at all. As was observed in *Gillies*,[14] it would be obviously wrong to send an offender to prison simply because he was wealthy enough for any fine to have a negligible effect.

13.15 As regards the means of the offender, or better, his capacity to pay, it is clear that the fine decided upon need not be within the offender's immediate means, but should be calculated in the context of his expected income during the period, also to be calculated, over which the court considers the payment should be spread.[15] It also may mean that it may still be appropriate to fine a man who is out of work with no assets provided that there is a reasonable expectation of him obtaining employment in the near future – again provided that he is given time to pay. This is an increasing problem, especially when the offender's means are so limited, as for example by being on supplementary benefit, that the fine which could reasonably be imposed on the principles stated above would be almost derisory in relation to the seriousness of the offence. In such a situation there may be no alternative but to impose a very small fine and make it clear in court that the amount of the fine is no realistic measure of the offence itself but is the most that in justice can be imposed because of the offender's means and is recognition that even a small fine is a substantial penalty for such an offender. Sometimes there may be an alternative. Dealing with this aspect of the problem, the fourth edition of the *Sentence of the Court* sensibly makes the following suggestions:

"Alternatively, the court may consider making a non-financial order. Where immediate punishment is not essential, and the offender may respond to the threat of further punishment on re-offending a conditional discharge may be appropriate. Where an immediate punitive sanction does seem called for, a community service order or (for young offenders) an attendance centre order might be more suitable provided that the offence is one punishable with custody."

What is emphasised and what the courts themselves have laid down on a number of occasions is that it is wrong to impose a sentence of imprisonment, whether it be immediate or suspended, simply because an offender does not have the means to pay the kind of fine that would otherwise have been imposed.[16]

13.16 When a court imposes a fine it normally must give the offender time to pay and in the case of the Crown Court at this stage, must fix a

14 [1965] Crim.L.R. 64.
15 *Little* (1976) C.S.P. J1.2(d).
16 *McGowan* (1974) C.S.P. J1.2(f); *Reeves* (1972) 56 Cr.App.R. 366.

term of imprisonment in default of payment.[17] By the Powers of Criminal Courts Act 1973 Section 31(3), the Crown Court must allow time to pay unless:

(1) In the case of an offence punishable with imprisonment, the offender seems to have sufficient money to pay the fine forthwith;

(2) The offender is of no fixed abode or likely to go abroad; or

(3) The court sentences him to, or he is already serving, a sentence of imprisonment, youth custody, detention in a detention centre or detention under the Criminal Justice Act 1982, Section 9.

Similar provisions exist in respect of magistrates' courts under the Magistrates' Courts Act 1980, Section 75.

13.17 Therefore, where an offender does have some means, two operations are involved: there has to be a realistic assessment first of the offender's means and secondly the relation of this and the proposed fine to the time to pay. Except in very simple cases, a more useful approach than the simple "time to pay" formula is to devise an instalment plan, the instalments being fixed by reference to such criteria as the work record of the offender, his income, the amount of his savings, his family responsibilities and outgoings, the permanence of his address, etc. It is self-evident that taking into account the means of the offender involves first establishing what his real means are, and often requires the employment of skilful techniques of examination. All this will take some time but it is well known that time so spent at this stage often saves a great deal of time and effort later when it comes to enforcing the fine. Some courts, it has been observed, take the view that the offender himself should make it clear what his means are and whether he is asking for time to pay, and there is some judicial authority for this position. Thus in *Wright*,[18] where it was complained on appeal that the sentencing court had failed to find out more about the appellant's financial position before making an order for costs, Lord Widgery, C.J. made the following remarks:

> ". . . It is of course a fundamental principle of sentencing that financial obligations must be matched to the ability to pay, and there is an overriding consideration that financial obligations are to be subjected to that test. But that does not mean that the court has to set about an inquisitorial function and dig out all the information that exists about the appellant's means. The appellant knows what his means are and he is perfectly capable of putting them before the Court on his own initiative. If

---

17 Exceptionally the Crown Court does not fix a term in default when it orders a fine in disposing of an appeal from a magistrates' court. Magistrates do not usually fix a term in default when they impose sentence but may subsequently do so if the fine is not paid.
18 (1976) C.S.P. J1.2(g).

as happened here, the Court is only given the rather meagre details of the appellant's means, then it is the appellant's fault."

That, of course, must be right in the case of the represented defendant, but with due respect to the then Lord Chief Justice, in the case of unrepresented defendants, it overlooks the state of mind of the offender himself at the time, for he is then not normally in the best position to look after his own interests, which to some extent it is the function of the court to do.

13.18 The Court of Appeal has held on a number of occasions, however, that the period of repayment should not be too long and that when an offender is allowed to pay a fine by instalments the amount ordered to be paid should be such that the instalments may be completed within about twelve months.[19]

13.19 It is important to remember in all this that whatever the method of calculation, fines based upon deterrence or retribution must be more than a simple cash transaction in respect of misconduct, a charge for breaking the law or a device for raising revenue; and for that reason "the tariff" may be thought to be an unfortunate description of the process. As the memorandum submitted by the Association of Chief Police Officers of England and Wales to the Royal Commission on the Penal System in England and Wales[20] observed:

"Fines and other forms of payment have the great merit that if sufficiently large they immediately demonstrate that crime does not pay. In general, they are easy to collect, but we still emphasise the desirability of considering this form of punishment even when fines will have to be paid by instalments over a long period. We consider that many fines are far too small; they should be a punishment and sometimes a hardship rather than an irritating annoyance. Where loss has been suffered the fine should generally exceed that amount, otherwise the offender, and the public, may consider that 'it was worth it'."

13.20 It is only necessary to look at the current amount of outstanding and unpaid fines to see that for various reasons fines can be a penal "failure" and equally, as indicated above, fines that do not "bite" are ineffective as deterrents. Frequently, it is claimed, fines are not paid by offenders but by parents or friends or if a group has committed the offence and only one has been caught, the rest of the group. Sometimes it is suspected that the courts tacitly acknowledge that this happens and in the case of juveniles the court is under a legal duty to order the fine or

---

19 *Knight* (1980) 2 Cr.App.R.(S) 82; *Nunn* (1983) 5 Cr.App.R.(S) 203; *Owen* (1984) 6 Cr.App.R.(S) 137.
20 Royal Commission on the Penal System in England and Wales, Written Evidence Vol. III (1967) H.M.S.O. p. 11.

other financial penalty to be paid by the parent or guardian unless that person cannot be found or it would be unreasonable in the circumstances to make such an order for payment. The parent or guardian must be given an opportunity of being heard before such an order can be made, but this requirement will be satisfied if he has been required to attend but has failed to do so: Children and Young Persons Act 1933, Section 55 (as amended by the Criminal Justice Act 1982 Section 26).

13.21 Otherwise it has been regularly held over the years by the Court of Appeal that a fine should not be determined on the basis that some person other than the offender will pay it or contribute to its payment. Thus in *Lewis*[21] the appellant, who was aged 30, was convicted of what appeared to be a minor part in a conspiracy to smuggle watches on a large scale. He had no previous convictions and was fined £10,000. Apparently, although the appellant could not pay the whole fine himself, his father had, through counsel, expressed his willingness to put him in a position to pay any fine imposed and the judge took the view that the public interest did not require him to be sent to prison. The Court of Appeal varied the fine to £5,000 giving on this occasion as a reason for the fine needing to be within the defendant's capacity to pay, the fact that otherwise he might be saddled with a fine he could not pay and have to go to prison. Also the impression might be given that he had been saved from a prison sentence by the wealth of his family or friends.[22]

13.22 Where an offender is convicted of a number of offences on the same occasion and the court decides that a fine is the appropriate penalty, it is important to observe the "totality principle". Under this principle it is for the court to determine a fine that is appropriate to the gravity of the offence as a whole rather than simply impose a fine on each constituent offence which might in aggregate be completely unrealistic. A good example of where the "totality principle" is most obviously to be applied is where the offender has pleaded or been found guilty of a large number of motoring offences arising out of the same basic incident. Similarly, the "totality principle" must be borne in mind when combining a fine with orders for costs and compensation.

13.23 A final element which ought to be briefly mentioned is the desirability of imposing fines which the offenders themselves think fair in terms of the amount. Apart from anything else it is possible that there is greater likelihood of a fine thought to be fair being paid, and accepted

21 [1965] Crim.L.R. 121.
22 See also *Curtis* (1984) 6 Cr.App.R.(S) 250.

as a deterrent. By the same token, a "fair" fine will reinforce any possible rehabilitative element that a fine might have where this method has been chosen in preference to a sentence of imprisonment.

The fine combined with other measures

13.24 For a large number of offences provision is made for a sentence of imprisonment and a fine to be imposed on the same offence at the same time – and where the offender is charged with more than one offence which is punishable with imprisonment it is possible to impose a sentence where he is faced with a combination of two types of penalty. It is clear that in such a situation there will be cases where the profit from the offence, the means of the offender and the otherwise serious circumstances in which the offence was committed, will be such that the court will be justified in imposing a sentence of immediate custody together with a substantial fine or other financial penalty at the same time. Thus in *Waterfield*[23] the appellant was convicted of a number of offences under the Customs and Excise Acts in relation to approximately 7,500 indecent films and 70,000 indecent books which had been imported from Denmark, many of them in a lorry carrying bacon. He was sentenced to three years' imprisonment and fined a total of £7,000. The sentence of imprisonment was reduced as the offences related to material which was indecent rather than obscene and did not therefore justify the maximum penalty, but the Court of Appeal refused to criticise the additional imposition of the fine, Lawton L.J. observing:

> "This court is firmly of the opinion that if those who take part in this kind of trade know that on conviction they are likely to be stripped of every penny of profit they make and a good deal more, then the desire to enter it will be diminished."

However, it has been held that a fine should not be imposed in order to deprive the offender of the profits of an offence unless that particular offence has either been proved or admitted.[24]

13.25 It has also been established that it is generally inappropriate that a fine should be imposed with a custodial sentence where the result will be to impose a financial burden on the offender on his release.[25] A likely consequence of added pressures of this kind is that the prospect of the released prisoner's adjustment to life outside, and therefore his chance of avoiding further offences, will be considerably decreased. Over-

---

23 (1975) C.S.P. J1.3(a).
24 *Ayensu and Ayensu* (1982) 4 Cr.App.R.(S) 248; *Johnson* (1984) 6 Cr.App.R.(S) 227; see para. 3.13 *supra*.
25 *McCormack* (1976) C.S.P. J1.3(c).

deterrence ceases to be a deterrent – once again, one might just as well be hanged for a sheep as a lamb.

13.26 It also is plainly unfair to impose a fine together with a custodial sentence where the offender has no means to pay and in consequence will probably serve a term of custody fixed in default of payment, consecutively to his original sentence.[26] Nevertheless, it has been held in a number of cases that there may be such a combination even where there is no evidence that the offender has the means to pay the fine, provided that the sentencer reduces the length of the term of custody which is appropriate to the offence by the length of the period which the offender will be required to serve in default. In *Savundra*[27] the appellant was convicted of conspiracy to defraud customers of an insurance company by fraudulently applying the proceeds of the premiums to his own benefit. He was sentenced to eight years' imprisonment and fined a total of £50,000, with two years' imprisonment in default. Giving the judgment of the court, Salmon, L.J. observed:

> "Having regard to the gravity of these offences, this Court does not consider that a sentence of ten years' imprisonment would have been too long . . . this Court cannot shut [its] eyes to the fact that when frauds are perpetrated on this scale it sometimes occurs that the criminal is conscious of the peril in which he stands of being prosecuted and takes the precaution of putting large sums of money out of the way of his creditors against the time when he comes out of prison . . . £50,000 is a very small proportion of this appellant's plunder and this Court can see nothing wrong with the decision of a judge that if the appellant does not or cannot produce that sum, his sentence should be one of ten years, which this Court certainly would not regard as being in any way excessive. If he does produce it, he will serve two years less."

See also *Lott-Carter*,[28] *Benmore and others*[29] and the new confiscation powers in respect of drug trafficking offences discussed in paras 15.23ff *infra*.

13.27 As regards suspended sentences, there is nothing wrong in adding a fine to a suspended sentence as an additional penalty, but it is wrong to impose a suspended sentence in conjunction with a fine in a case where a fine alone would provide an adequate penalty.[30]

26 *Millington* (1975) C.S.P. J.1.3(b).
27 (1968) 52 Cr.App.R. 637.
28 (1978) 67 Cr.App.R. 404.
29 (1983) 5 Cr.App.R.(S) 468.
30 *Ankers* (1975) 61 Cr.App.R. 170.

Enforcement

13.28 Enforcement of all fines rests with the magistrates' courts, but as indicated above, the Crown Court in ordering a fine must fix a term of imprisonment in default of payment. The current scales set out in Powers of Criminal Courts Act 1973 Section 31(3A) (as amended) are as follows:

An amount not exceeding £50		....	7 days
An amount exceeding £50	but not £100	....	14 days
£100	£400	....	30 days
£400	£1,000	....	60 days
£1,000	£2,000	....	90 days
£2,000	£5,000	....	6 months
£5,000	£10,000	....	9 months
£10,000	....		12 months

13.29 The term in default may be ordered to run concurrently with or consecutively to any custodial sentence being served or imposed at the same time.

13.30 Fines ordered to be paid by instalments should be enforced by the fixing of a single term of imprisonment in default of payment of the whole fine outstanding and not by periods in default of non-payment of the instalments.[31]

13.31 The actual mechanics of fine enforcement are governed by the Magistrates' Courts Act 1980, Sections 75 to 91 and the Attachment of Earnings Act 1971. They are essentially concerned with procedural matters and accordingly fall outside the scope of this work.

COMPENSATION

13.32 The notion of compensation has become increasingly popular in recent years[32] as a means both of responding appropriately to crime and, to some extent, of reconciling the victim with the offender. In the

---

31 *Aitchinson and Bentley* (1982) 4 Cr.App.R.(S) 404; *Power* (1986) 8 Cr.App.R.(S) 8.
32 See *e.g. Compensation and Support for Victims of Crime*, First Report of the Home Affairs Committee of the House of Commons, Session 1984–85 (1984) H.C. 43. The Government's reply was *Compensation and Support for Victims of Crime* (1985) H.M.S.O. (Cmnd 9457).

latter sense it is seen as "constructive" and, of course, it is perhaps not unduly cynical to observe that it is a measure that costs the Exchequer nothing. Courts have accordingly been seen as "soft" on compensation. Perhaps not surprisingly therefore the courts have been enjoined to use compensation orders more freely and in order to encourage this to be done, by virtue of the provisions of the Criminal Justice Act 1982, Section 67 (amending the Powers of Criminal Courts Act 1973, Section 35) a compensation order is now a sentence in its own right rather than ancillary to other sentences. It is also provided that when both compensation and a fine are considered appropriate, but the offender's means are inadequate to meet both, the former takes precedence over the latter.

13.33 Traditionally, the courts have taken the view that the order for compensation was a useful measure and that it may be important for "good moral reasons" to make an order (for payment by instalments) to "remind the defendant of the evil he has done",[33] but that the essence of the order was that it provided a quick and simple machinery which should only be used for dealing with claims in simple and straightforward cases.[34] Again, as Scarman, L.J. put it in *Inwood*,[35] such orders are

> "a convenient and rapid means of avoiding the expense of resorting to civil litigation when the criminal clearly has the means which would enable the compensation to be paid."

It is also perhaps useful as a means of obtaining an early interim payment where civil litigation will be rather slow to produce results. Although it seems from *Chappell*[36] that for a compensation order to be made by a criminal court, it is not necessary for the offender to be liable in the sense required in a civil action (and the court need only consider whether injury, loss or damage was the result of the offence), it was not intended that compensation orders should necessarily replace actions in the civil courts. In the civil courts, there is already a system for dealing with claims for damages based upon personal injury and loss or damage to goods. The county courts are nowadays relatively accessible and although it would be undoubtedly convenient always to finalise all matters and claims at one hearing, by the very nature of things this would be impossible for the more serious cases where complex issues of pecuniary and non-pecuniary loss are likely to take a long time and

---

33   *Miller* (1976) 63 Cr.App.R. 56.
34   *Daly* (1973) 58 Cr.App.R. 333; *Donovan* (1981) 3 Cr.App.R.(S) 192.
35   (1974) 60 Cr.App.R. 70.
36   [1984] Crim.L.R. 574.

require a good deal of technical expertise to resolve. Such cases should obviously be left to the civil courts.

13.34 On the other hand, as the Report of the Advisory Council on the Penal System *Reparation by the Offender* (1970) observed:

> "If the victim has a substantial civil claim, and the offender has some assets which could properly be applied as a contribution towards meeting the victim's loss, and which might be dissipated before a civil claim could be heard, a criminal court should, we think, be able to make a compensation order without attempting to quantify the loss. Such an order would, we think, be justified on the footing that the amount of the order is demonstrably less than the total loss, and that the victim can pursue a civil action for the balance if he wishes."

Such cases may well be reasonably easy to deal with in practice and not call for lengthy investigation or argument.

13.35 Another problem is the extent to which compensation orders are seen as providing offenders with a "soft option". As Scarman, L.J. said in *Inwood*:[37]

> "Compensation orders were not introduced into our law to enable the convicted to buy themselves out of the penalties of crime."

13.36 Accordingly in attempting to provide compensation for the victim the court must be careful not to give the impression that a different standard will be applied to offenders with means than to those who are unable because of lack of means to do so. In some cases it will be difficult to strike the right balance between the public interest and the needs of justice on the one side and the interests of the offender and the expectations of the victim on the other.

Basic legal provisions

13.37 By the Powers of Criminal Courts Act 1973, Section 35(1) (as amended), the court may deal with an offender, either instead of or in addition to any measure, by making a compensation order in respect of any injury, loss or damage suffered by the victim of an offence. It is not necessary for the victim to make application for compensation and the offences for which an order can be made include offences taken into consideration. There are no formal limits on the amount of the order that may be imposed by the Crown Court but as far as magistrates'

---

37 Note 35 *supra*. See also *Stapleton and Lawrie* [1977] Crim.L.R. 366, and *Copely* (1979) 1 Cr.App.R.(S) 55.

courts are concerned limits are laid down by the Magistrates' Courts Act 1980, Section 40(1) (as amended) *i.e.* £2,000 in respect of any one offence. Where offences are taken into consideration, the total amount ordered to be paid still cannot exceed the maximum that could be ordered on the offences which are actually charged. Accordingly the extent of injury, loss or damage and the scale and range of compensation available to the Court, including compensation in respect of offences taken into consideration, will be matters that justices will wish to take into account in deciding whether or not to commit the accused to the Crown Court for sentence or trial. When an order is made, the court should make it clear what amounts of compensation are specifically directed to the charges and what to the offences taken into consideration, and a "global figure" order should not be fixed.[38] However, where all charges involve the same victim, it seems that a single sum may be ordered.[39]

13.38 The problems when the charges or offences taken into consideration reveal several competing claimants for the available funds so far as the offender or offenders are concerned, may be considerable in terms of the priority and proportionality of the claims where the funds are insufficient to meet the claims in full. Normally the approach to be adopted by the court in such cases is to apportion the total compensation made on a *pro rata* basis unless there are strong grounds for not doing so.[40] Thus in *Amey*[41] it was held that, where in the case of one large claim and several other smaller ones, *pro rata* apportionment would lead to inadequate compensation of the latter, the court could select some of the claimants and order their compensation to the exclusion of others. But it is a procedure that is unlikely to satisfy everyone.

Relationship of injury to offence

13.39 Section 35(1) requires that the injury, loss or damage should result from the offence, which seems to give the court a wide discretion in its approach to making an order. In *Rowlston v. Kenny*[42] it was stated that the test was not whether a particular loss results solely from the offence charged but whether it can be said fairly to have resulted from the offence.[43] Again in *Howell*[44] it was stressed that it is not necessary

38 *Oddy* (1974) 59 Cr.App.R. 66.
39 *Wharton* [1976] Crim.L.R. 520.
40 *Miller* (1976) 63 Cr.App.R. 56.
41 (1982) 4 Cr.App.R.(S) 410.
42 (1982) 4 Cr.App.R.(S) 85.
43 See also *Thompson Holidays* [1974] 1 All E.R. 823.
44 (1978) 66 Cr.App.R. 179.

that the injury, loss or damage should be the direct result of the offence but in this case, which concerned the innocent buyer of stolen goods, it was held that it was enough that it was part of the whole design of the offender to dispose of the goods by sale to an innocent buyer.

13.40 It is clear from *Bond*[45] that the courts may seek to compensate distress, anxiety, inconvenience, disappointment and "pain and suffering", and that damage to clothing or spectacles for example in the course of an assault are covered without the need for a charge of criminal damage to be included. However it was held in *Berkeley v. Orchard* [46] that a compensation order could not be made in respect of a person made ill by a drug formerly in the possession of a person convicted only of unlawful possession, on the basis that the injury could not be said to have resulted from the offence charged. Whether it would be otherwise if the offender had been convicted of supplying the drug to the user would obviously depend upon the facts of the case. However, in general terms it is perhaps questionable whether it would be in the public interest to make orders for compensation as between persons equally involved in illicit trading in controlled drugs.

13.41 So far as property is concerned, if there is no damage or loss of value to goods, then no compensation may be ordered.[47] The point is not whether or not the offender has profited from the offence but whether and to what extent the victim has suffered loss.[48]

13.42 As already indicated above, the courts have frequently said that compensation orders should only be made where the offender's legal liability is clear, which probably means that complex issues of causation and liability are more appropriately considered by the civil courts. In *Kneeshaw*,[49] where the offender pleaded guilty to burglary, the property listed as having been stolen included four rings which he denied ever taking and which were the only items of property not recovered. The victim made no application for compensation but an order was made and on appeal compensation in respect of the rings was set aside. The reason for doing so was that where there was a denial of the theft of particular items, the court should not consider making a compensation order unless there was an application supported by evidence of theft, and even then the court in the exercise of its discretion, should hesitate

45 [1983] 1 W.L.R. 40.
46 [1975] Crim.L.R. 225.
47 *Sharkey* [1976] Crim.L.R. 338; *Cadamarteris* [1977] Crim.L.R. 236; *Hier* (1976) 62 Cr.App.R. 233.
48 *Ford* [1977] Crim.L.R. 114; *Maynard* [1983] Crim.L.R. 821.
49 [1975] Q.B. 57.

to embark upon an investigation of complicated issues of fact. Again it is a matter of degree, and questions of remoteness have sometimes been considered by the criminal courts.[51]

13.43 One major area of inquiry that is largely excluded by the Act from compensation in the criminal courts is that "arising out of the presence of a motor vehicle on the road or other public place" (Section 35(3)). The exception to this general rule is damage arising from an offence under the Theft Act 1968, but then in effect only in respect of the motor vehicle which has been stolen or taken without authority; see *Quigley v. Stokes*.[52]

13.44 Furthermore, no compensation may be ordered in respect of loss suffered by dependants of a person as a result of his death (Section 35(3)).

Evidence of injury

13.45 Although the section makes it clear that it is not necessary for the victim of crime to make application for compensation, orders may not be made arbitrarily by the courts. As already explained, *Kneeshaw*[53] makes it plain that where the offender disputes the loss or damage *etc.*, and applications are made, they should be supported by evidence. But more generally, when the new Section 35(1A) to the 1973 Act was introduced by the Criminal Justice Act 1982, Section 67, providing that compensation

> "shall be of such amount as the court considers appropriate having regard to any evidence and to any representations that are made by or on behalf of the accused or the prosecution."

it was thought that this would remove the limitations imposed by *Vivian*,[54] which held that personal injury, loss or damage must be either agreed or proved. This latter rule was, of course, justified on the basis that an order for compensation is part of the criminal process and enforced by imprisonment in default. *Vivian* was distinguished in

---

50 *Schofield* [1978] 2 All E.R. 705; *Hammerton Cars Ltd v. London Borough of Redbridge* [1974] 2 All E.R. 216.
51 Powers of Criminal Courts Act 1973, s. 35(2) and (3).
52 (1976) 64 Cr.App.R. 198.
53 Para. 13.42 and note 51 *supra*.
54 [1979] 1 All E.R. 48.

Bond[55] on the ground that it applied not to personal injury but only to physical damage, and in *Davies*[56] it was made clear that if there is no suggestion that injuries are caused other than by the offence, an order will be made, *i.e.* disputes as to extent of injury will not prevent an order, only disputes as to causation. Then in *R. v. Horsham Justices, ex parte Richards*[57] it was held that representations alone by the prosecution were not enough and that the prosecution had to prove loss by evidence *and* representations. Once more if there is a dispute as to cause of loss, this should be dealt with by the civil courts. In *Swann*[58] the Court of Appeal said that the new Section 35(1A) was intended only

> "to ameliorate the strict requirements laid down in the cases of the burden of proof required before compensation orders could be made."

The order

13.46 By Section 35(4) of the Powers of Criminal Courts Act 1973 in making an order the court must have regard to the means of the offender. The effect of such a provision is likely to be that the courts will interpret it restrictively and will err on the side of safety so far as the offender is concerned to the disadvantage of the victim.

13.47 Thus in *Harrison*[59] it was held that it is generally wrong in principle to make an order which would inevitably mean the sale of the offender's home.[60] However in *Workman*[61] it was held to be legitimate to expect household items bought with the proceeds of the crime to be sold to pay compensation.

13.48 It is of interest to note that the police have no power to retain a defendant's money on the basis that it will then be available for the satisfaction of a compensation order should one be made.[62]

13.49 The courts have sometimes sought to mitigate the strictness of Section 35(4) and it was held in *Bradburn*[63] that the fact that an offender has no means or only limited means does not imply that no order can be made against him, Lord Widgery, C.J. observing:

55 [1983] 1 W.L.R. 40.
56 [1982] Crim.L.R. 243.
57 (1985) 7 Cr.App.R.(S) 158.
58 (1984) 6 Cr.App.R.(S) 22.
59 (1980) 2 Cr.App.R.(S) 313.
60 See also *Heath* (1984) 6 Cr.App.R.(S) 397, and *Butt* [1986] Crim.L.R. 755.
61 (1979) 1 Cr.App.R.(S) 335.
62 *Malone* [1979] 1 All E.R. 256.
63 (1973) 57 Cr.App.R. 948.

"We think that as long as a man has his normal physical health and is, therefore, capable of earning something, it is perfectly proper to make a compensation order against him although the amount may well be restricted by reason of the probability that his earnings will be comparatively small. It is not right to restrict compensation orders to cases where the defendant can easily pay."

In *Workman* the court made the point that it would be "contrary to propriety and justice" *not* to make an order, despite the offender's low income, the defendant having "sought to feather her nest by stealing."

13.50 It is sometimes questioned whether in times of high unemployment it is right to order compensation at all when the chances of obtaining work are negligible. In *Webb and Davis*[64] and in *Mortimer*[65] it was held that it is no use making such an order where there is no realistic possibility of it being paid. However, in these cases the courts were concerned with large orders and it is suggested that small amounts of compensation can realistically be ordered to be paid from social security benefits in appropriate circumstances and do something to reassure the victim that he or she is not forgotten in the criminal justice system. Many assaults could be made the subject of relatively modest orders, and more orders made in respect of damage done or loss suffered in burglary, in the taking of motor cars and so on. It is true that many such orders are made annually but the present interest in compensation could be utilised to stimulate wider use of the order as a constructive approach to crime and, on occasion, reconciliation between victim and offender. Sentencers should also bear in mind the fact that a victim can only apply to the Criminal Injuries Compensation Board if the award is going to be £550 at least.

13.51 One answer to the above problem is to allow time to pay or direct payment by instalments under Section 34 of the 1973 Act and the Magistrates' Courts Act 1980, Section 75(1). However it is clear from the cases that an order must not be oppressive,[66] nor should it become a millstone around the offender's neck.[67] Accordingly it is clear that both the amount and the length of time ordered for payment must be "reasonable". What is reasonable, however, is likely to be the subject of some disagreement as the decisions show – the best that one can say is that orders which require instalments for longer than two to three years

---

64 (1979) 1 Cr.App.R.(S) 16.
65 [1977] Crim.L.R. 624.
66 *Miller* (1976) 63 Cr.App.R. 56.
67 *Inwood* (1974) 60 Cr.App.R. 70.

are likely to be held to be unreasonable. In *Daly*[68] an order requiring payment over six years was reduced to three years (with a reduced amount), and in recent cases it has been held that, as with fines, amounts of compensation that would take more than a year to pay off are "wrong in principle".[69] More recently in *Scott*[70] Watkins, L.J. laid down guidelines for the Crown Court when making compensation orders, saying that "the court had endeavoured, as the authorities showed, to impress upon judges that compensation orders should not be made without careful inquiry by the court into the defendant's ability to pay". He added that once the court was satisfied about this ability the period of time given to the defendant to pay should not be excessive.

13.52   In *Bradburn*[71] the court observed that it was "generally much better that these orders should be sharp in their effect rather than protracted".

13.53   The attitude of the courts towards contributions from other persons has not always been consistent. There is a certain attraction in the rough justice of ordering compensation against one offender in the expectation that others not brought to book will contribute – especially where each is wholly liable as a joint tortfeasor. However, it has been held that the promises of friends and families should be disregarded when considering the offender's means.[72]

Combining compensation with other measures

13.54   As has already been stated above, by Section 35(1) of the Powers of Criminal Courts Act 1973 a compensation order may be made either instead of or in addition to dealing with an offender in any other way, Section 12(4) making it clear that it can be combined with a probation order or a discharge, and Section 14(8) expressly providing that it can be made with community service. But while there is nothing wrong in principle with a compensation order and a fine being imposed at the same time, Section 35(4A) makes it clear that when both are considered appropriate but the offender has insufficient means to pay

---

68 (1973) 58 Cr.App.R. 333.
69 *Holden* (1985) 7 Cr.App.R.(S) 7; *Hills* [1986] Crim.L.R. 756.
70 (1986) *The Times*, 2 April.
71 (1973) 57 Cr.App.R. 948; para. 13.49 *supra*.
72 *Inwood* (1974) 60 Cr.App.R. 70; *Hunt* [1983] Crim.L.R. 270.

both at appropriate levels, then the court shall give preference to compensation, although it may still impose a fine as well.

13.55   Again while it is not wrong in principle to combine compensation with an immediate custodial sentence or with a suspended sentence of imprisonment, it must not be done in an oppressive manner and the cases suggest that it is seldom appropriate to do so when imposing an immediate custodial sentence[73] unless there is evidence of the offender's possession of the proceeds of crime or unless he has assets out of which an order can be made.[74] The point frequently made is that discharged prisoners are often short of money and it is hardly in the public interest that they should be tempted to commit further crime in order to fund an existing order for compensation.[75] However, a contrary view was taken by the court in *Workman*[76] where the Court of Appeal upheld an order of £2,118 compensation to be paid in instalments of £10 per week after the offender's release from a six months' sentence, although it recognised that the order

> "might put upon her so heavy a burden as to tempt her to commit other offences in order to meet the obligation under it."

The justification for this approach was that the offender had used stolen money to buy expensive household goods and to help purchase the house where she would continue to live after her release.

13.56   Accordingly it seems that whether compensation and immediate custody should be ordered at the same time will depend upon the circumstances such as the length of sentence, means and assets of the offender and their sources.

13.57   So far as the suspended sentence is concerned, when considering whether to combine it with compensation, the court shoud also take into account the question whether activation of the suspended sentence would affect the capacity to pay on the lines suggested above.[77]

Payment of compensation where there are joint offenders

13.58   Generally the rule about equal guilt applies to awards of compensation against joint offenders, so that they pay in equal propor-

---

73   *Wilkinson* [1980] 1 W.L.R. 396; *Shenton* (1979) 1 Cr.App.R.(S) 81.
74   *Morgan* (1982) 4 Cr.App.R.(S) 358.
75   *Oddy* (1974) 59 Cr.App.R. 66; *Miller* (1976) 63 Cr.App.R. 56; *Wylie* [1975] R.T.R. 94; *Morgan* (note 75 *supra*).
76   (1979) 1 Cr.App.R.(S) 335.
77   *Whenman* [1977] Crim.L.R. 430; *McGee* [1978] Crim.L.R. 370.

tions unless the evidence indicates to the contrary or their capacity to pay is entirely different.[78] Joint and several orders should not be made.[79]

Compensation by children

13.59 As in the case of fines, compensation in respect of an offence committed by a child must be paid by the parents or guardians unless the court is satisfied:

(1) That the parent or guardian cannot be found; or

(2) That it would be unreasonable to make an order for payment having regard to the circumstances of the case.

Enforcement and review

13.60 Compensation orders are enforceable as fines. For the powers of magistrates' courts to review compensation orders see the Powers of Criminal Courts Act 1973, Section 37.

COSTS

13.61 The procedure for ordering the payment of costs in criminal cases is now governed by Part II of the Prosecution of Offences Act 1985. This Act replaces the Costs in Criminal Cases Act 1973, and with the introduction of the Crown Prosecution Service abolishes payment of prosecution costs (except in the case of private prosecutions) from central funds. As a theoretically self-funding body the Crown Prosecution Service will accordingly in all appropriate cases seek to obtain the full costs of prosecution from convicted defendants. However, although this changes the emphasis so far as applications for costs are concerned, it does not of course make any change in the discretion of the courts to make orders for costs when it is considered appropriate to do so. The practice, however, is different to the extent that courts are now asked to specify amounts of costs to be awarded. The procedure for making awards of costs from central funds to acquitted defendants remains substantially unchanged although the number of situations in which it may now be done has been enlarged. The procedure by which costs could be awarded directly against the prosecution is abolished.

---

78 *Amey* (1982) 4 Cr.App.R.(S) 410.
79 *Grundy and Moorhouse* [1974] 1 W.L.R. 139.

Prosecution costs

13.62 In default of any guidance to the contrary, it is suggested that the approach that the courts should employ in deciding whether or not to order costs against the defendant under the 1985 Act should be in principle the same as that employed under the previous law. Thus in deciding whether to order prosecution costs to be paid by the offender, the court may take into account all the circumstances of the case, including the strength of the case against him and his knowledge of that case where he has pleaded not guilty.[80] This, however, is not as straightforward as it may appear, for although copies of the statements and depositions of witnesses are provided to the defendant when he is committed for trial on indictment, the position is different in summary trial and until recently it was not unusual for a defendant or his solicitor to know none of the details of the case against him, except those contained in the charge or summons itself, until he got to court. Now under the Magistrates' Courts (Advance Information) Rules 1985, the prosecution is bound if requested to provide at least a summary of its case to the defence prior to summary trial of an offence triable either way. Even with full disclosure of the prosecution case, it is not always clear until the trial is under way just how strong the evidence is or in some cases whether an offence has actually been committed. In *Singh*[81] the approach was rather different and it was emphasised that the ordering of costs against a convicted person was not automatic but rather a means of indicating disapproval of the manner in which the defence had conducted the case as, for example, fighting an evidently hopeless case or pleading not guilty where the truth of the matter must have been known to the defendant. This comes perilously close to penalising a defendant for exercising his right to plead not guilty and to undermining the principles of the burden of proof in criminal cases.

13.63 In a similar way it has been held in *Dawood*[82] to be wrong in principle to order an offender to pay costs simply because he has been convicted following jury trial, although this may be a factor if the decision to elect jury trial was "extravagant and unreasonable". Again it is difficult to see how in principle electing jury trial, even in the most minor shoplifting case, could be "extravagant and unreasonable" if there is a legal right to do so. Once more it is difficult to accept that an offender should be penalised for exercising it. If it is thought that it is

---

80   *Yoxall* (1973) 57 Cr.App.R. 263.
81   [1982] Crim.L.R. 315.
82   [1974] Crim.L.R. 486.

inappropriate to have the right to choose jury trial for such minor matters, then the proper approach is to abolish the right to do so.

13.64 What the courts have held, and with this one can have less quarrel, is that if it is appropriate to order costs against the offender, the costs of jury trial are inevitably greater than trial in the magistrates' courts and the order should realistically reflect the greater expense.[83]

13.65 A plea of guilty does not automatically exclude the ordering of costs against an offender but it is a factor which will be taken into account, although weight has to be given to the nature of the case and the stage at which the plea is entered.[84]

13.66 A change of plea at the last moment in the Crown Court can have little effect upon the expenses of a jury trial unless it actually saves several days of trial, a factor which could reduce if not prevent an order for costs. On the other hand a plea tendered at the earliest possible moment in circumstances where a defendant had always indicated an intention to plead guilty, is likely to be a persuasive point on costs as well as good mitigation of sentence.

13.67 It may be seen to be appropriate that where a person enters a written plea of guilty under procedures provided by the Magistrates' Courts Act 1980, Section 12, no costs should be ordered against him – indeed it could even be counterproductive in nullifying the advantage to the accused of procedures which are also administratively advantageous. Furthermore, it is doubted by some whether it is legally permissible under these procedures for an application for costs to be made at all.

13.68 In the past, although magistrates' courts have routinely made orders for costs against convicted defendants, the emphasis in the more serious cases was upon ordering costs to be paid out of central funds, thus leaving the courts to decide the appropriate financial penalty in terms of compensation and fines. As indicated above, with the abolition of the payment from central funds of costs of prosecutions conducted by public authorities (which includes the new Crown Prosecution Service as well as central and local government agencies and nationalised industries), the main difference is that in all appropriate cases there are now

---

83 *Hayden* (1975) 60 Cr.App.R. 304; *Bushell and others* (1980) 2 Cr.App.R.(S) 77.
84 *Maher and others* (1983) 5 Cr.App.R.(S) 39.

applications for costs in specific amounts against individual defendants which the courts will have to consider.

13.69 Section 18 of the Prosecution of Offences Act 1985 makes it plain that applications may be made as follows:
(a) On conviction in a magistrates' court or the Crown Court; and
(b) On dismissal by the Crown Court of an appeal against conviction or sentence.[85]

In such cases the court "may make such order as to the costs to be paid by the accused to the prosecutor as it considers just and reasonable". The actual amount to be paid has to be specified in the order.

13.70 The ordering of costs to be paid by the accused remains a matter of discretion for the court. Apart from the considerations already outlined above in relation to the defendant's knowledge and conduct of his case, the courts will no doubt take into consideration such factors as the particular penalty imposed, the means of the offender where the latter are limited and the priority of different financial orders. As already discussed in this chapter, compensation orders take priority over other financial orders but there is no guidance about whether the fine should be considered before costs or *vice-versa*. That they are likely to be linked is made plain by Section 18(4) and (5) (see para. 13.77 below). It is also plain that an order for costs ought to be related to the offender's means and any other financial penalty imposed at the same time.[86] There is undoubtedly a problem of consistency as between different courts and benches throughout the country but one view is that, subject to means, the fine ought to be the measure of the gravity of offences punished in this way and in many cases it would reduce fines to derisory levels if the full economic cost of the prosecution were to be ordered to be paid first. Against this is the argument, which is likely to be supported by the Crown Prosecution Service, that it is in the public interest that the full cost of prosecutions should be made clear and should be paid to the prosecuting authority where means allow. It is perhaps a difference that may only be resolved by a Practice Direction.[87]

---

85 Powers to order costs in respect of committals for sentence are set out in the Costs in Criminal Cases (General) Regulations 1986 (SI no. 1335) r. 14.
86 *Rowe* [1975] R.T.R. 309.
87 In an address to the Somerset and South Avon Branch of the Magistrates' Association on 14 November 1986 Lord Hailsham, L.C. gave support to the Association's policy (most recently set out in *The Magistrate* (1987) *43* No. 2 at p. 30) that the fine should take precedence over costs except where a prosecution is brought privately.

13.71 As already indicated above, what is clear is that in fixing the amount to be paid in costs regard should be had to the offender's means.[88] It has also been held that where a defendant is sentenced to a substantial custodial sentence, he should not be ordered to pay costs as well unless he has private capital, and it has been pointed out that on his release his earnings will be necessary for rehabilitation.[89] In *Maher* it was also held that it was desirable in appropriate cases for the prosecution to be in a position to give a real estimate of the costs rather than for an over-estimate to be made.

13.72 However, it is suggested that where an offender is sentenced to a non-custodial penalty which is also non-financial the payment of costs, subject to means, becomes particularly appropriate.

13.73 In assessing the fairness and reasonableness of a particular application for costs (and this is likely to apply mainly to the Crown Court after a lengthy trial) the court may usefully consult the standard fees for counsel and solicitors in the preparation and presentation of cases applied in legal aid taxation. In the magistrates' courts the Crown Prosecution Service itself will seek costs according to guidelines which will be generally available, on the basis of a particular sum for guilty pleas and for contested hearings respectively in the different categories of case, plus a further sum for each five minutes of hearing time.

13.74 So far as the justices are concerned, the Divisional Court will act by way of *certiorari* if they exercise their jurisdiction in the calculation of costs wrongly, or apply unreasonably high figures in the calculations, so far as to produce orders which are so harsh and oppressive as necessarily to involve an error of law.[90]

13.75 The general rule that as a test of reasonableness, costs, like fines and compensation, should be payable within one year was applied in the case of *R. v. Nottingham Justices, ex parte Fohmann*[91] when an order to pay £600 costs at £10 per week (in addition to a £400 fine) was quashed when the offender was known to be in receipt of supplementary benefit.

---

88 *Whalley* (1972) 56 Cr.App.R. 304; *Mountain and Kilminster* (1978) 68 Cr.App.R. 41.
89 *Judd* (1971) 55 Cr.App.R. 14; *Gaston* (1971) 55 Cr.App.R. 88; *Maher and others* (1983) 5 Cr.App.R.(S) 39.
90 *R. v. Tottenham JJ. ex p. Joshi* (1982) 4 Cr.App.R.(S) 19.
91 (1986) *The Times*, 27 Oct.

13.76 In *Neville v. Gardner Merchant Ltd*[92] it was held that *prima facie* costs ordered should include an amount in respect of the time of an investigating officer spent on the case.

13.77 In making an order, a magistrates' court shall not by Section 18(4) order a person convicted of an offence to pay any costs where it has ordered a sum not exceeding £5 to be paid as a fine, penalty, forfeiture or compensation, unless in the particular circumstances of the case it considers it right to do so. Furthermore by Section 18(5), any costs ordered by such courts to be paid by a convicted defendant under the age of 17 shall not exceed the amount of any fine imposed on him.

13.78 By Section 18(2) the Court of Appeal, in dismissing an appeal or application for leave to appeal (including an application for leave to appeal to the House of Lords), may order the accused to pay costs to the person named in the court's order. The court may make such order as it considers just and reasonable and may include the reasonable costs of a transcript obtained for the purposes of these proceedings (Section 18(6)).

Appeals

13.79 There may be an appeal against an order for costs made in the Crown Court (Criminal Appeal Act 1968, Section 50(1)), but there is no right of appeal against an order for costs imposed by a magistrates' court (Magistrates' Courts Act 1980, Section 108(3)).

Enforcement

13.80 An order for costs against an offender made by a magistrates' court is enforceable as a sum adjudged to be paid on conviction (Administration of Justice Act, 1970, Section 41).

Private prosecutions

13.81 The opportunity for private prosecutors to have their costs paid out of central funds in respect of indictable offences only is preserved by Section 17(1) of the Prosecution of Offences Act 1985. Exceptionally central funds are also available for summary offences in respect of proceedings in Divisional Court of the Queen's Bench Division and the House of Lords. A private prosecutor will be able to recover any

92 (1983) 5 Cr.App.R.(S) 349.

expenses properly incurred by him in the proceedings, excluding loss of earnings and investigation expenses such as the hire of a private enquiry agent.

13.82 By Section 17(3) the court may order the payment of less than the full amount of the private prosecutor's costs out of central funds where the circumstances of the case make it inappropriate that he recover the full amount, as for example, when conviction is secured on less than the full number of counts charged. Where the court does order less than the full amount it is required to specify that amount; otherwise, unless the prosecutor agrees the amount to be paid, there will be a determination in accordance with the Costs in Criminal Cases (General) Regulations 1986.[93]

Where a case privately prosecuted is subsequently taken over by the Crown Prosecution Service, costs up to that time only may be recovered.

Defendant's costs orders

13.83 By Section 16 of the 1985 Act a "defendant's costs order" may be made out of central funds in favour of an acquitted defendant or a successful appellant. The significant change introduced by this section is that it now allows costs out of central funds to be made in respect of summary cases as well as "either way" and indictable offences. Included are cases not proceeded with, or where the defendant is discharged following committal proceedings, as well as where the defendant is acquitted on any count of an indictment, and where on appeal a "less serious punishment" is imposed—although no guidance is given as to what constitutes the latter. Also included are successful appeals in the Court of Appeal against conviction, a verdict of not guilty by reason of insanity, a finding that the accused is unfit to plead under the Criminal Procedure (Insanity) Act 1964, Section 4 and the substitution of a verdict of guilty of another offence and certain other findings and conclusions. A defendant's costs order may also be awarded on the determination of any appeal, whether favourable to the defendant or not, to a Divisional Court of the Queen's Bench Division, or the House of Lords, or in respect of the determination of any application for leave to appeal to the House of Lords.

13.84 Section 16(6) specifies that the award should be "such amount as the court considers reasonably sufficient" to compensate the defendant

93 SI no. 1335.

for properly incurred expenses in the proceedings, which again excludes loss of earnings. Section 16(7) allows the amount to be reduced to what is "just and reasonable" where the court is of the opinion that there are circumstances which make it inappropriate for the defendant to recover the full amount. Thus where a defendant is acquitted in part on indictment, it may well be that the court will decide to exercise the power to order payment of less than the full amount. By Section 16(8), in calculating a defendant's costs order, expenses incurred under legal aid orders are to be disregarded.

13.85 Where the court does not specify the amount, or where the defendant does not agree the sum specified, there will be a determination in accordance with the Costs in Criminal Cases (General) Regulations 1986.

13.86 It is suggested that in practice the discretion to awards costs under Section 16 will be exercised in a way similar to that followed under the Costs in Criminal Cases Act 1973, Section 3. The general principles to be followed have been set out in a number of practice notes and directions including the Practice Direction of 5 November 1981,[94] where it was observed that the exercise of the powers to order costs in such circumstances is "in the unfettered discretion of the court in the light of the circumstances of each particular case" and that it should be accepted as "normal practice" that payment of costs should be made to acquitted defendants out of central funds "unless there are positive reasons for making a different order". Examples of such reasons were listed as follows:

"(a) (no longer applies)
(b) where the defendant's own conduct has brought suspicion on himself and has misled the prosecution into thinking that the case against him is stronger than it is . . .;
(c) where there is ample evidence to support a conviction but the defendant is acquitted on a technicality which has no merit . . ."

13.87 It is emphasised that an acquitted defendant can no longer recover costs against the prosecution, but under Section 19 and the Costs in Criminal Cases (General) Regulations 1986, rule 3, there may be awards between parties in respect of costs thrown away by one party due to some unnecessary or improper act or omission on the part of his opponent.

94 [1981] 3 All E.R. 703.

Awards of costs in other circumstances

13.88 Under the Costs in Criminal Cases (General) Regulations 1986, Part V, payment of defence and private prosecutor's witnesses', interpreters' for the accused and medical practitioners' expenses may be ordered out of central funds.

CHAPTER 14

Discharges and Bind-overs

ABSOLUTE AND CONDITIONAL DISCHARGES

14.01 By the Powers of Criminal Courts Act 1973, Section 7, if the court considers, having regard to all the circumstances of the case including the nature of the offence and the character of the offender, that it is inexpedient to inflict punishment, and that in addition it is inappropriate to make a probation order, it may make an order discharging him either absolutely or on condition that he commits no other offence within a specified period of time up to three years from the date of the order.

14.02 In *O'Toole*[1] it was held that an absolute discharge was appropriate where there was no moral blame attached to the person convicted. In this case an ambulance driver who was answering an emergency call drove along a main road at between 50 and 60 m.p.h. with his blue lights flashing and his siren sounding continuously. Unfortunately another vehicle pulled across his path from a garage forecourt and a collision resulted. Both drivers were convicted of dangerous driving, fined £50 and disqualified, in the case of the appellant for 12 months. Sachs, L.J., giving the judgment of the court, made the following observations:

> "Each case falls to be determined on its own facts and of course nothing in this judgment is intended to suggest that driving which is careless or reckless can in any circumstances be condoned by the courts. On the other hand it is for courts when imposing sentences in cases such as the present one to recognise that balance which must be maintained in the interests of the public between the essential element of not unnecessarily impeding the answering of the calls of humanity in emergencies and that of not involving road users in unnecessary risks. Great care has to be applied in determining on which side of the line a case falls. The tensions under which drivers of ambulances and fire engines have to work must not be overlooked and it is within the knowledge of the Court from other cases that any imposition of ill-judged penalties naturally tends, in detriment of the public interest, to cause unrest in the services on which everyone depends for rescue."

1   (1971) 55 Cr.App.R. 206.

He went on to say that the imposition of disqualification in the present case was ill-judged and substituted an absolute discharge for the penalty originally imposed.

14.03 It is suggested that an absolute discharge could also be used to signify that the offence was so technical or trivial that no penalty was justified; or where in the light of the character of the offender, no rehabilitation or reform was necessary, either because it had already occurred, and did not need the reinforcement of a mild deterrent like a conditional discharge, or because neither the support of probation nor supervision was necessary.

14.04 A conditional discharge on the other hand is a mild deterrent. It is a recognition that the circumstances of the offence are such that a retributivist approach or a sentence of general deterrence is not justified but that the avowed good intentions of the offender not to repeat his offence need some kind of legal reinforcement which falls short of the kind of support that probation and supervision would provide. It is therefore particularly appropriate for the first offender. It has also been held in *Wood*[2] to be appropriate where an offender's conduct does not justify a sentence of imprisonment, whether immediate or suspended, but he has no resources from which to pay a fine. In this case the appellant, who was a chronically sick man unable to work, was convicted of handling the sum of £2.23 by assisting in its retention. His son was arrested in connection with a burglary, and was allowed to get a coat from a room in the house; he took the money from a pocket in the coat and gave it to his father to look after for him. The appellant had been sentenced to nine months' imprisonment, suspended for two years: a conditional discharge was substituted.[3]

14.05 By Section 7(3) before making an order the court shall explain to the defendant in ordinary language that if he commits another offence during the operational period of the conditional discharge, he will be liable to be sentenced for the original offence.

14.06 The procedure to be followed to bring a person in breach of a conditional discharge back before the court is set out in Section 8. Once a court is satisfied that he is in breach it may then proceed to deal with him for the original offence in any manner in which it could deal with him if he had just been convicted by or before the court for that offence,

2 (1974) C.S.P. D1.3(c).
3 See also *McGowan* [1975] Crim.L.R. 113, and *Whitehead* [1979] Crim.L.R. 734.

save that a Crown Court dealing with an offender conditionally discharged by a magistrates' court is limited to the latter court's powers (Section 8(8)). A magistrates' court upon convicting an offender of an offence committed during the operational period of a conditional discharge imposed by the Crown Court may commit him in custody or on bail to appear before the Crown Court but cannot itself deal with the original offence (Section 8(6)).

14.07 Where a juvenile offender has been made the subject of a conditional discharge in respect of an offence only triable on indictment in the case of an adult, any court dealing with him subsequently for the original offence after he has attained the age of 17, may only use the powers which would have been available for an either-way offence tried summarily (Section 9(1) as amended).

14.08 Orders for an absolute or conditional discharge may be combined with ancillary orders such as orders for costs, compensation, or restitution,[4] recommendations for deportation[5] and disqualification and endorsement.[6]

BINDING-OVER

14.09 In this section will be covered the power to bind over persons appearing before the court to keep the peace and/or be of good behaviour, the power to order a parent to enter into a recognisance in respect of the care and control of a child, and finally the power of the Crown Court to bind over an offender to come up for judgment.

Binding over to keep the peace and be of good behaviour

14.10 The powers of a magistrates' court to bind over a person to keep the peace and/or be of good behaviour arise either on complaint[7] or on its own motion without complaint in respect of *any* person appearing before the court. These are ancient powers said to be derived from the common law as well as various statutes of which the oldest and most widely known is the Justices of the Peace Act 1361.

---

4 Powers of Criminal Courts Act 1973, s. 12(4).
5 *Akan* (1972) 56 Cr.App.R. 716.
6 Road Traffic Act 1972, s. 102.
7 For which the procedure is set out in the Magistrates' Courts Act 1980, s. 115. Detailed examination falls outside the scope of this book.

14.11 The use of these powers is essentially an aspect of preventive justice, for as Blackburn, B. observed in *ex parte Davis*:[8] "A binding of a party is a precautionary measure to prevent a future crime, and is not by way of punishment for something past. . . ." However, although a bind-over is not a sentence in itself, it is an order that may be made on conviction either instead of a sentence[9] or in addition to a sentence or indeed, following an acquittal. The Justices of the Peace Act 1968, Section 1(7) is declaratory of the fact that the powers are possessed by the Crown Court as well as the magistrates' courts.

14.12 Perhaps the most common situation where a person is bound over in the Crown Court is in the case of an indictment for assault where the evidence is not strong and the injuries are so minor that a full trial is not thought in the circumstances to be justified. In such a case where the complainant is satisfied by this course, the defendant may agree to be bound over on the prosecution offering no evidence. It is particularly appropriate where there is a dispute between neighbours.

Requirements of an order

14.13 By the order a person is required to enter into his own recognisance or find sureties for his good behaviour, or both, for a specified period, usually not more than 12 months. The person to be bound over must consent to the order but if he fails to do so he may be imprisoned for up to six months. There is no power under the 1361 Act to include any additional requirement such as a requirement for an offender to return to his country of origin.[10]

Procedure

14.14 The power to bind over arises in respect of a person who (or whose case) is before the court but it is obviously elementary justice that where the court is minded to require a person who has not been charged, such as a witness, to be bound over, it should give him an opportunity to make such representations on the matter as he may think fit.[11] It is to be noted that a person who has been brought

8 (1871) 35 J.P. 551.
9 It is to be noted that some Clerks to Justices take the view that a bind-over is an ancillary order and may not be imposed on conviction in the magistrates' courts instead of a sentence.
10 *Ayu* (1958) 43 Cr.App.R. 31; *R. v. East Grinstead JJ. ex p. Doeve* [1968] 3 All E.R. 666.
11 *Sheldon v. Bromfield JJ.* [1964] 2 Q.B. 573.

to court to give evidence but has not been called as a witness may not be bound over.[12]

14.15 Where an acquitted defendant is to be bound over, it is not essential that he should be given an opportunity to address the court first, but it is good practice to do so. Thus in *R. v. Woking Justices, ex parte Gossage*[13] Lord Widgery, C. J. observed:

> "It seems to me that a very clear distinction is drawn between, on the one part, persons who come before the justices as witnesses, and on the other, persons who come before the justices as defendants. Not only do the witnesses come with no expected prospect of being subjected to any kind of penalty, but also the witnesses as such, although they may speak in evidence, cannot represent themselves through counsel and cannot call evidence on their own behalf. By contrast, the defendant comes before the court knowing that allegations are to be made against him, knowing that he can be represented if appropriate, and knowing that he can call evidence if he wishes. It seems to me that a rule which requires a witness to be warned of the possibility of a binding-over should not necessarily apply to a defendant in that different position . . . .
> That is not to say that it would not be wise, and indeed courteous in these cases for justices to give such a warning; there certainly would be absolutely no harm in a case like the present if the justices, returning to court, had announced they were going to acquit, but had immediately said, 'We are however contemplating a binding-over; what have you got to say?' I think it would be at least courteous and perhaps wise that that should be done, but I am unable to elevate the principle to the height at which it can be said that a failure to give such a warning is a breach of the rules of natural justice."

14.16 Where the amount of the recognisance in which the court proposes to bind over a person is a substantial amount of money, he should be allowed to address the court on the question of his means and other personal circumstances.[14] A court has the power to bind over a juvenile with his consent, notwithstanding the fact that he could not be imprisoned for failure to agree or for breach of the recognisance.[15]

Effect of breach

14.17 On breach of a bind-over the person concerned may be required to forfeit the amount of the recognisance, but there is no power to commit such a person to prison unless he is in default of payment following an order for forfeiture.[16]

---

12   *R. v. Swindon Crown Court ex p. Pawittar Singh* (1983) 5 Cr.App.R.(S) 422.
13   [1973] 1 Q.B. 48.
14   *R. v. Central Criminal Court ex p. Boulding* (1983) 5 Cr.App.R.(S) 433.
15   *Conlan v. Oxford* (1983) 5 Cr.App.R.(S) 237.
16   *Gilbert* (1974) C.S.P. D9.3(a).

Bind-over of parent or guardian

14.18 Where a child is convicted of homicide or a child or young person is convicted of any offence, the court[17] may order a parent or guardian with the latter's consent to enter into a recognisance to take proper care of him and exercise proper control of him under the Children and Young Persons Act 1969, Section 7. By this section the period of the bind-over must not exceed three years or until the juvenile attains the age of 18 years, whichever is the sooner. The amount of the recognisance must not exceed £1,000.

Bind-over to come up for judgment

14.19 The Crown Court has the power derived from that possessed by the former courts of assize and quarter sessions, to release an offender without sentencing and bind him over on recognisance to come up for judgment if required to do so. Conditions may be imposed with which the offender must comply during the period of the bind-over on the basis that if he complies he will either not be sentenced or if he is, there will only be a nominal penalty. An offender must give his consent to the bind-over.[18] If he is in breach of any undertaking, he runs the risk of forfeiting the amount of the recognisance as well as being sentenced. It follows that once a person has been sentenced he cannot be bound over to come up for sentence again.[19]

14.20 The existence of such means of disposal as conditional discharges, probation orders and community service orders has to a large extent nullified the use of the bind-over to come up for judgment, which is now mainly limited to cases where the court wishes the offender to leave the country but cannot make a recommendation for deportation.[20] Where a condition to leave the United Kingdom is included, it should normally be used only to ensure that the defendant goes to a country of which he is a citizen or habitual resident.[21]

---

17 This includes an adult court.
18 *Williams* (1982) 4 Cr.App.R.(S) 239.
19 *Ayu* (1958) 43 Cr.App.R. 31.
20 *Hodges* (1967) 51 Cr.App.R. 361.
21 *Williams* (note 18 *supra*).

CHAPTER 15

Other Ancillary Orders

15.01 In this chapter we discuss a number of other ancillary orders available to the sentencer as follows:
  (1) Forfeiture and confiscation;
  (2) Restitution;
  (3) Recommendations for deportation; and
  (4) Disqualification from driving and endorsement of driving licences.

FORFEITURE AND CONFISCATION ORDERS

15.02 Forfeiture and confiscation orders may be seen primarily as deterrent measures designed not only to pursue and confiscate the direct proceeds of crime, such as the profits made from unlawful activity like drug trafficking, but also sometimes the valuable means of committing certain forms of crime, as in the use of motor cars. Forfeiture may also be regarded as preventive in the sense of ensuring the confiscation and destruction of those means themselves, as in the case of offensive weapons, housebreaking implements, counterfeiting equipment, controlled drugs and so on.

15.03 The legislation empowering such orders may be divided into two kinds: first there are the general powers to order forfeiture under the Powers of Criminal Courts Act 1973, Section 43, and secondly, specific powers of forfeiture under a number of individual statutes such as the Prevention of Crime Act 1953, Section 1, and the Misuse of Drugs Act 1971, Section 27, and confiscation under the Drug Trafficking Offences Act 1986.

General powers of forfeiture

15.04 The Powers of Criminal Courts Act 1973, Section 43 allows for the making of a forfeiture order in the following circumstances:
  (1) on conviction of any offence punishable on indictment with imprisonment for two years or more;

(2) where the property was in the offender's possession or control at the time of his apprehension; and

(3) where the property has been used for the purpose of committing or facilitating the commission of any offence *or* was intended to be used for that purpose.

The order may be made either by a magistrates' court or the Crown Court. By Section 43(2) "facilitating the commission of an offence" includes "the taking of any steps after it has been committed for the purpose of disposing of any property to which it relates or of avoiding apprehension or detection".

15.05 Whether property falls within the scope of Section 43 is a matter of fact for the tribunal. In most cases there is likely to be no difficulty and the property concerned will be easily identified as being used for criminal purposes. The sawn-off shotgun, the housebreaking implements found at the offender's premises on his arrest at home are unambiguously for the purposes of crime and will properly be confiscated under Section 43. However, problems have arisen with respect to property that could be used for innocent purposes such as motor vehicles, with which many of the decided cases have been concerned.

15.06 The first limitation on the use of this power is that the property concerned must be in the possession or control of the offender *at the time of his apprehension*, and in *Hinde*[1] it was made clear that this was a limitation which will be interpreted strictly. In this case the offender's car, containing stolen goods, was seized at the scene of the burglary but he himself escaped. He was arrested four days later. On appeal a forefeiture order in respect of the car was quashed on the basis that it had not been in his possession or control at the time of his apprehension. Bridge, L.J., giving the judgment of the Court of Appeal, explained that the concept of possession was a difficult one, but went on to say that any concept of possession "must include either an element of physical possession or an element of right to possession". Here it was plain that the offender had not been in physical possession or control of the car on his arrest because it was in police custody, and because on ordinary principles it was lawfully seized by the police, he could not *de jure* be entitled to any immediate right to possession. This, the court readily conceded, led to a result which appeared to be entirely without merit, and it concluded with this traditional statement of the role of the courts in such situations:

> "it is no function of this court, when considering criminal statutes, to strain the meaning of plain words in order to embrace what may appear to be a

1   (1977) 64 Cr.App.R. 213.

case which the statute ought to have dealt with. Parliament has quite deliberately used this unambiguous phrase 'in his possession or under his control at the time of his apprehension'. This car was not within that phrase and we have no alternative but to allow the appeal and quash the order under section 43 . . . ."

A similar conclusion was reached in *McFarlane*.[2] It follows that if there is no apprehension, as where proceedings are initiated by means of summons without arrest, there can be no forfeiture under Section 43: see *Bramble*.[3]

15.07   Whether or not an item of property was "used for the purpose of committing or facilitating the commission of any offence, or was intended to be used for that purpose" has produced some difficulty. In *Lucas*[4] the appellant with others gave a girl a lift in his car; she consented to "certain familiarities" and the appellant drove her to some waste land where she was indecently assaulted. On appeal a forfeiture order with respect to the car was quashed on the basis that it was independent of the offence and that it had not been proved that any offence was intended when the journey started. However in *Attarde*[5] a forfeiture of the car used to steal petrol from other vehicles by means of a petrol pump operated from the dashboard of the offender's car, was upheld.

15.08   Probably one of the most common ways of using a car for the purposes of crime (apart from simply as a means of conveyance) is to transport stolen goods. In *Lidster*[6] the Court of Appeal held it was entirely appropriate to order the confiscation of a car used by the offender to transport stolen goods. Forbes, J. observed:

"It is a case where the use of the motor car was an integral part of the offence. This offence could not have been committed by this appellant had it not been for the motor car and it is quite clear that the use of the motor car was the reason why the appellant was asked to commit the offence and why he did commit the offence. He committed it because he had a motor car which was suitable for dealing with the goods in this manner."

However in *Buddo*[7] Park, J. commented that the court is not required to make a forfeiture order in every case in which a vehicle is used in the

2   (1982) 4 Cr.App.R.(S) 264.
3   *Bramble* (1984) 6 Cr.App.R.(S) 80.
4   [1976] Crim.L.R. 79.
5   [1975] Crim.L.R. 729.
6   (1975) C.S.P. J4.2(b). See also *Brown* (1974) C.S.P. J4.2(b).
7   (1982) 4 Cr.App.R.(S) 268.

commission of a crime. In *Scully*,[8] where the offender had broken into a house and stolen goods worth £1,239 which he removed from the scene in his car, the Court of Appeal held the forfeiture order in respect of the car (worth approximately £10,000) combined with a sentence of nine months' imprisonment suspended, and a fine of £5,000, was too heavy a burden and the forfeiture order was quashed. It seems to be clear that forfeiture of the car was not in principle inappropriate in this case; it was simply that in combination with the other penalties imposed for the same offence, it was too severe a sentence overall and the totality principle had been offended. In *Thompson*[9] the appellant allowed his motor car worth approximately £8,500 to be removed from his garage and made a false claim on his insurance, stating that it had been stolen. He pleaded guilty to obtaining £8,500 by deception and was sentenced to fifteen months' imprisonment, suspended, fined £5,000 and ordered to forfeit the car and pay £500 costs. Roskill, L.J., giving the judgment of the court, assumed that the car came within Section 43 but said that it was wrong in principle to make a forfeiture order in this type of case. He then went on to point out that the effect of the various financial penalties imposed on top of the suspended sentence, was to require the offender to lose some £14,000, which was out of proportion to the offence itself. The forfeiture order was accordingly quashed.

15.09 Nor should a forfeiture order be made where by *itself* it creates undue hardship. In *Tavernor*[10] an order in respect of the offender's car used to transport stolen drugs was quashed on the basis that it was too severe a penalty. The car had been purchased out of compensation arising from an accident in which he had suffered injuries and was needed for his transport because of the injuries.

15.10 It has been emphasised that a forfeiture order under Section 43 is an *additional* penalty and that it is wrong to make such an order merely so that the property forfeited may be sold and the proceeds applied to the payment of a fine or a separate order of compensation made at the same time.[11] All that an order under Section 43 does is "to deprive the offender of his rights, if any, in the property to which it relates"; thereafter the property is required to be taken into the possession of the police (Section 43(3)).

8 (1985) 7 Cr.App.R.(S) 119.
9 (1977) 66 Cr.App.R. 130.
10 (1974) C.S.P. J4.4(b).
11 *R. v. Kingston-upon-Hull JJ. ex p. Hartung* (1980) 2 Cr.App.R.(S) 270. See also *Thibeault* (1983) 76 Cr.App.R. 201.

15.11   It is also clear that a forfeiture order should not be made where the property concerned is the subject of joint ownership or in respect of which there are other encumbrances. In other words, as the decision in *Troth*[12] makes clear, forfeiture orders should only be made in "simple, uncomplicated cases". In this case the appellant was convicted of theft of coal, using a tipper lorry which was co-owned by himself and his partner and used in the course of their joint business as coal merchants. There was no suggestion that the partner was involved in the theft and on appeal a forfeiture order, depriving the appellant of his rights in the lorry, was quashed.

15.12   The power to make a forfeiture order does not apply to real property, so, for example, it has been held in *Khan*[13] that the courts have no jurisdiction to make such an order in respect of an offender's house.

15.13   In considering whether to make an order under Section 43, the court may act on its own initiative or on the application of the prosecution, but there must be a full and proper investigation, with evidence put before the court by the prosecution specifically to the point if necessary. In *Pemberton*[14] the appellant pleaded guilty to burglary and was sentenced to imprisonment with a forfeiture order in respect of five motor cars. It was agreed on appeal that there had been no adequate examination prior to the making of the order of the circumstances relating to the five cars. Giving the judgment of the court, Kilner Brown, J. said:

> ". . . It is incumbent upon the prosecution to justify the application (for forfeiture) and it is incumbent upon the trial judge to put the prosecution to proof if they simply state baldly, without any supporting evidence, that they seek an order for forfeiture. This applies equally, whether or not the article, usually a motor car, was used for the purpose of committing crime or whether it was purchased directly out of the proceeds of a crime previously committed."

15.14   Where there are several offenders equally responsible for an offence, an order made against one only may create unjustifiable disparity in their respective sentences and accordingly should not be made in such circumstances. In *Ottey*,[15] the appellant was convicted with others of conspiracy to defraud and was driving his car when

12   (1979) 71 Cr.App.R. 1.
13   (1982) 4 Cr.App.R.(S) 298.
14   (1982) 4 Cr.App.R.(S) 328.
15   (1984) 6 Cr.App.R.(S) 163.

arrested. The offences had taken place over several months and involved a total of £7,578. On appeal, a forfeiture order in respect of the car was quashed on the basis that where several offenders were equally involved, it was wrong to impose on one the additional penalty of forfeiture.

Forfeiture orders under Section 43 Powers of Criminal Courts Act 1973 combined with other measures

15.15   As already indicated in *R. v. Kingston-upon-Hull Justices ex parte Hartung*,[16] a forfeiture order is an additional penalty. However, it has been held that because of that it could not be combined in one charge with an absolute discharge,[17] or indeed with a conditional discharge,[18] because the court makes one of the two latter orders where it is of "opinion . . . that it is inexpedient to inflict punishment" (Powers of Criminal Courts Act 1973, Section 7(1)).

15.16   The same reasoning would appear to apply to its use with a probation order, which is "instead of sentencing" the offender (Powers of Criminal Courts Act 1973, Section 2(1)).

Forfeiture under other statutes

15.17   As has already been mentioned, several statutes enable the courts to make orders of forfeiture in respect of their subject-matter. One of those most commonly invoked is the Misuse of Drugs Act 1971, Section 27, which in respect of someone convicted of a drugs offence allows the forfeiture of anything shown to be related to the offence, including such items as drugs, money used in unlawful trading in drugs, equipment like scales, and so on. Under this section, property forfeited may be ordered to be destroyed or "dealt with in such other manner as the court may order", which allows the sentencer a very wide discretion.

15.18   By Section 27(2) the court may not make an order where another person, claiming to have an interest in the property, makes application to the court without giving that person a hearing and a chance to show cause why the order should not be made. But that is the only limitation and it does not prevent the court making an order in respect of property claimed by another person once his claim has been

---

16 (1980) 2 Cr.App.R.(S) 270; para. 15.10 *supra*.
17 *Hunt* [1978] Crim.L.R. 697.
18 *Savage* (1983) 5 Cr.App.R.(S) 216.

rejected. As it happens, there are not many claimants for drugs seized by the Customs or police!

15.19 It has been held that before such an order may be made, it must be shown that the property sought to be forfeited must be related to the particular offence committed under the Act and not related to intended future offences. Thus in *Morgan*[19] the appellant pleaded guilty to possession with intent to supply and other offences, and was sentenced to imprisonment with an order for forfeiture of £393 found in his possession at the time of his arrest. On appeal, although it was accepted that the money was part of his working capital for the purpose of his trade in drugs, it was pointed out that he was convicted of possession with intent to *supply* and would not have required the money to sell them. The court went on to hold that there was insufficient evidence to justify the conclusion that the money related to the offence of which he was convicted, and quashed the forfeiture order. This may be seen to be an unnecessarily restrictive interpretation of the words "related to the offence", but in any event it would seem that the confiscation of "working capital" would be covered by the Powers of Criminal Courts Act 1973, Section 43 (see para. 15.04 above).

15.20 Similarly in *Ribeyre*[20] it was held that it would be straining the construction of Section 27 to hold that money admitted to be the proceeds of *past* drugs sales was related to a conviction for possession with intent to supply.

15.21 It has also been held in *Cuthbertson*[21] that the power to order forfeiture under the Misuse of Drugs Act 1971 does not apply to offences of conspiracy to commit an offence under the Act.[22]

15.22 Powers were also introduced by the Drug Trafficking Offences Act 1986 to "follow the assets" of drug dealers and strip traffickers of the profits of their activities by the making of confiscation orders.

---

19 [1977] Crim.L.R. 488.
20 (1982) 4 Cr.App.R.(S) 165.
21 (1980) 2 Cr.App.R.(S) 214.
22 It was also held in *Cuthbertson* that to be subject to a forfeiture order under s. 27, property must be within the jurisdiction of the English courts.

15.23 Thus where a person appears before the Crown Court to be sentenced[23] in respect of one or more drug trafficking offences defined by Section 38(1),[24] before and in addition to passing whatever sentence the court thinks is appropriate, it must determine whether the offender has benefited from drug trafficking by receiving any payment or reward from it. If he has, the court must make a confiscation order.[25] The amount of the order will be the sum assessed as the value of the proceeds of the offender's whole drug trafficking career and not just the proceeds of the offences with which he is charged on the present occasion.[26] In making the assessment the court is empowered to assume that all the offender's property and everything owned in the previous six years is or represents the proceeds of drug trafficking unless it is shown otherwise, but the order should not exceed the offender's current assets.[27] The Act provides for the tendering of statements relating to the offender's alleged benefit from drug trafficking and states, *inter alia*, that when an allegation is accepted by either side it shall be conclusive of the matters to which it relates.[28] Powers of enforcement are set out at Sections 6 to 13 and fall outside the scope of this work, but it is to be noted that confiscation orders are enforceable as fines in terms of the periods of imprisonment ordered to be served in default of payment (see para. 13.28 *supra*, as amplified by Section 6). The Act also provides for the imposition by the High Court of "restraint orders" prohibiting any person dealing with any realisable property, and charging orders in respect of land, securities etc. Powers are also available for the appointment of a receiver in respect of realisable property.

15.24 Specific powers of forfeiture under other legislation includes the following:
Incitement to Disaffection Act 1934, s. 3
Prevention of Crime Act 1953, s. 1
Obscene Publications Act 1964, s. 1

23 On conviction on indictment or committal for sentence under the Magistrates' Courts Act 1980, s. 38, but not on committal under s.37 or committal under the Criminal Justice Act 1967, s. 56. By s. 1(1) Drug Trafficking Offences Act 1986 the procedure is not required to be followed in the case of an offender who has "previously been sentenced or otherwise dealt with", *i.e.* on appeal to the Crown Court or on breach proceedings in respect of probation, community service, or a suspended sentence or for revocation of a parole licence. For further details see Bucknell and Ghodse on *Misuse of Drugs* (1st Supplement 1986).
24 Including producing, supplying and possession with intent to supply controlled drugs of all classes, offences of importation contrary to Misuse of Drugs Act 1971, s. 3, and attempting, conspiring, inciting or aiding the commission of any such offences.
25 Drug Trafficking Offences Act 1986, s. 1.
26 S. 2(1) and (4).
27 S. 2(2), (3) and (4).
28 S. 3.

Firearms Act 1968, s. 52
Immigration Act 1971, s. 25(6)
Customs and Excise Management Act 1979, ss. 139-144
Forgery and Counterfeiting Act 1981, s. 24
Prevention of Terrorism Act 1984, ss. 1 and 10.

RESTITUTION

15.25 A restitution order requires the return of a specific item (or in certain limited circumstances its value in money) to the loser from whom it has been unlawfully obtained. Since the more general introduction of compensation, which is more flexible in its operation, it has become a less significant form of reparation so far as the victim is concerned.

15.26 The present rules for restitution are contained in the Theft Act 1968, Section 28 (as amended) by which, where it is established before a court:

(1) that the goods in question have been stolen, and either

(2) a person is convicted of any offence with reference to the theft (whether or not the stealing is the gist of the offence), or

(3) a person is convicted of any other offence but an offence in (2) is taken into consideration in determining sentence, the court may order anyone having possession or control over the goods to restore them to the loser. Where the offender is no longer in possession of the stolen goods but has other goods which directly or indirectly represent the lost goods as the proceeds of their disposal or realisation, the court may on application order the transfer of such goods to the person entitled to them. A sum not exceeding the value of the "stolen" goods may also be ordered to be paid by the court from sums found on the offender on his arrest. If the last two orders are combined, the court must, of course, ensure that the loser does not receive more than the value of the goods stolen.[29] The advantage of making a restitution order over a compensation order from money found in the defendant's possession on arrest is, of course, that the police can ensure that the money is actually handed over to the victim. Whether or not a person is entitled to stolen goods or goods or monies representing them in the possession of the offender is a matter of civil law. Accordingly it is plain that restitution orders should only be made in cases where the situation is clear and not where there is

---

29 *Parsons and Haley* (1976) C.S.P. J3.2(f).

any question of the property or money concerned belonging to a third party.[30] In *Calcutt and Varty*,[31] Woolf, J. made the point directly when he said:

> ". . . this court has repeatedly emphasised that a restitution order should only be made where it is clear that the money or goods in question fall within the statutory provisions to which we have just referred. It is important that if there is doubt the court should not make an order, since injustice can be caused, particularly to third parties who have no rights to intervene in the criminal proceedings. Furthermore, the criminal courts are not the appropriate forum in which to satisfactorily ventilate complex issues as to the ownership of such money or goods. In cases of doubt it is better to leave the victim to pursue his civil remedies or, alternatively, to apply to the Magistrates' Court under the Police (Property) Act 1897. On the other hand, in appropriate cases where the evidence is clear, it is important that the court should make proper use of the power to order restitution since this can frequently avoid unnecessary expense and delay in the victim receiving the return of his property."

15.27 All this stresses the importance of establishing the factual basis for the order. It was also held in *Church*[32] that a restitution order should not be made unless the evidence on which it is based is given before sentence is imposed, and not merely added on to the sentence as an afterthought.

RECOMMENDATIONS FOR DEPORTATION

15.28 The court's powers to made recommendations for deportation are now governed by the Immigration Act 1971, as amended by the British Nationality Act 1981. By Section 6(3) of the 1971 Act a recommendation may be made in respect of any person who is not a British citizen who is aged 17 or over and is convicted of an offence punishable with imprisonment as an adult. A British citizen (*i.e.* a person with the right of abode in the United Kingdom) is defined by the 1981 Act, but by Section 7 of the 1971 Act a Commonwealth citizen or a citizen of the Irish Republic shall not be recommended for deportation if he was resident in the United Kingdom when the 1971 Act came into force and has been ordinarily resident there for the five years prior to conviction. In view of the passage of time, few defendants will any longer be able to benefit from this exception. In this connection periods of six months or more spent in prison or in detention do not count

---

30 *Ferguson* (1970) 54 Cr.App.R. 410.
31 (1985) 7 Cr.App.R.(S) 385.
32 (1970) 55 Cr.App.R. 65.

towards the five years (Section 7(3)). Temporary absence on holiday will be disregarded. In cases of dispute the onus is on the offender by Section 3(8) to show that he is a British citizen or is otherwise exempted under the Act, but by Section 6(2) a court shall not make a recommendation for deportation unless seven days' written notice is given, if necessary the court adjourning after conviction for this to be done or for the seven days to elapse. It has been held that where the court is considering making a recommendation for deportation, it should bring the matter to the attention of the defence so that representation may specifically be made and mitigation advanced as to why such a recommendation should not be made.[33] In *Nazari*[34] the further point was made that no court should make an order recommending deportation without a full inquiry into the circumstances and not "as has sometimes happened in the past, by adding a sentence as if by an afterthought . . ."

Exercise of the discretion to recommend deportation

15.29 The decision whether or not to make an actual deportation order rests with the Home Secretary and is obviously a very grave step so far as the offender is concerned. It follows that the making of a recommendation by the court is something which should be exercised with the greatest care, not least perhaps because it would bring the administration of justice into disrepute if the courts habitually made recommendations which were not acted upon by the Home Secretary.

15.30 In recent years the Court of Appeal has given guidance on the general principles to be applied. In the first place, the court should consider whether the continued presence of the offender in the United Kingdom will be to the detriment of the community. As Lawton, L. J. put it in *Nazari*:

> "This country has no use for criminals of other nationalities, particularly if they have committed serious crimes or have long criminal records. That is self-evident. The more serious the crime and the longer the record the more obvious it is that there should be an order recommending deportation. On the other hand, a minor offence would not merit an order recommending deportation. In the Greater London area, for example, shoplifting is an offence which is frequently committed by visitors to this country. Normally an arrest for shoplifting followed by conviction, even if there were more than one offence being dealt with, would not merit a recommendation for deportation. But a series of shoplifting offences on

33 *Antypas* (1972) 57 Cr.App.R. 207.
34 (1980) 2 Cr.App.R.(S) 84.

different occasions may justify a recommendation for deportation. Even a first offence of shoplifting might merit a recommendation if the offender were a member of a gang carrying out a planned raid on a departmental store."

15.31 The effect of European Economic Community law, and in particular the principles contained in Articles 3 and 9 of the Council Directive 64/221/EEC, on the right of member countries under their domestic laws to order the deportation of E.E.C. citizens, were considered in *re Bouchereau*[35] and in *R.v. Secretary of State, ex parte Santillo*.[36] Summarised, these decisions lay down that an offender who is an E.E.C. citizen should not be recommended for deportation solely because he has a criminal record but that such a recommendation may be made if the court considers that his record together with the offence of which he is convicted, makes it likely that he will re-offend. These cases also decide that reasons for recommendations should be given.

15.32 In *Kraus*[37] the Court of Appeal upheld the recommendation for deportation of a West German citizen who had pleaded guilty to two offences of theft of sums totalling over £2,000 from his employer. The appellant was also sentenced to six months' imprisonment. It was argued on his behalf that he did not constitute a threat to the fundamental interests of society, as was required by the decision in *Bouchereau*, as his only offences were against property, and that there was no evidence that he was likely to commit any offences against public policy in the future. However on his own admission the appellant had committed a serious offence as a result of blackmail in relation to his membership of the Nazi party in Germany, which was itself an illegal organisation. Watkins, L. J. observed:

> "There is in our view a reasonable apprehension that he will, or may be the subject of further acts of blackmail by the British Movement which holds beliefs similar to those which he himself had held when he belonged to the Nazi party in Germany. There is no guarantee whatsoever that he has surrendered these beliefs himself. We are entitled to take notice, so we think, that members of parties such as the Nazi party are notorious for their unswerving allegiance to the objectionable cause they seek to serve and for the ruthlessness with which they seek to achieve their aims, including blind subservience to those who control the party from all the other members of it, where ever seemingly they may be."

For these reasons, the court concluded that the appellant's presence in the country constituted, in the words used in *Bouchereau*, "a genuine

35 (1977) 66 Cr.App.R. 202.
36 (1980) 2 Cr.App.R.(S) 274.
37 (1982) 4 Cr.App.R.(S) 113.

and sufficiently serious threat to the requirements of public policy affecting one of the fundamental interests of society."

15.33 It has been held that the fact that an offender is living on social security is not a factor which should be taken into account when making a recommendation for deportation, as not being of sufficient detriment.[38] Also where a person of previous good character in the United Kingdom is convicted even of a relatively serious offence, a recommendation for deportation will seldom be appropriate if it appears unlikely that further offences will be committed by the offender in the future.[39] In *Tshuma*[40] the appellant pleaded guilty to arson in setting fire to a chalet where a man with whom she had had an affair was staying and causing £3,000 worth of damage. The Court observed that it was a very serious offence but was committed under the stress of emotion and was unlikely to be repeated. Accordingly the recommendation was set aside.

15.34 It has been held that in deciding whether or not to make a recommendation for deportation the court should not take into account the political situation of the offender's country of origin. In *Nazari*[41] Lawton, L.J. made the point and the reasons for it crystal clear:

> "The courts are not concerned with political systems which operate in other countries. They may be harsh; they may be soft; they may be oppressive; they may be the quintessence of democracy. The court has no knowledge of these matters over and above that which is common knowledge; and that may be wrong. In our judgment it would be undesirable for this Court or any other court to express views about regimes which exist outside the United Kingdom of Great Britain and Northern Ireland. It is for the Home Secretary to decide in each case whether an offender's return to his country of origin would have consequences which would make his compulsory return unduly harsh. The Home Secretary has opportunities of informing himself about what is happening in other countries which the courts do not have."

However the court may consider difficulties of a personal nature which will affect the offender on his return, or the effects of deportation upon innocent people not before the court, such as the members of the offender's family. Thus in *Walters*[42] a recommendation for the deportation of a youth of 17 was set aside where its effect would be to send him

38 *Serry* (1980) 2 Cr.App.R.(S) 336.
39 *David* (1980) 2 Cr.App.R.(S) 362 (theft of a passport).
40 (1981) 3 Cr.App.R.(S) 97.
41 Paras. 15.28 and 15.30; note 34 *supra*.
42 (1977) C.S.P. K1.5(b).

back to a country which he hardly knew and which his parents had since left. The consequences of sending him back in such circumstances, it was observed, would be very severe indeed.

15.35 In *Fernandez*[43] a recommendation for deportation was also quashed where the appellant, a Spanish national, had lived in England for about ten years. His two children had been born in this country and English was their first language. Lawton, L. J. said that the Court "had no wish to break up families or impose hardship on innocent people".

15.36 It has been held that where an offender who has committed a grave offence is subject to a degree of mental instability which makes the commission of further grave offences likely, a recommendation for deportation may be appropriate.[44]

15.37 Persons entering the country by fraudulent means must expect to be recommended for deportation.[45] But those who fail to comply with a landing condition will not necessarily be made the subject of such a recommendation by the court, although it will remain open to the Secretary of State to make such an order if he thinks fit.[46]

Relationship between a recommendation and the sentence

15.38 It was held in *Edgehill*[47] that a recommendation for deportation was not part of the punishment for an offence and accordingly the offender should first be sentenced in the manner thought to be appropriate according to normal principles. Nor should the sentence be mitigated on the ground that the offender has been recommended for deportation. It seems, however, that there is nothing wrong in principle in combining a conditional discharge with a recommendation for deportation.[48] However, in view of the more recent decisions cited above, it might be difficult to find the right combination of gravity of offence and predisposition to commit future offences in relation to past conduct, to justify such a combination in practice.

---

43 (1980) 2 Cr.App.R.(S) 84.
44 *Dissanayake* (1980) 2 Cr.App.R.(S) 84.
45 *Uddin* (1972) C.S.P. K1.5(d).
46 *Akan* (1972) 56 Cr.App.R. 716.
47 (1963) 47 Cr.App.R. 41.
48 *Akan* (note 46 *supra*).

DISQUALIFICATION AND ENDORSEMENT

15.39 Disqualification from driving is an important weapon in the sentencers' armoury in dealing with certain motoring offences. It may be seen as acting retributively, as a deterrent and as a protection of the public. However the consequences for the offender can be very considerable in affecting not only his way of life in the short term but also his means of earning a living. Accordingly, the principles which govern the way in which it is used by the courts must be carefully examined. Furthermore, as driving whilst disqualified is itself an offence, it is an order which in some cases if not used sensitively and with restraint may be considered to be directly counter-productive.

15.40 Endorsement of driving licences is required to be ordered on conviction for a wide range of motoring offences (see Road Traffic Act 1972 Section 101(1)) and its significance for the offender and for the courts lies principally in the accumulation of penalty points within the statutory period which itself results in obligatory disqualification (see below).

15.41 Disqualification, which may be obligatory or discretionary depending on the circumstances, may be said to arise in the following four main situations:
  (1) Obligatory disqualification for certain grave offences;
  (2) Obligatory disqualification on the basis of the accumulation of penalty points;
  (3) Discretionary disqualification for other motoring (or associated) offences; and
  (4) Discretionary disqualification where motor vehicles have been used in the course of committing certain non-traffic offences.

15.42 In addition there is the power to order disqualification until the offender has passed a further driving test and a magistrates' court may also disqualify in the interim an offender convicted of an appropriate offence who is committed to the Crown Court for sentence.[49]

Obligatory disqualification

15.43 The offences which call for obligatory disqualification are the common law offence of manslaughter (by the driver of a motor vehicle)

---

[49] For a detailed discussion of endorsement and disqualification see Halnan and Spencer, *Wilkinson's Road Traffic Offences* (12th edn 1985), Chs. 19 and 20.

and the following offences under the Road Traffic Act 1972:

(1) Causing death by reckless driving, contrary to Section 1;

(2) Reckless driving when previously convicted of a similar offence or of causing death by reckless driving committed within the previous three years, contrary to Section 2;

(3) Driving or attempting to drive when unfit through drink or drugs, contrary to Section 5(1);

(4) Driving or attempting to drive with excess alcohol, contrary to Section 6(1)(a);

(5) Failing or refusing to provide specimens for analysis when driving or attempting to drive, contrary to Section 8(7); and

(6) Motor racing or speed trials on the highway, contrary to Section 14. On conviction for one of the above offences, the court *must* disqualify the offender for a minimum of 12 months (*vide* Section 93(1)), subject to the provisions of Section 93(4).[50]

15.44 Those convicted as aiders and abettors, counsellers or procurers of an offence where disqualification is otherwise obligatory, need not themselves be disqualified but must have ten penalty points endorsed on their licences. Furthermore where a court makes a hospital order or a guardianship order under the Mental Health Act 1983, Section 37(3) in respect of an offender "without convicting him" there would presumably be no need to order disqualification as there had been no conviction. But an offender ordered to perform community service or made the subject of an absolute or conditional discharge or a probation order must be disqualified unless there are special reasons (Powers of Criminal Courts Acts 1973, Section 14(8) and Road Traffic Act 1972, Section 102(1)).

15.45 Disqualification runs from the moment of pronouncement, i.e., it can no longer be imposed consecutively.[51]

15.46 If a person has a previous conviction in the ten years preceding the *commission* of a second similar offence for one of the following:

(1) Driving or attempting to drive when unfit through drink or drugs; or

(2) Driving or attempting to drive with an alcohol concentration above the prescribed limit; or

(3) Refusing to give a specimen for analysis or laboratory test (*when the accused had been driving or attempting to drive at the relevant time*),

---

50 See para. 15.46 *infra*.
51 *Higgins* [1973] R.T.R. 216; *Meese* [1973] R.T.R. 400; see also Transport Act 1981, Sch. 9, para. 2, which repealed Road Traffic Act 1972, s. 93(3) and (5).

he is bound to be disqualified for a minimum of three years unless there are "special reasons" for not doing so (Road Traffic Act 1972, Section 93(4)). These provisions do not apply when the conviction is merely for being drunk in charge of a motor vehicle.

Special Reasons

15.47 It may seem trite to say so, but the finding that there are "special reasons" gives the court a discretion in what would otherwise be cases of obligatory disqualification. Similarly there may be given a discretion not to endorse, and by not endorsing obligatory disqualification as the result of the accumulation of penalty points may be avoided. The phrase "special reasons" has not been defined by statute but in *Crossan*[52] it was held:

> "A special reason . . . is one which is special to the facts of the particular case, that is special to the facts which constitute the offence. It is, in other words, a mitigating or extenuating circumstance, not amounting in law to a defence to the charge, yet directly connected with the commission of the offence and one which the court ought properly to take into consideration when imposing punishment. A circumstance peculiar to the offender as distinguished from the offence is not a 'special reason'. . ."

This formulation was approved by Lord Goddard, C. J. in *Whittall v. Kirby*,[53] and in *Wickins*[54] it was held that to amount to a "special reason" a matter must:

(1) Be a mitigating or extenuating circumstance;

(2) Not amount in law to a defence to the charge;

(3) Be directly connected with the commission of the offence; and

(4) Be one which the court ought properly to take into consideration when imposing sentence.

In *Chatters v. Burke*[55] Taylor, J. stated:

> "In the course of this case Watkins, L. J., indicated seven matters which ought to be taken into account by justices if a submission is made that special reasons exist for the defendant not being disqualified. First of all they should consider how far the vehicle was in fact driven; second, in what manner it was driven; third, what was the state of the vehicle; fourth, whether it was the intention of the driver to drive any further; fifth, the prevailing conditions with regard to the road and the traffic on it; sixth, whether there was any possibility of danger by contact with other road users; and, finally, what was the reason for the vehicle being driven at all."

---

52 [1939] 1 N.I. 106.
53 [1946] 2 All E.R. 552.
54 (1958) 42 Cr.App.R. 236.
55 [1986] 3 All E.R. 168.

Obligatory penalty points disqualification

15.48 The detailed rules governing the imposition of penalty points may be found in other more specialised works of reference[56] but in general one may say that the penalty point system is designed to deal with the repeated offenders, whose offences by themselves do not justify individual disqualification, but whose conduct over a period requires disqualification to be imposed.

15.49 Under arrangements that came into operation on 1 November 1982, every endorseable offence attracts a fixed or variable number of penalty points (Transport Act 1981 (as amended), Section 19 and Schedule 7). A penalty points disqualification arises when an offender is convicted of any endorseable offence where the number of penalty points, accumulated in respect of offences committed within three years of the commission of the offence for which the offender appears before the court, reaches twelve or more (Section 19(3)). Unlike the "totting up" disqualification under the 1972 Act, Section 93(3) which it replaces, a penalty points disqualification does not run consecutive to any other disqualification – it takes effect from the moment it is made. In addition, where an offender is dealt with for one or more offences not *committed* on the same occasion, each offence committed on different occasions involves the imposition of penalty points.

15.50 Disqualification[57] wipes the slate clean in the sense that it removes from the offender's licence any previous penalty points but continues to count as a disqualification for the purpose of increasing the period of a subsequent penalty points disqualification (see below).

15.51 The statutory minimum for penalty points disqualification is six months, but by Section 19(4), where there has been a previous disqualification within the three years immediately preceding the latest offence in respect of which penalty points are to be taken into consideration, the minimum period is 12 months – similarly, if there have been two previous disqualifications within that time, the minimum period is two years.

15.52 By Section 19(5), when an offender is convicted on the same occasion of more than one offence involving discretionary or obligatory

---

56 *E.g. Wilkinson, op. cit.* (note 49 *supra*).
57 Any disqualification except interim disqualification under the 1972 Act, s. 103, disqualification where a vehicle was used to commit an offence under the Powers of Criminal Courts Act 1973, s. 44 (see paras. 15.59–65 *infra*), and disqualification under the Transport Act 1981, s. 21.

disqualification, the court is required, in determining the period of disqualification, to take into account "all the offences". It seems clear from the fact that the period under Section 19(2) is expressed as a "minimum period" that the court should take into account the number, if any, of penalty points that will be "wiped clean" and the number of penalty points that but for disqualification would be incurred.

15.53 A court is obliged to impose the minimum period of penalty points disqualification unless "having regard to all the circumstances there are grounds for mitigating the normal consequences of the conviction."

Mitigating circumstances

15.54 A number of grounds are excluded by Section 19(6). Para. (a) excludes "any circumstances that are alleged to make the offence or any of the offences not a serious one." However, although this prevents arguments against disqualification on this ground, it does not, it seems, prevent it being argued that a licence should not be endorsed on this ground and, of course, if there is no endorsement, penalty points are not imposed and the question of penalty points disqualification does not arise. Para. (b) excludes from consideration "hardship, other than exceptional hardship." What amounts to "exceptional hardship" is a matter of fact for the court do decide. It is also clear from *Cornwall v. Coke*[58] that the court may take into account hardship caused to the public and, it is suggested, to innocent third parties such as employers, employees or family. The burden of establishing "exceptional hardship" is, or course, on the defendant, and is to be established by evidence.

15.55 Finally, the court is expressly prevented by Para. (c) from considering circumstances taken into account on a previous occasion either for not disqualifying or for disqualifying for a lesser period than the minimum prescribed. How the court can decide that a matter has or has not been taken into account by another court in such circumstances is more difficult to say, given that even if court registers are available, the statement of the grounds for not disqualifying may not be as detailed as the subsequent court might wish. Once again the evidential burden of establishing that the mitigating reasons have not been employed before rests upon the defendant. However, the obligation for setting out the reasons in sufficient detail rests with the court.

---

58 [1976] Crim.L.R. 519.

Discretionary disqualification

15.56 All the offences in respect of which there is the power of discretionary disqualification are those offences which are required to be endorsed. Disqualification cannot be ordered, however, in the defendant's absence when he has pleaded guilty by post under the Magistrates' Courts Act 1980, Section 12, unless he has been given an opportunity to attend an adjourned hearing specifically for the purpose of considering disqualification. However, if notice of this has been duly served, disqualification may then be ordered if he does not attend. Again where the defendant has been summonsed and the matter is proved in his absence, the case must then be adjourned for him to attend as regards disqualification (1980 Act, Section 11(4)). Orders for disqualification, whether discretionary or obligatory, made in breach of this rule are invalid, even where the defendant knew that he would be disqualified.[59] If the offender fails to attend the adjourned hearing, he may then be disqualified. An absent defendant represented by barrister or solicitor is deemed not to be absent (Magistrates' Court Act 1980, Section 122).

15.57 Where the defendant has been convicted under the Construction and Use Regulations[60] for the dangerous condition of his vehicle, dangerously unsuitable use, insecure load, defective brakes, steering or tyres, *etc.*, he may not be disqualified if he did not know and had no reasonable cause to suspect that the facts of the case were such that the offence would be committed (1972 Act, Schedule 4, Part 1, offences contrary to Section 40(5), column 5).

15.58 Disqualification may also not be imposed when an order is made under the Mental Health Act 1983, Section 37(3).

Disqualification where vehicle used for crime

15.59 This power is now contained in the Powers of Criminal Courts Act 1973, Section 44 and can only be exercised by the Crown Court on conviction of a defendant of an offence punishable on indictment with two years' imprisonment or more, or on committal for sentence having been convicted of such an offence.

15.60 It is not an endorseable offence and accordingly does not count as a conviction for the purpose of a penalty points disqualification under

---

59 *R. v. Bishops Stortford JJ. ex p. Shields* (1968) 113 S.J. 124.
60 Road Vehicle (Construction and Use) Regulations 1986 (SI no. 1078).

the Transport Act 1981, Section 19. It also does not wipe the offender's licence clean and does not count as a disqualification for the purposes of increasing the minimum period of a penalty points disqualification under Section 19(9).

15.61 In order for a disqualification to be imposed under Section 44 it is necessary for the vehicle to have been used to commit the offence of which the offender has been convicted.[61] There is no power to make an order for disqualification under Section 44 for the offence of conspiracy to steal.[62] Before an order under Section 44 is made counsel should be given the opportunity of addressing the court on the question of disqualification.[63] Where an offender is sentenced to imprisonment he should not be disqualified under Section 44 for such a period as would prevent him from obtaining employment on release.[64]

Disqualification until the passing of a driving test

15.62 Where an offender is convicted of any endorseable offence the court may order him to be disqualified until he passes a driving test (1972 Act, Section 93(7)). It is clear that if a person is disqualified for a period *and* until he passes a driving test, he cannot take out a provisional licence until the period of ordinary disqualification is completed.

15.63 It has been held that Section 93(7) is not meant to be punitive but should be used where the offender is aged, infirm or inexperienced and where the circumstances are such that the public interest requires that the offender should be ordered to pass a driving test first.[65]

15.64 In *Guilfoyle*[66] the Court of Appeal reduced to 12 months a three-year disqualification of a lorry driver aged 19 convicted of causing death by dangerous driving, but upheld an order that he also be disqualified until he had taken a test, on the basis that an interruption of 12 months in his driving career was a substantial time for someone with

---

61 *Parrington* (1985) 7 Cr.App.R.(S) 18.
62 *Riley* [1984] R.T.R. 159.
63 *Powell and Carvel* (1984) 6 Cr.App.R.(S) 354; *Lane and others* [1986] Crim.L.R. 574.
64 *Wright* (1979) 1 Cr.App.R.(S) 82.
65 *Donnelly* (1975) 60 Cr.App.R. 250 (approving *Ashworth v. Johnson* [1959] Crim.L.R. 735); *Charlesworth v. Johnson* [1959] Crim.L.R. 735; *Banks (John)* [1978] R.T.R. 535.
66 [1973] R.T.R. 272.

his lack of experience. Generally it seems that the longer the disqualification, the more important is the requirement to take a test.[67]

15.65 A court should also not impose an order under Section 93(7) where the offender is not incompetent but suffers instead from disease or disability rendering his driving a danger to the public. In such a case the court should notify the Secretary of State for Transport under the 1972 Act, Section 92.[68]

Disqualification on committal for sentence

15.66 By the 1972 Act, Section 103(1), where a magistrates' court commits an offender to the Crown Court for sentence under the Magistrates' Courts Act 1980, Section 38 for an endorseable offence, it may disqualify him from driving until the Crown Court deals with him. Similar provisions apply to committals for offences committed during the currency of a probation order, conditional discharge or sentence of suspended imprisonment (Powers of Criminal Courts Act 1973, Section 24), and for committals under the Magistrates' Courts Act 1980, Section 56.

---

67 See also *Heslop* [1978] R.T.R. 441.
68 *Hughes v. Challes* [1984] R.T.R. 285.

CHAPTER 16

The Future of Sentencing

16.01 Crystal-ball gazing is not really the function of lawyers, nor perhaps of writers of books such as this. On the other hand it is difficult to see how the sentencing process can be improved over the years to come unless lawyers of all sorts – in Parliament, in court and in the law schools – give a little more time to the consideration of sorely-needed improvements. The contribution of the legal profession to the discussion of sentencing problems has over the years been piecemeal and minimal. There is possibly some excuse for the piecemeal nature of the contribution, for by and large Parliament has legislated in a piecemeal fashion after being advised by advisory bodies that had dealt with one or a few topics at a time. As a result the views of the legal profession have been sought on a limited number of sentencing points at any one time. There is perhaps less excuse for the minimal amount of interest shown by the profession.

16.02 There have been many criticisms of the judiciary over the years in connection with its difficult sentencing task. Many have come from legislators who might be said to speak from privileged glass houses when they throw their stones at the judges who cannot respond. However, whilst the Court of Appeal has striven manfully in recent years to introduce more order into the tangle of problems under the leadership of Lord Lane, C. J. and Lawton, L. J., and with guideline decisions, the formal contribution of Parliament, as we have seen, has not been particularly helpful. Statutes with sentencing provisions in them have been flung at the courts, recently in quick succession, with little consideration of how the new provisions were to fit in with existing ones, or how they were to be interpreted. Not that Parliament's task is an easy one either. As Hood has pointed out:[1]

> "The question of how sentencing legislation can be formulated is a tricky one, and one which has not had a successful history in this country."

One of the essentials for any significant improvement in the future is that our legislators must also devote more time, energy and thought to the complex problems of sentencing.

---

1   R. Hood, *Tolerance and the Tariff* (1974) NACRO, p. 13.

16.03 Over the years various suggestions have been made about the replacement of the present sentencers by a tribunal made up of various experts such as psychiatrists, probation officers, prison governors, police officers, together with judges and possibly a leavening of lay members. The experience of the Parole Board has been that a mixed panel of this kind can work very well; that sensible discussions by members with different backgrounds lead to good results, and that there is no danger of the judges attempting to overpower their colleagues in any way. The latter point is scarcely surprising, since lay magistrates have certainly not felt overawed by their professional judicial colleagues when sitting in the Crown Court.[2] However there is now an increasing awareness that merely switching sentencing decisions from judges and magistrates to others would not make the problems go away. Many of those who in the past were critical of the present system and enthusiastic about the idea of mixed sentencing tribunals, would probably now agree with the conclusion of James, L.J.:[3]

"On the other hand, an efficient sentencing practice does not require the sentencer to be a doctor, psychologist, or criminologist. Ability to understand, to evaluate and, in the appropriate circumstances, to give effect to the evidence of such experts is what is required. The established training programme for new magistrates, the conferences arranged by the Magistrates' Association branches, and the seminars and conferences for Recorders and Judges, arranged under the direction of the Lord Chancellor and Lord Chief Justice, have ensured, and continue to ensure, that the sentencing process is in the hands of those qualified to carry it out. Looking ahead then to the last quarter of this century, the writer concludes that there are good cogent reasons for leaving the courts as the sentencing authority. Such disadvantages as can be pointed to in the present practice do not seriously detract from the cogency of those reasons."

16.04 A more recent proposal for a new sentencing body was that put forward by Ashworth. It differed from the earlier ones in that it left the courts to pass sentence as now, but proposed a new sentencing council with significant powers:[4]

"My proposal is for a sentencing council, chaired by the Lord Chief Justice himself and producing recommendations which would be issued as practice directions with the full authority of the Lord Chief Justice. Its membership would draw on persons with considerable experience of the

---

2 G. Hawker, *Magistrates in the Crown Court* (1974) Institute of Judicial Administration, U. of Birmingham.
3 A. James, "The Sentencing Process: Present Practices and Future Policy"in L. Blom-Cooper (ed.), *Progress in Penal Reform* (1974) Oxford U.P., p. 170.
4 A. Ashworth, "Reducing the Prison Population in the 1980s: The Need for Sentencing Reform," in *A Prison System for the 80s and Beyond* (1983) NACRO, p. 14. See also K. Pease and M. Wasik (eds.), *Sentencing Reform: Guidance or Guidelines?* (1987) Manchester U.P.

penal system, from magistrates, to a circuit judge sitting at second- and third-tier centres, to a probation officer, a prison governor, a Home Office official and an academic. . . . A court which departed from the guidance ought to give its reasons for doing so. The Court of Appeal would retain its present role, subject to a duty to apply the guidance in practice directions and with a power to authorise reasons for departing from them."

16.05   Various suggestions have been made for the improvement of the present system by adding to the contributions which could be made by persons other than the judge or magistrate. From time to time probation officers have claimed that they ought to play a more important role in sentencing by, for example, sitting on the bench as assessors or technical advisers. We have seen that the idea of victim participation has been explored in the United States; in this country there is certainly an increasing feeling that the victim should be taken more into account. The suggestion is sometimes made that the victim's views should be ascertained as a matter of course before sentence is passed. Furthermore, as we have mentioned earlier, magistrates' clerks feel from time to time that their role is too much of an ancillary one, and that as experienced lawyers they ought to participate more in sentencing decisions.

16.06   There is one great disadvantage to be borne in mind when considering an addition to the number of participants in the sentencing stage, or changing the roles of those already involved to some extent. Research has shown that probation officers' recommendations are often followed, particularly in the lower courts. It must be borne in mind that not all probation officers have the same views – any more than all judges or all magistrates – about the various objectives of the system or the methods of achieving them. Bottomley has drawn attention to the fact that the divergent views of probation officers increase the problem of disparity. Judicial disparities, he pointed out,[5] are

"compounded by the apparent way in which magistrates follow the recommendations of equally 'individual' probation officers."

It is easy to see how the problem of disparity would be further aggravated by letting victims participate if one considers the example of two rape victims expressing their views to the court. One might say that she had forgiven the defendant and did not want to see him punished, even though he was a total stranger who had acted brutally and without any encouragement; whilst the other might say that she wanted her

5   A.K. Bottomley, *Decisions in the Penal Process* (1973) Martin Robertson, p. 167.

defendant flayed and imprisoned for life at the very least – despite encouragement on her part and the absence of any aggravating features. Should the courts be required to fine the first defendant and imprison the second for life? If not, how much weight should be given to the views of individual victims? Parliament would have to think very hard before introducing the victim or other participants into the sentencing stage in a formal way.

16.07 A similar suggestion has sometimes been made in relation to counsel for the prosecution, notably by Zellick, who has suggested that they should be given an enhanced role. This suggestion would seem to have a great deal to commend it. Zellick drew attention to the fact that sentencing is becoming increasingly complex, and that the judge needs all the help he can get. He wrote:[6]

> "To bring in the prosecutor would go some way towards making the sentencing of the offender, if not scientific, at least more disciplined; for it is essential that it be as rational as the present state of knowledge will allow."

16.08 No-one suggests that counsel for the prosecution should demand the maximum penalty, or claim that the offence in question was one of the worst he had ever encountered, but it might well help if he were able to address the court on the real alternatives open and if he were able to cite any relevant Court of Appeal decisions, whether of a guidelines nature or otherwise. The sentencing process would be lengthened, but the results might well be better, with fewer appeals based on the judge's failure to recall what the Court of Appeal had said on a given topic. Counsel would be obliged to make better mitigation speeches also, for an accurate summary of the relevant law and practice by counsel for the prosecution would have to be followed by a speech which dealt properly with the relevant matters placed before the court. Furthermore, the raising of the level of competence at the mitigation stage would in due course improve sentencing by judges as the experienced advocates reached the bench. That would be in addition to the immediate improvement in sentencing decisions.

16.09 There has been some reluctance on the part of the Court of Appeal to listen to the citation of previous decisions. As Thomas pointed out:[7]

---

6 G. Zellick, "The Role of Prosecuting Counsel in Sentencing" [1979] Crim.L.R. 493.
7 D. Thomas, "Sentencing Discretion and Appellate Review," in J. Shapland (ed.), *Decision-Making in the Legal System* (1983) British Psychological Society, p. 68.

"Counsel was praised for citing the 'clang of the gates' cases in *Smith*,[8] but citation of what were probably the same cases led to criticism of counsel in *Routley*"[9].

The reluctance to hear cases cited is diminishing, partly because the guideline cases are obviously designed to guide all sentencers, including those in the Court of Appeal, and partly because – thanks largely to Thomas – sentencing cases are now properly reported. Furthermore, there seems to be an increasing appreciation of the fact that consistency of approach cannot be achieved unless one looks at other decisions. The judiciary used to be similarly reluctant to allow the citation of earlier decisions in personal injuries cases when counsel first attempted to refer to the damages awarded in other cases. The reasons then given for shutting out earlier decisions have been heard in the sentencing debate also:

(1) Each case turns on its own complex facts;

(2) The brief reports of earlier decisions were not sufficently detailed to be useful;

(3) The time taken for trials would be unduly lengthened by the citation of a large number of cases.

In personal injuries most judges nowadays welcome the citation of earlier decisions, proper reports having become available over the years, thanks largely to the pioneering work of David Kemp, Q.C. A little reflexion will show that points (1) and (3) tend to melt away as point (2) is tackled. It seems likely that judges will similarly increasingly welcome the citation of previous sentencing decisions.

16.10 In response to Zellick's suggestion, King pointed out that counsel appear much less in the magistrates' courts than in the Crown Court; many defendants are not represented at all there, whilst others are represented by solicitors.[10] The particular problems of the lower courts would have to be borne in mind, but an improvement of the system in the Crown Court and in the Court of Appeal should be made if at all possible, if only because that is where the major decisions are made. That fact also perhaps justifies affording some professional assistance to the Lord Chief Justice and to Lords Justices who preside regularly over criminal appeals. Although English lawyers are some-times rather scathing about American judges having law clerks, it must

---

8 [1982] Crim.L.R. 469.
9 [1982] Crim.L.R. 383.
10 M. King, "The Role of Prosecuting Counsel in Sentencing – What about Magistrates' Courts?" [1979] Crim.L.R. 775. A useful publication which can help magistrates at the sentencing stage is K. Barker and J. Sturges, *Decision-Making in Magistrates' Courts* (1986) Fourmat.

be conceded that we possibly ask too much of our unaided senior judges.

16.11 The above improvement relating to prosecuting counsel could be introduced without legislation: probably all that is required is a practice direction from the Lord Chief Justice giving his blessing to counsel for *both* sides addressing the court on sentencing and to the citation of authority (even if not binding)."

16.12 Most important changes, however, can only be brought about by legislation. One of the matters which should be considered by Parliament is whether all the various sentencing powers of the courts are really needed, or whether the system could be simplified. Have the suspended sentence and the partly suspended sentence really been more of a boon than a nuisance? Is the extended sentence entitled to a further reprieve? In view of the matters we have discussed briefly above, can it really be said that that particular provision has been of much use? Also, would it not be possible to have a simpler method of dealing with alternatives to custody, with one universal obligation (a) not to commit any other offence during the relevant period, and (b) not to breach any requirement of the order, together with one method of dealing with breaches? Thomas has said of the present parole legislation:[12]

> "The extension of the parole scheme under the Criminal Justice Act 1982, s. 33, has in my view reduced the process of custodial sentencing in the Crown court to a complete farce."

Whilst this may be overstating the position, the legislature has clearly not to date given adequate consideration to the fact that, in sentencing matters as elsewhere, what the right hand does inevitably affects the left.

16.13 Sentencing legislation, as a glance at the various statutes will confirm, has been of a haphazard nature, with piecemeal attempts to improve the system. Whilst the Court of Appeal has in the past often said that it will not tinker with sentences, that is, make minor alterations, the legislature happily tinkers away from time to time, with barely a glance at its earlier contributions. Since the public, the police, the legal profession, the probation service and the reform lobbies have differing views about the appropriate measures to be used for different offenders, there should be ample time for consultation before any

---

11   The Lord Chief Justice has twice stated that he would welcome participation by the Crown at the sentencing stage, in *Dempster* (1987) The Times 10 April, and in *The Times* 9 May 1987, p. 24.
12   D. Thomas, "Parole and the Crown Court" (1985) 149 J.P. 344.

further legislation is passed. Lord Hailsham pointed to the best way to secure those various views:[13]

> "The Law Commission publishes its tentative conclusions as a Working Paper before it delivers a report, and a period of a year or two years of public discussion usually precedes the final consideration of the Working Paper by the Commission. This tends to prevent the kind of hysterical outburst which greeted the report of the Criminal Law Revision Committee."[14]

16.14 If a drastic revision of sentencing laws should ever be contemplated by Parliament, whether as a part of a Criminal Code or otherwise, not only should the various European penal codes be consulted, but also the various alternative approaches tried in the United States and the Commonwealth.[15] Whatever changes are made in the future, it will be important for the legislation to strike the right balance between depriving the courts of their discretion altogether and leaving the courts without any adequate expression of the legislature's intentions. In the meantime the judiciary and the legal profession should give the important questions of sentencing the attention they deserve. Those questions are not necessarily pure questions of law, but they certainly require the earnest consideration of the lawyers who are jointly responsible for the most important sentencing decisions of all, those affecting the liberty of the subject.

13 Lord Hailsham, *The Door Wherein I Went* (1975) Collins, p. 285.
14 *Eleventh Report: Evidence (General)* (1972) H.M.S.O. (Cmnd 4991).
15 See *e.g.* Judge R. Puglia, "Determinate Sentencing in California," in *The Future of Sentencing* (1982) U. of Cambridge Institute of Criminology; L. Wilkins, "Sentencing Guidelines to Reduce Disparity?" [1980] Crim.L.R. 201; *Revised Draft Sentencing Guidelines* (1987) U.S. Sentencing Commission; *Sentencing Reform: A Canadian Approach* (1987) Report of the Canadian Sentencing Commission.

Bibliography

References are to paragraphs at which the work is mentioned or discussed.

Anon—"Disparity in Sentencing" (1986) 150 J.P. 196 – 13.10

Archbold—*Pleading, Evidence and Practice in Criminal Cases* (eds. Stephen Mitchell and P.J. Richardson) (42nd edn. 1985) Sweet & Maxwell – 3.33, 8.13

Ashworth A.—"Justifying the First Prison Sentence" [1977] Crim.L.R. 553 – 9.06

Ashworth A.—"Judicial Independence and Sentencing Reform" in *The Future of Sentencing*, (1982) Cambridge University Institute of Criminology – 6.05

Ashworth A.—"Reducing the prison population in the 1980's: the need for sentencing reforms" in *A Prison System for the 80s and Beyond* (1983) National Association for the Care and Resettlement of Offenders, 1.15, 16.04

Ashworth A.—*Sentencing and Penal Policy*, (1983) Weidenfeld & Nicolson – 1.40, 1.70, 3.17

Ashworth A.—"Techniques of Guidance on Sentencing" [1984] Crim.L.R. 519 – 1.43, 2.15, 7.34, 9.26

Ashworth A. *et al*—*Sentencing in the Crown Court*, (1984) Oxford Centre for Criminological Research Paper No. 10 – 4.20

Ashworth A. and Gostin L.—"Mentally Disordered Offenders and the Sentencing Process" [1984] Crim.L.R. 209 – 5.12

Baldwin J. and McConville N.—*Negotiated Justice; Pressures to Plead Guilty,* (1977) Martin Robertson – 2.28

Barker K. and Sturges J.—*Decision making in Magistrates' Courts* (1986) Fourmat: 16.10

Bean P.—*Punishment*, (1981) Martin Robertson – 1.74

Bottomley A.K.—*Decisions in the Penal Process* (1973) Martin Robertson – 16.06

Bottomley A.K.—*Criminology in Focus* (1979) Martin Robertson – 1.49

Bottoms A.E.—"Reflections on the Renaissance of Dangerousness" (1977) Howard Journal 16, p. 70 – 1.80

Bottoms A.E.—"The Advisory Council and the Suspended Sentence" [1979] Crim.L.R. 437 – 6.34

Bottoms A.E. and McClean J.D.—*Defendants in the Criminal Process* (1976) Routledge & Kegan Paul – 2.28

Brody S.R.—*The Effectiveness of Sentencing* (1976) HORS No. 35 HMSO – 1.72

Brody S.R. and Tarling R.—*Taking Offenders out of Circulation* (1981) HORS No. 64 HMSO – 1.77

Bucknell P. and Ghodse H.—*Misuse of Drugs* (1986 with 1st supplement) Waterlow – 15.23

Burney, E.—"All Things to All Men: Justifying Custody under the 1982 Act" [1985] Crim.L.R. 284 – 10.22

Burns J.M. and Mattina J.S.—*Sentencing* (1978), National Judical College (U.S.) – 1.86, 7.14

Carlen P. and Powell M.—"Professionals in the Magistrates' Courts" in H. Parker (ed.) *Social Work and the Courts* (1979) E. Arnold – 4.39

Clarke Hall and Morrison on Children (10th Ed.) Richard A.H. White (ed.) Butterworths – 12.45

Code of Conduct for the Bar (1980)—4.09, 5.01, 5.14, 7.38

Code For Crown Prosecutors, Law Society Gazette (1986), p. 2308 – 2.05

Croft I.J.—letter in (1985) Br. J. of Criminology 25, p. 320 – 1.72

Dell S.—*Silent in Court* (1971) Bell – 2.28

Devlin K.—*Sentencing Offenders in Magistrates' Courts* (1970) Sweet & Maxwell – 7.13, 7.39, 9.51

Fielding, Henry—*The History of Tom Jones* (Penquin Ed. 1966) – 5.20

Floud J. and Young W.—*Dangerousness and Criminal Justice* (1981) Heinemann – 1.80

Frankel, Judge M.—*Criminal Sentences: Law without Order* (1973) Hill & Wang – 1.71, 5.10

Glaser D.—*The Effectiveness of a Prison and Parole System* (1969 abridged edn.) Bobbs-Merrill – 6.11

Godsland J.H. and Fielding N.G.—"Young Persons Convicted of Grave Crimes" (1985) Howard Journal 24, p. 282 – 7.29

Goldstone, Judge P.—"A fresh look at Community Service Orders", The Magistrate (May 1982) – 12.09

Hailsham Lord—*The Door Wherein I Went* (1975) Collins – 2.14, 16.13

Hailsham Lord—Letter to *The Times* (26 June 1975) – 1.11

Hailsham Lord—Address to Somerset and South Avon Branch of the Magistrates' Association (14 November 1986) – 13.70

Hall Williams J.E.—*The English Penal system in Transition* (1970) Butterworths – 9.40

Hall Williams J.E.—"The Contribution of the Judiciary" in N. Walker and E. Giller (eds.) *Penal Policy-Making in England* (1977) Cambridge Institute of Criminology – 1.39

Halnan and Spencer—*Wilkinsons Road Traffic Offences* (12th edn. 1985) – 15.42, 15.48

Hawker G.—*Magistrates in the Crown Court* (1984) Institute of Judicial Administration, University of Birmingham – 6.10, 16.03

Henham R.—"The Influence of Sentencing Principles on Magistrates' Sentencing Practices" (1986) *Howard Journal* 25 p. 190 – 1.36, 2.25

Hill M.D.—in Wines E.C. (ed.) *Transactions of the National Congress on Penitentiary and Reformatory Discipline* (1871) Weed, Parsons – 1.07

Hogarth J.—*Sentencing as a Human Process* (1971) University of Toronto Press – 1.22, 1.75, 6.04

Home Office (*see also under* Reports)—Circular no. 230/1972 on Criminal Justice Act 1972 – 12.05

Home Office—*Criminal Justice Act 1982: Summary of Young Offender Powers* (1983) – 1.26

Home Office—*Compensation and Support for Victims of Crime* (1985) Cmnd 9457 – 13.32

Home Office—*The Sentence of the Court* (3rd ed. 1978) – 12.05; *ibid.* (4th ed. 1986) – 1.23, 1.67, 12.05, 13.15

Home Office—*A Review of Criminal Justice Policy* (1976) – 1.23

Home Office—*The Reduction of Pressure on the Prison System: Observations* (1980) Cmnd 7948 – 1.25

Home Office—New guidelines on cautioning issued in Feb. 1985 with H.O. Circular 14/1985 – 1.46

Home Office—*Research and Planning Unit Bulletin* (1986) No. 21 – 9.38

Hood R.—*Tolerance and the Tariff* (1974) National Association for the Care and Resettlement of Offenders – 1.71, 16.02

Hood R.—*Freedom on licence* (1981) Quartermaine House – 1.71

Hood R. and Sparks R.—*Key Issues in Criminology* (1970) Weidenfeld and Nicholson – 1.51, 6.04

Hough M. and Lewis H.—*Penal Hawks and Penal Doves: Attitudes to Punishment in the British Crime survey*, Home Office Research and Planning Unit, Research Bulletin (1986) No. 21, p. 5 – 1.65

Hough M. and Mayhew P.—*The British Crime Survey* (1983) HORS No. 176, HMSO – 1.65

Hough M. and Mayhew P.—*Taking Account of Crime* (1985) HORS No. 85, HMSO – 1.65

Howard League Working Party Report—*Freedom on Licence* (1981) Quartermaine House – 1.71

James, Sir Arthur—*A New Approach to the Criminal Process*, The Riddell Lecture (1974) Institute of Legal Executives – 1.46

James, Sir Arthur—"The Sentencing Process: Present Practice and Future Policy" in L. Blom-Cooper (ed.), *Progress in Penal Reform* (1974) Oxford U.P. – 16.03

Jardine E. *et al.*—"Community Service Orders, Empolyment and the Tariff" [1983] Crim.L.R. 17 – 12.16

Justices' Clerks' Society, *Sentencing in the 1980s* (1980) – 1.33

Kemshall H.—"The Justice Model in Warwicks" (1985) Probation Journal 33, p.106 – 4.21

King M.—*Bail or Custody?* (1971) Cobden Trust – 5.05

King M.—The Role of Prosecuting Counsel in Sentencing – "What about Magistrates' Courts?" [1979] Crim.L.R. 775 – 16.10

Kittrie N.N. and Zenoff E.H.—*Sanctions, Sentencing and Corrections* (1981) Foundation Press – 1.31

Lane, Lord—Address to the Annual Meeting of the Central Council of Probation Committees 1981 – 1.28, 4.25

MacKay R.D.—"Psychiatric Reports in the Crown Court" [1986] Crim.L.R. 217 – 4.35

MacKenna B.—"General Deterrence" in L. Blom-Cooper (ed.) *Progress in Penal Reform* (1974) Oxford U.P. – 1.55, 1.61

Magistrate, The—(1987) 43 No. 2 p. 30 – 13.70

Martinson R.—"What Works?" in *The Public Interest* (Spring Issue 1974) – 1.72

Mitra C.L.—"The Pre-Trial Social Inquiry Report" (1984) 148 J.P. 22 – 4.22

Mohr J.W.—in Brian A. Grosman (ed.) *New Directions in Sentencing* (1980) Butterworths – 1.83

Morris N.—*The Future of Imprisonment* (1974), University of Chicago Press – 1.57

Morris N.—*Madness and the Criminal Law* (1982), University of Chicago Press – 1.32; 5.12

Morris N. and Hawkins G.—*The Honest Politician's Guide to Crime Control* (1969) University of Chicago Press – 1.44

Morrish P. and McLean I.—*The Crown Court: An Index of Common Penalties* (11th edn. 1983) Barry Rose – 8.09

Napier H.—"Probation Officers and Sentencing" (1978) *Probation Journal* 25, p. 122 – 4.24

National Association for the Care and Resettlement of Offenders—*Black People and the Criminal Justice System* (1986) – 5.08

Nicholson, C.G.B.—*The Law and Practice of Sentencing in Scotland* (1981) W. Green & Son – 1.53, 2.29, 9.13

Parliamentary All Party Penal Affairs Group: "Life Sentence Prisoners" (1981) Barry Rose – 9.48

Packer H.L.—*The Limits of the Criminal Sanction* (1968) Stanford U.P. – 1.68

Page L.—*Crime and the Community* (1937) Faber – 1.55

Pease K.—"Community Service and the Tariff" [1978] Crim.L.R. 269 – 12.16

Pease K. *et al*—*Community Service Orders* (1975) HORS No. 29, HMSO – 12.07

Pease K. *et al*—*Community Service Assessed in 1976* (1977) HORS No. 39, HMSO – 12.07

Pease K. and McWilliams W. (eds.)—*Community Service by Order* (1980) Scottish Academic Press – 12.07

Pease K. and Wasik M. (eds.)—*Sentencing Reform: Guidance or Guidelines?* (1987) Manchester U.P. – 16.04

Puglia, Judge R.—"Determining Sentencing in California" in *The Future of Sentencing* (1982) Cambridge Institute of Criminology – 1.32, 16.14

Registrar of Criminal Appeals Guide (1983) 77 Cr.Ap.R. 138 – 7.13

Report of the Committee on Social Services in Courts of Summary Jurisdiction (Cmnd. 5122) (1936) HMSO – 12.34

Report of the Royal Commission on Capital Punishment (1953) HMSO (Cmnd. 8932) –1.54

Report of Advisory Council on the Treatment of Offenders, *Alternatives to Short Terms of Imprisonment*, (1957) HMSO – 1.09, 13.02

Report of the Royal Commission (Chairman: Lord Wolfden) on Homosexuality and Prostitution (1957) HMSO (Cmnd. 247) – 1.03, 3.23

Report of the Interdepartmental Committee (Chairman: Streatfeild J.) on the Business of the Criminal Courts (1961) HMSO (Cmnd. 1289) – 1.23, 1.70

Report of the Departmental Committee (Chairman: Morison) on the Probation Service (1962) HMSO (Cmnd. 650) – 12.26: 12.28

Report of the Interdepartmental Committee (Chairman: Lord Donovan) on the
   Court of Criminal Appeal (1965) (Cmnd. 2755) HMSO – 1.39
Report of Advisory Council on the Penal System, *Reparation by the Offender*
   (1970) HMSO – 13.34
Report of Advisory Council on the Penal System (Chairman: Baroness
   Wootton): *Non-Custodial and Semi-Custodial Penalties*, (1970) HMSO –
   12.05
Report (11th) of Criminal Law Revision Committee: Evidence (General) (1972)
   HMSO (Cmnd. 4991) – 16.13
Report (First) of Criminal Law and Penal Methods Reform Committee of South
   Australia (1973) – 1.12
Report of the Committee (Chairman: Lord Butler) on Mentally Abnormal
   Offenders (1975) HMSO (Cmnd. 6244) – 4.34, 11.14, 11.57
Report of Advisory Council on the Penal System, *The Length of Prison
   Sentences: Interim Report* (1977) – 1.14, 1.26, 6.13
Report (15th) from the Expenditure Committee: *The Reduction of Pressure on
   the Prison System* (1978) HMSO – 1.24
Report of Advisory Council on the Penal System (Chairman: Baroness Serota):
   Sentences of Imprisonment: a review of maximum penalties (1978) HMSO –
   1.50, 1.56, 1.67, 9.30
Report of the Committee (Chairman: May, J.) of Inquiry into the U.K. Prison
   Services (1979) HMSO (Cmnd. 7673) – 1.73
Report of a National Association for the Care and Resettlement of Offenders
   Working Group, *Social Reports in the Juvenile Court* (1984), – 4.42
Report (1st) of the Home Affairs Committee of the House of Commons Session
   1984-1985 (1984) H.C.43, *Compensation and Support for Victims of Crime*
   (HMSO) (Cmnd. 9457) – 13.32
Report of the Panel of Inquiry into the circumstances surrounding the Death of
   Jasmine Beckford, *A Child in Trust*, (1985) London Borough of Brent –
   7.38
Report of the Committee (Chairman: Farquharson J.) on the Role of
   Prosecution Counsel (1986) Counsel 1, p. 28 – 2.08
Report of the Canadian Sentencing Commission: *Sentencing Reform: A
   Canadian Approach* (1985).
Reynolds, F.—"Magistrates' Justification for making Custodial Orders on
   Juvenile Offenders" [1985] Crim.L.R. 294 – 10.22
Rosett A. and Cressey D.R.—*Justice by Consent* (1976) Lippincott – 2.28
Royal Commission on the Penal System in England and Wales, Written
   Evidence Vol. III (1967) HMSO – 13.19
Rutter M. and Giller H.—*Juvenile Delinquency: Trends and Perspectives* (1983)
   Penguin – 1.48

Savage. S.—"Conditions in Probation Orders" (1985) 149 J.P. 105 – 12.33
Scarman, L.—*Control of Sentencing* (1974) Howard League – 1.33, 1.44, 1.61
Shapland J.—*Between Conviction and Sentence* (1981) Routledge and Kegan
   Paul – 4.28, 5.08, 5.14
Shaw, S.—*Community Service – A Guide for Sentencers* (1983) Prison Reform
   Trust – 12.07
Skinner, Mr. Justice. (1985) The Magistrate 41, p. 146 – 2.25

Smith D. et al—*Reducing the Prison Population* (1984) Home Office Research and Planning Unit Paper No. 23 – 9.02

Sprott, W.J.H.—"Sentencing Policy" in P. Halmos (ed.) *Sociological Studies in the British Penal Services* (1965) University of Keels – 1.52

Stockdale E.—*The Court and the Offender* (1967) Gollancz – 5.13, 6.39

Stockdale, E.—"The Courts as Sentencers" in H. Jones (ed.) *Society Against Crime* (1981) Penguin – 1.64

Stockdale E.—*The Probation Volunteer* (1985), The Volunteer Centre – 5.08

Sussex J.—*Community Service by Offenders – Year One in Kent* (1974) Barry Rose – 12.07

Tarling R.—*Sentencing Practice in Magistrates' Courts* (1979) HORS No. 56 HMSO – 1.34, 13.10

Thomas D.A.—"The Case for Reasoned Decisions" [1963] Crim.L.R. 243 – 7.13

Thomas D.A.—"Parole and the Crown Court" (1985) 149 J.P. 344 – 6.50: 16.12

Thomas D.A.—"Principles of Sentencing (2nd ed. 1979) Heinemann – 4.38

Thomas D.A.—"Sentencing Discretion and Appellate Review" in J. Shapland (ed.) *Decision making in the Legal System* (1983) British Psychological Society –   1.40: 4.37: 16.09

Thomas D.A.—*Encyclopaedia of Current Sentencing Practice*, Sweet & Maxwell vii – 4.11, 9.13, 9.23, 11.20

Thorp J.—*"Social Inquiry Reports: A Survey* (1978) HORS No. 48 – 4.20

Turner M.—*Safe Lodging: The Road to Norman House* (1961) Hutchinson – 1.41

Tutt N. and Giller H.—"Doing justice to great expectations" *Community Care*, 17 January, 1985 – 4.21

United States Sentencing Commission—*Revised Draft Sentencing Guidelines* (1987) – 16.14

Walker N.—*Sentencing: Theory, Law and Practice* (1985) Butterworths – 6.18, 6.48, 7.17, 9.43, 12.05

Walker N. and Marsh C.—"Do Sentences Affect Public Disapproval?" (1984) *British Journal of Criminology* 24, p. 27 – 1.59

Wasik N.—Letter in [1982] Crim.L.R. 152 – 6.21

Wasik N.—"Sentencing and the Divisional Court" [1984] Crim.L.R. 272 – 1.36

West D.—*Delinquency: Its Roots, Careers and Prospects* (1972) Heinemann – 1.48

Wheeler S. (ed.)—*Controlling Delinquents* (1968) Wiley – 1.75, 4.38

Whitehead P. and MacMillan—"Checks or Blank Cheque?" (1985) *Probation J.* 32, p. 87 – 7.20

Wilcox A.E.—*The Decision to Prosecute* (1972) Butterworths – 1.84

Wilkins L.—"Sentencing Guidelines to Reduce Disparity?" [1980] Crim.L.R. 201 – 16.14

Willis A. et al—"Community Service and the Tariff" [1978] Crim.L.R. 540 – 12.16

Worrall A. and Pease K.—"The Prison Population in 1985" (1986) Br. J. Criminology 26, p. 184 – 6.51

Wootton, B.—"Official Advisory Bodies" in N. Walker and E. Giller (eds.)
  Penal Policy-Making in England (1977) Cambridge Institute of
  Criminology – 1.09
Wright, M.—*Making Good* (1982) Burnett Books – 1.91
Young W.—*Community Service Orders* (1979) Heinemann – 12.16

Zander M.—*Diversion from Criminal Justice in an English Context*, Report of a
  National Association for the Care and Resettlement of Offenders Working
  Party (1975) Barry Rose – 1.46, 8.03
Zellick G.—"The Role of Prosecuting Counsel in Sentencing" [1979] Crim.L.R.
  493 – 16.07
Zimring F.E. and Hawkins G.J.—*Deterrence* (1973) University of Chicago
  Press – 1.68

Index